121. II La Chanson de Guillaume: edition and translation

Critical Guides to French Texts

EDITED BY ROGER LITTLE, WOLFGANG VAN EMDEN, DAVID WILLIAMS

LA CHANSON DE GUILLAUME

(*La Chançun de Willame*)

edited and translated by

Philip E. Bennett

Reader in French

University of Edinburgh

Grant & Cutler Ltd
2000

ISBN 0 7293 0421 3

DEPÓSITO LEGAL: V. 4.647 - 2000

Printed in Spain by
Artes Gráficas Soler, S.A., Valencia
for
GRANT & CUTLER LTD
55–57, GREAT MARLBOROUGH STREET, LONDON W1V 2AY

Contents

For Helen

Bone fud l'ore que jo te pris a per

Preface

This edition was first mooted many years ago as a companion volume to a Grant & Cutler Critical Guide, since at that time there was no readily available student edition of the *Chançun de Willame* (referred to thus throughout, though the conventional 'Guillaume' has been retained in the title, to avoid confusion). Since then François Suard has published his edition with a translation into modern French and Andrea Fassò has reissued Duncan McMillan's text with a translation into Italian. There is, however, still no readily available edition for English-speaking students on medieval or comparative literature courses, and it is to them that the current work is addressed. The edition remains as faithful as possible to the one extant manuscript witness to the poem, and the accompanying introduction, translation and notes are meant to elucidate the text while keeping closely in touch with what is at times an idiosyncratic original.

Inevitably with a work that has been over ten years in gestation many people, both colleagues and students, have contributed (consciously or unwittingly) to its growth. To all of them I express my gratitude. I also owe particular thanks to the late Professor Duncan McMillan for his immense intellectual and personal generosity as my work on 'his' text developed, to Professor Wolfgang van Emden, whose close reading of my work and very perceptive comments on it have helped me avoid many a pitfall, and to Mr Raymond Howard of Grant & Cutler for keeping faith with a project which has been overlong in coming to fruition.

I also wish to record my thanks to the British Academy for financial support during the early stages of the work, and to the Research Committee of the Faculty of Arts, University of Edinburgh, for financial support during its closing stages.

Philip E. Bennett
Edinburgh

Introduction

The *Chançun de Willame* is one of the most enigmatic of *chansons de geste*. Its opening sequence in which Vivien and count Tedbalt of Bourges[1] face a pagan invasion contains some of the earliest known French epic materials not related to any of the three 'established' cycles of the King, of Garin de Monglane (ancestor of Guillaume d'Orange) or revolt (for a description of these cycles see Suard, 1993, Chapter IV). Moreover, its first 2,000 lines have elements that must be contemporary with the *Chanson de Roland* in the Oxford version (Wathelet-Willem, 1975, p.652). At the same time it presents allusions and references to almost every other major poem from the cycle of Garin de Monglane, and in the form in which it has come down to us must date from between 1150 and 1175. No less of a puzzle is its poetic form and the language in which it is written. There can be no doubt that the earliest parts of the poem are of Continental, probably western French origin and composed in the mono-assonanced *laisses* of decasyllabics with a caesura after the fourth syllable which are typical of Old French epic poems before 1200. The text we have is written in lines of very variable length, with an unstable caesura, and in *laisses* which often present more than one assonance, although lines are usually grouped together to provide mono-assonanced blocks. The language of the surviving poem is that of Anglo-Norman England in the period 1170 to 1250. How can these puzzles be resolved?

---

[1] Throughout I will use the forms of personal names found in the poem, to emphasise that we are dealing with literary, not historical characters. Where spelling varies in the poem I will generalise the most common form. Where geographic sites have recognisable equivalents in the 'real world' the common modern English form will be used, as it is likely that the poets intended their audience to make such identifications.

1. The Poem in the Manuscript

The *Chançun de Willame* exists in only one manuscript in the British Library (Additional 38663), a small volume of 25 folios measuring 27cms x 16.5cms — rather smaller than an A4 sheet. The text is copied in two columns per page with initials coloured alternately red and blue to mark the start of each *laisse*. The poem begins with a large, coloured capital, but otherwise, although the text is on the whole carefully copied in a clear hand, the manuscript is unadorned, and has no miniatures or historiations. This, together with the indifferent quality of the vellum, suggests that it was not prepared for a wealthy collector. Full descriptions of the manuscript and accounts of its provenance can be found in McMillan, 1949–50, I, pp.ix-xxii and Wathelet-Willem, 1975, pp.27–42. The copy was made in England in the middle of the thirteenth century.

The manuscript, which offers neither title[2] nor *explicit*, presents a continuous text with each line of verse on a separate line and the first letter of each line off set left by one space. The manuscript does not use punctuation in the modern sense, but employs a point to separate out some elements of a line (e.g. Roman numerals or items in a list) and an inverted semi-colon which serves as an exclamation mark. This punctuation may actually be related to chant or recitation rather than to the syntactic content of the lines. Apart from the coloured initials which mark the start of *laisses* there are no structuring markers in the text. This fact has led many commentators and even editors to consider the poem as one continuously composed unit and to analyse it structurally and thematically on that basis (Adler, 1969; Robertson, 1965). This, as we shall see, tends to ignore some very sharp textual problems, involving both changes of linguistic and prosodic usage (Bennett, 1987) and contradictions within the narrative line, which are well-known and have been frequently discussed, with no consensus as to

---

[2]The 'title', in English at the head of the text, 'Romance of Guillaume au Courtney', is clearly eighteenth- or nineteenth-century in origin.

their significance (McMillan, 1949–50, II, p.130; Wathelet-Willem, 1975, pp.391–95; Suard, 1991, pp.xv–xx). The most important of these concerns lines 1979–82. At the end of *laisse* 130 we read:

> Lores fu mecresdi:
> ore out vencu sa bataille Willame!

while the next line, beginning a new *laisse*, reads:

> Li quons Willame chevalche par le champ.
> Tut est irez et plein de maltalant...

in which it requires ingenuity to find the signs of the victory that has just been announced.

The nub of the question concerns the status we are prepared to assign to the person or persons, presumably working between ca 1150 and ca 1200 (since no part of the existing manuscript text is free of those errors which reveal it to be a copy of a previous version) responsible for the current state of the poem. Wathelet-Willem, 1975, pp.66–78, envisaged a series of scribes to be blamed for unconsciously defacing a fine monument of French poetry, although it is equally possible to discern the activity of a single redactor or editor deliberately conjoining two traditions to produce a new work (Lejeune, 1960). Indeed the modern distinctions between 'author', 'editor' and 'scribe' are not always easy to apply in a medieval context (Kennedy, 1970), so it would not necessarily be inappropriate to treat the results of a scribe's labours as if we were dealing with a poet's. However, this does beg some fundamental questions about the nature of text production in the twelfth and thirteenth centuries (particularly in the case of the epic) and even more about the mode of dissemination of those works. Even if we discount recomposition in performance as a means of generating the *Willame* text, it is clear from references in contemporary poems (Beroul, *Tristran*, ll. 1265–68 [Ewert, 1967]; Chrétien, *Erec et Enide*, ll. 9–22 [Fritz, 1992]) that people were aware of a galaxy of material underlying the poem they were hearing. This mutability or *mouvance* (Zumthor, 1991, pp.41–49) of the medieval text will have reduced the audience's sense of the homogeneity of the artefact. Equally the fact that the vast majority of the poem's audience received the text aurally will have imposed its own sense of discontinuity, since it is, in fact, most unlikely that any audience ever heard the entire song at a sitting, and comparatively unlikely that 'serial' singing or reciting of the song occurred with sufficient regularity to allow any 'recipient' of the text to get the overview of it that we have today studying it in a critical edition. Consequently, when dealing with a text such as the *Willame*, in which the 'seams' are clear to see, we are doing the poem no disservice if we consider it as a compilation, and analyse the parts before we try to evaluate the sum of those parts.

2. The Poem in the Episodes

The clearest division into episodes in the poem is that which separates the adventures of the giant Reneward from those of the other heroes. Although some scholars have, as indicated above, made light of this division, it is so marked that Rita Lejeune (1960) and Jeanne Wathelet-Willem (1952) labelled the two parts of the poem *G1* and *G2*, and Hermann Suchier (1911) cut short his edition of *La Chançun de Guillelme* at line 1980, where Willame's victory is announced. The reasons for considering the second part of the poem as a separate entity have been much debated, and one can add to them the structural distinction that while *G2* presents a homogeneous and continuous narrative, *G1* is itself an episodic construct with some sharp disjunctions between its constituent elements. Three episodes actually make up the part of the poem referred to as *G1*: the battle in which Vivien dies (ll. 1–932); the second battle in which Girard and Guischard die (ll. 933–1401); the third battle in which Deramé[3] is killed and Willame is victorious with the help of his youngest nephew, Gui (ll. 1402–1980).

[3] In the first 1,000 lines of the poem the pagan commander is called 'Deramed'. From there to the end of the poem his name is given in the phonetically more modern form 'Deramé'. Since there is no sign of a change of scribe in the manuscript, this might be a

The exact limits of the episodes are not clear, and a certain amount of rewriting to accommodate the insertions has gone some way to hiding the joins. Nor is it totally clear in which order the new elements were added. The confusion over the fates of the characters called 'Gui/Guiot/Guielin', and of Girard and Guischard suggests that *G2* may have been added first, since it seems not to know of the deaths of Girard and Guischard. However, it is unlikely that later hands would have left line 1980 untouched if it had appeared in the middle of a poem being further modified. Similarly, while the opening of the 'Gui' episode (ll. 1402ff.) seems to depend on the defeat suffered in the 'Girard-Guischard' episode, ll. 1787–88 ('Cist nus querrat ço que Girard nus quist, / Quand il Willame nus amenat ici') refer back to the first, 'Vivien' episode and seem to ignore the second expedition to l'Archamp. Since an analysis of the versification of the two episodes covering ll. 933–1980 reveals that, as we read them now, they were probably composed by the same Anglo-Norman hand (Bennett, 1987, pp.274–76), the safest conclusion is that these lines, reworked from pre-existing and possibly independent materials, were inserted as a block into *G1* between 1150 and 1170, by a redactor wishing to parody the old poem and aware of the still autonomous 'Reneward' material. *G2* will have been added, along with *laisse* 115 to co-ordinate data between *G1* and *G2*, also after 1150 and certainly before 1185 (the earliest date for the extant version of *Aliscans* (Régnier, 1990, I, 40).

The song opens with a single *laisse* as prologue summarising the contents of the poem. Notably no mention is made of Reneward, and the victory over Deramed is attributed solely to Willame. The text is announced unequivocally as 'la chançun de Willame' (l. 11), which makes it unique among *chansons de geste*, and rare in medieval literature, in being assigned something resembling a modern title.

---

further indication of the separate origins of the Vivien episode and the rest of the poem as currently constituted.

    The only hero mentioned in the prologue along with Willame
is Vivien, and it is to him that we immediately pass. Vivien, who is
identified only as a valiant knight and Willame's nephew with no
attribution of a fief, is in company with Tedbalt, count of Bourges,
and his nephew, Esturmi. Also present are seven hundred knights
apparently under Vivien's command, whose presence is not explain-
ed, but who may form one of the troops of *bachelers* under training
which were a regular part of military establishments in the twelfth
century. They are in the count's capital, returning from vespers,
although the already drunken state of Tedbalt and Esturmi does not
evoke religious devotion. A messenger arrives announcing an
invasion by pagans led by Deramed of Cordoba, who are attacking
Munt Girunde[4] and devastating the country. Tedbalt, acting as a
responsible feudal overlord, asks advice from his household. Vivien
counsels summoning a host and enlisting the help of the veteran
Willame; Esturmi, inspired by envy, urges immediate action to
secure glory. With cups of wine, in a ritualistic gesture from which
Vivien dissociates himself, Tedbalt and Esturmi pledge themselves
to fighting. On the battlefield next day, however, things take a
different turn and when they see the size of the enemy forces
Tedbalt and Esturmi flee in ignominy, leaving Vivien and his loyal
troop, plus those of Tedbalt's forces who joined the army overnight
and who prefer glorious death to shameful life, to defend an
impossible position. Vivien, rightly pointing out that no oath binds
the other knights to himself, releases them, saying that his vow to
God not to flee in the face of the enemy obliges him to fight and die
alone if necessary. They accept his leadership, as a representative of
Willame's clan, and he is further joined by his cousin, Girard
(Tedbalt's squire), who symbolically strips his master of his arms
and unhorses Esturmi before returning to the field, where the
unequal contest rapidly leads to the total destruction of the Frankish
army. Vivien, his duty done, then sends Girard to summon Willame
and reinforcements. Girard departs across a desert-like wasteland

---

[4] For a full discussion of the problems associated with this identification of the site of
Deramed's invasion see the note to line 14.

and Vivien, having offered up prayers reminiscent of those of Christ in Gethsemane, is hacked down and his body placed under a tree, off the path, to prevent Christians finding it.

Although within a 'Proto-Guillaume' the Vivien material must have formed part of a diptych of heroic death and revenge similar to that of the *Chanson de Roland* (the prologue announces Willame's ultimate victory as well as Vivien's death), within the existing text it shows several features which give it the air of an autonomous poem. The opening in Bourges in the presence of Tedbalt and Esturmi may well be borrowed from an earlier song dealing with the death of Vivien, count and lay-abbot of Tours, in battle against the Bretons in 851. If so, the story has been so completely assimilated to the thematics of the nascent Guillaume Cycle with its focus on war against the 'pagans' of 'Spain' that no trace is left of material otherwise alien to the Old French epic tradition.[5] The ritual heroic boasting of Tedbalt and Esturmi, which belongs to an ancestral, pagan tradition, is devalued and presented as drunken bravado in contrast to Vivien's ascetic vow to face the enemies of Christendom in spite of all (Bennett, 1984, p.487). This reinterpretation of heroic endeavour as Christian duty gives the episode a spiritual dimension at odds with the other parts of the poem, even with the second episode with its facile contrast of Girard's death in the faith and Guischard's death as a renegade. The importance of the atmosphere of suffering and renunciation in the first part of the poem can be measured by the almost total lack of descriptions of fighting, as the poet concentrates on reviewing the suffering of the injured and dying. Such an 'anti-chivalric' approach sets the episode apart not only from the rest of this poem, but also from the rest of the Old French epic tradition, where death (rather than suffering) is seen as a natural ingredient of heroic knightly activity, and when portrayed

---

[5] The *Chanson d'Aiquin*, which dates from ca 1200 (Jacques, 1979, pp.xxii–xxiv) and tells of a fictional conquest of Brittany by Charlemagne, places Bretons in the imperial army, and makes the enemy pagan 'Sarrasins', as usual.

is presented as the culmination, even the consecration, of the warrior's career in the service of his lord.[6]

The second episode, which begins at line 933, provides the first serious problem in assessing the construction of the poem. The first seventy lines of the episode, recounting Girard's arrival in Barcelona, where he finds Willame, just returned himself from a major battle, and his wife, Guiburc, a convert to Christianity, probably survive from the original song, or just possibly form part of the reworking by the *remanieur* responsible for the extant Gui episode. The 'Girart-Guischard' episode proper seems to start at the beginning of *laisse* 83, or, more probably, at the end of that *laisse*, where Guiburc unexpectedly offers her nephew, not mentioned in Vivien's message, as a member of Willame's army. The couple present a picture of placid harmony looking over the land from an upper window after hearing vespers and reflecting on their years together. Girard delivers his message repeating in detail Vivien's appeal for help from Willame and from Vivien's young brother Gui. After a momentary manifestation of despair, which the poet tells us is designed to test Guiburc, Willame agrees to go to Vivien's aid, accompanied not by Gui, who disappears from the text at this point, but by Guiburc's nephew Guischard, a convert, like his aunt, from 'paganism'. After a hearty meal and a night's sleep Girard is formally equipped as a knight and the army departs. At l'Archamp the Frankish army finds the Saracen fleet becalmed and, thanks to its initial surprise, has some success. The pagans soon regroup however, and three days of fighting are summarised in four lines (1120–23) at the end of which only Willame, Girard and Guischard remain alive. The refrain, which in the first episode with its constant allusion to 'lunsdi al vespres' functions as a timeless lyric incantation all the more poetic because of the imprecision of its reference, here, with its reference to 'joesdi al vespre' (l. 1127)

---

[6] Although parallels between plastic arts and literature can be misleading, it may be worth indicating the similarity between the 'normal' approach to death in battle of the Old French epic and the representation of Christ Crucified in 'pre-gothic' art, in which the figure on the cross is shown in perfect repose, with no sign of the suffering which is a hallmark of later art.

becomes a mundane index of narrative chronology. The deaths of the two young men are described in strictly parallel terms, and with identical details, except that, while Vivien's erstwhile companion dies a Christian martyr's death (ll. 1134–75), Guischard renounces the Christian God, averring that if he had been faithful to Mahomet he would be safely at home in Cordoba drinking wine (ll. 1176–1201). The manner of his death obliges Willame to take home the corpse of a renegade, since he has promised Guiburc that he will return her nephew to her after the battle. As Willame leaves the field the poet points out with embarrassing precision that his hero is not fleeing, merely going away (l. 1225). As stated above, the indications are that this episode and the one that follows are by the same hand, and the satirical edge on the lines describing Willame's departure from the field would fit that view, even though the blatant didacticism of the 'Girard-Guischard' material sits ill with the spritely humour of the 'Gui' episode. Since Guischard is a constant and valiant participant in the battle along with Girard and Gui in *G2* and *Aliscans*, and like them belongs to the Narbonnais clan, we are confronted with a complex series of modifications to the original song, which appears to be designed to leave the spotlight firmly on young Gui in the last episode of *G1*.

This episode also opens in Barcelona, where the prescient and active Guiburc has raised a further 30,000 knights from her own vassals (ll. 1229–35) and, when Willame returns, insists on opening the gates to him in person. There follows a poignant interview over Guischard's body before Guiburc takes Willame in to a hearty meal, and, offering suitable lies to her vassals about the real situation at l'Archamp, persuades them to join Willame on a further expedition (ll. 1275–1435). Despite his voracious appetite, which Guiburc sees as a sign of his valour, Willame has not fully recovered his spirits and worries about who will look after Guiburc and his lands after what he seems to envisage as an almost inevitable defeat. This signals the unexpected entrance at l. 1436 of young Gui, abandoned since the first episode. He rises from the fire, both a phoenix representing the unquenchable ardour of the clan and a *Cendrillon* type hero. By the wisdom of his answers (and his refusal to show

undue deference) to his uncle he is soon named as Willame's heir
and protector of his wife, on condition that he remains behind. He
has no difficulty, however, in persuading Guiburc that without his
aid she will never see Willame again, a judgement the poet fully
supports. He also proves himself a worthy pupil of his aunt by
saying that he can lie effectively to his uncle and convince him that
he escaped by force. Equipped with suitably small armour, and
riding one of Guiburc's palfreys, he soon joins the army. Willame
harangues his troops and notices the particularly small warrior
among the squires. He makes a joke about the need for men of
anyone bringing such a small follower to the field, and is chagrined
when he learns it is his own nephew (ll. 1615–25). The battle starts
as a carbon copy of the previous one, except that for the first time
Deramé appears on the scene, accompanied by a train of fifteen
kings with conventional pagan names (ll. 1705–29). The main
purpose of these lines seems to be that of providing a link to *G2*, by
recounting the capture of a number of warriors who will play a part
in that section, including the previously dead Guischard, and
Bertram (another nephew of Willame not mentioned in the *Willame*
before this point). As predicted by Willame, Gui soon starts
suffering from hunger and Willame sends him to the pagans' ships
to find food. Again the refrain is used to mark the passage of time:
the reference back from a 'real' Wednesday of narrated time when
Gui leaves to look for food to a 'real' Monday on which the battle
started (ll. 1771–80) has the same effect as the shift from 'lunsdi' to
'joesdi' in the second episode of 'depoeticising' what in the original
poem appears as pure lyric invocation. During Gui's absence
Willame finds himself in considerable difficulties, and is on the
point of being killed when Gui rescues him; the fleeing pagans call
Gui a thunderbolt, while suggesting that Vivien has returned from
the dead. Gui offers Willame his horse, stating truthfully that it has
been lent him by Guiburc (ll. 1869–70). This throws Willame into a
rage, but Gui retorts with his 'catch phrase' ('I never heard the
like'), urging his uncle to get on with things. Willame, however
cannot pursue the fleeing enemy, as his feet hang below the
shortened stirrups. At this point Deramé, forgotten since his first

appearance, is found lying in a mess of blood and sand. He leaps to his feet, however, and into the saddle, and there follows a burlesque duel in which Deramé charges in conventional fashion and Willame holds his sword precariously across his saddle bow, as if intending to impale him on it. As Deramé gallops past him Willame cuts off his leg, and the pagan king falls ignominiously to the ground. Willame offers Gui the pagan king's horse, an offer that is accepted provided the saddles are swapped. Willame agrees to this condition, and while he is performing the functions of a groom Gui beheads Deramé. Willame protests against his nephew's unchivalrous behaviour, but with his usual wisdom the young man points out that Deramé had only lost a leg, not his genitals, and could have produced heirs to seek revenge and carry on the war. Willame approves this judgement, signalling the poet's disapproval of the fashionable aristocratic view of war as a sporting contest between gentlemen (especially where the enemies of the faith are involved) and announces that Willame has won his battle (l. 1980).

If, as defined in *La Chanson de Roland* for example, this is taken to mean that Willame and Gui are masters of the field even if all their own army has been annihilated, the battle has clearly not been won in epic terms. Although Willame succeeds in finding Vivien still alive in an idyllic setting and giving him communion before he dies (ll. 1988–2053), he cannot take his body home, since fifteen more pagan kings suddenly appear to imprison Gui, who has been following his uncle at a distance and was absent from the final scene with Vivien (ll. 2069–77); he now joins the other warriors captured in *laisse* 115 only to disappear from the poem, as unlike them he is not released by Reneward.[7] Yet another king, Alderufe, also emerges, with whom Willame replays his duel with Deramé, but in more conventional terms, and without assistance (ll. 2091–209). After swapping arms (and horses) with Alderufe, Willame returns to his capital, no longer Barcelona but Orange. There Guiburc is again alone except for a gate-keeper, and refuses

---

[7] For a full discussion of the problems associated with these captures and releases see the note to *laisse* 115.

to admit her disguised husband until he has proved himself by rescuing Christian prisoners from a passing band of marauding pagans. This he achieves, as his arms convince them that they are being attacked and punished by Alderufe, angry at their non-attendance at the battle of l'Archamp (ll. 2210–98). Guiburc still refuses to admit her husband, however, since 'so many men resemble each other in prowess' (a concept alien to the epic), and obliges him to reveal the wound to his nose received in battle against Tedbalt (thus linking the account of the battle for Orange with that contained in Vivien's message in *G1* (ll. 666–78) while contradicting the versions of the *Couronnement de Louis* (Lepage, 1978, *Rédaction AB*, ll. 1035–46), for the wound to the hero's nose, and of the extant *Prise d'Orange*, from which Tiebaut-Tedbalt is absent). Willame is at last admitted, laments his losses in a series of questions and answers exploiting the *ubi sunt?* motif, and the feast scene is replayed, with the master and mistress again at a low table, as in the Gui episode, but in a great hall devoid of knights, to which Willame addresses a formal lament (ll. 2299–409). His suggestion that it is time to retire into religious life is vigorously rebutted by Guiburc, who tells him to go to Laon to get aid from the emperor. In answer to her husband's worry about who will defend the town in his absence, Guiburc replies that she has seven hundred ladies capable of doing it.

Willame thus sets out and rides to Laon, where he is greeted by greedy young courtiers used to receiving the treasures of Spain from him (ll. 2410–74). When they realise that he is destitute they abandon him. Lowis welcomes him, however, but is reluctant to give material support until Willame threatens to renounce his fief and defy the king, at which point the rest of the Narbonnais clan, who are present, calm things down and large numbers of troops are pledged for the war. Lowis now seems prepared to lead an army in support of Willame, until the queen, Willame's sister, accuses Guiburc of being a witch who will poison Lowis and have Willame crowned. This throws Willame into a rage, and in violently crude terms he accuses his sister of leading a life of debauchery. Nemeri de Nerbune, Willame's father, again restores peace, and the army is summoned to march south (ll. 2496–635). At this point a shambling, ragged figure emerges from the kitchens bearing across his shoulders the yoke he habitually uses for carrying buckets. This is Reneward, another *Cendrillon* and also a 'disguised hero' who will prove his heroic status, to the detriment of Willame, by winning the final battle virtually single-handed. He persuades Willame to let him go to l'Archamp with him, but has first to dispose of his 'boss', Lowis's head cook, and several kitchen boys, who play violent pranks on him. Reneward's riposte is equally violent, exploiting a sort of cartoon humour, burning and braining people with gay abandon, but causing no sign of dismay to the world at large (ll. 2648–717). Reneward also shows himself habitually unable to remember the yoke which he vows will be his only weapon, refusing a sword from Willame, although he later accepts one from Guiburc. The magical link between the implement and its owner is shown by the inability of anyone else even to move it, while it virtually gives itself into Reneward's hand (he is not at this stage formally identified as the giant he will become in other parts of the tradition).

After the army's return to Orange, where Guiburc recognises Reneward as her brother, but without enlightening him (following the established model of the 'Fair Unknown' story-type he must earn his recognition as hero, not have it bestowed on him), the army set out for l'Archamp a fourth time. In the intervening night there is a third 'replay' of the feast scene, enlivened by a repetition of Reneward's cooking the meal as he had done at Willame's camp, but this time with his knight's sword at his side, and a repetition of the brutal exchange of pranks between the 'unrevealed' hero and the kitchen boys. Additionally Reneward refuses to sleep in a bed, paralleling his dislike of those other symbols of chivalric civilisation, swords and horses, and uses his yoke to give a rude awakening to reluctant warriors by almost demolishing the great hall of the castle round their ears (ll. 2790–928). The following scene on the battlefield is exactly what it has been at the start of the previous two episodes, with the becalmed pagans picnicking and indulging in tourism while waiting for a favourable wind. Again the start of the battle echoes closely the beginning of the Girart-Guischard and Gui

episodes; again, like Gui, Reneward suffers from hunger, but unlike
Gui, when he goes down to the ships he finds not food but the
Christian prisoners, whom he releases (ll. 3006–79). Bertram, the
first to be released, justifies the name of 'timonier' ('steersman')
given to him in *Aliscans* and the 'Siège d'Orange' episode in MS *E*
of the *C(E)* redaction of *La Prise d'Orange* by claiming to be an
expert in the handling of ships, and helping Reneward manœuvre
alongside other vessels where prisoners are held. These are soon
released and reunited with Willame (including Girart, who was not
listed among the captured at the end of *G1*, and who now replaces
Reiner). The *G2* poet's embarrassment is revealed by his adapting
the formulaic epithet, 'Girart quis cadele', used by Alderufe in his
allusion to the capture scene (ll. 2098–10), to 'Girart fiz cadele',
giving him what amounts to an Anglo-Norman patronymic.

The victory is now swift, being produced by a series of
burlesque combats between Reneward and monstrous pagans armed
as unconventionally as himself. For the last of these, against the
Emir of Balan who fights with a flail, a rustic implement to match
Reneward's culinary one, Reneward arms himself with seven
halberks and piles seven helmets on his head. His trusty yoke breaks
and he 'miraculously' finds the sword given him by Guiburc, and it
is with this, a knight despite himself, that he kills the emir and wins
the battle (ll. 3157–342). There follows a rapid return to Orange,
where Reneward is ignored at the victory feast. Acting out
Guischard's threat he sets off for Spain to reclaim his kingdom,
whence he threatens to return to wreak vengeance on Willame. The
messengers sent first to bring him back are violent and rude, and he
scatters them, using a roof-tree torn from a cottage to replace his
yoke. Willame and Guiburc, unconcernedly kissing and cuddling,
observe this and go themselves. Guiburc persuades her brother to
accept Willame's reparations for his insult, Reneward is baptised,
tells the story of how he came to be in Lowis's kitchen, and is
finally enlightened as to his relationship to the lord and lady of
Orange. On hearing this he avers that, had he known he was
Willame's brother-in-law, he would have exerted himself even
harder at l'Archamp (ll. 3347–554). On which note the poem ends.

3. *The Structures of the Poem*

Although the poem is essentially episodic and has reached its present condition by a series of accretions, which are revealed among other things by changes in vocabulary (e.g. the use of 'alferant' and 'destrer' in the Gui and Reneward episodes rather than the universal 'cheval' of the earlier sections; see Wathelet-Willem, 1975, pp.416–23) and by the resuscitation of previously killed characters,[8] the resulting text is not without a certain organic unity.

François Suard has shown how this is worked out in the pairing and contrasting of characters (1991, pp.xliv–lii). Another simple structuring device is the use of the refrain, which unites the Vivien and Reneward episodes by the constant use of the incantatory 'lunsdi al vespre' against the purely chronological 'lunsdi al vespre'/'joesdi al vespre' of the Girart-Guischard episode and 'lunsdi al vespre'/'lores fu mecresdi' of the Gui episode. Since *Aliscans* does not have a refrain it is likely that the refrain in *G2* was added to his source text by the redactor responsible for adding *G2* to *G1*. Whether by accident or design, however, tension is also introduced into the fabric of the poem, since the identity of the refrain in lines 1–933 and 1981–3554 is set against a sharp disparity of tones in the two sections. The first, at least after the flight of Tedbalt de Burges and Esturmi, is marked by its lyrico-elegiac nature, in which the emphasis is on suffering and the enemy is a threatening absence observed mainly in the results of the slaughter perpetrated, while the last episode is a blood and thunder burlesque in which the mighty scullion, Reneward, joyously slaughters all, pagan or Christian, who offend him, transforming a poem rejecting traditional heroic values into one celebrating the most banal heroics.

---

[8] The common presupposition among scholars that the multiple Guis, Guischards and Girarts of the poem must be different characters is based on the 'logic' of post-Romantic realism, as is the assertion that Vivien did not 'die' at the end of *G1*, despite several statements to that effect in the text, because he is 'alive' at the beginning of *G2*. This view is belied by the difficulties that the *G2* poet in particular has in handling these returning characters.

The complexity of the relationship between the parts of the song is further assured by the presence of cowards in the army at the beginning of the first and last battles, as well as in the scene where Reneward finally throws away the ridgepole that has replaced his yoke (ll. 3470–73). The difficulty of determining how far this is a deliberate reference back to Tedbalt and Esturmi is shown by its being attached to a reference to Reneward's days in the king's kitchen, so that it is not improbable that the original circle being closed derived not from our *Chançun de Willame* but from the lost opening to the 'Song of Rainouart'. Even within the extant poem the abandoning of this weapon, which links Reneward to his scullion persona, marks his apotheosis as hero, anticipating his baptism, marriage and entry into the properly founded feudal hierarchy.

The refrain also acts as a marker within a framework which places this song firmly under the aegis of darkness. In this way it contrasts starkly with the *Roland* (Frappier, 1968; Bennett, 1977), which throughout is dedicated to the light. All the journeys to and from the battlefield, except the first, occur under cover of night, and the last one in particular starts so early that the French knights complain to Reneward, who has awoken them, that the cock has as yet crowed but twice. This could be an allusion to the Gospel story of Peter's denial of Christ (Matthew 26. 69–75), with a comic transfer of the triple action from the saint to the cock, or it could simply be an indication that, as it is not yet 'prime' (daybreak), it is too early to rise. Since the latter interpretation in a song dominated by the reference to the liturgical office of vespers would also carry religious connotations, either view would support the opinion of Micheline de Combarieu du Grès about *Aliscans* (1993, pp.55–77) that, in the Rainouart tradition, night reigns spiritually as well as physically over the established Christians, who need to be redeemed from their darkness by the converts, Guibourc and Rainouart.

This is certainly true for Tedbalt and Esturmi, whose drunkenness at the office is a prelude to their defection on the battlefield. In the context of the original poem the contrasting picture of Willame and Guiburc leaving vespers in Barcelona must have signalled the rescuing of the Christian cause by the saintly commander of the armies which had conquered the Spanish March at the beginning of the ninth century, transformed by tradition into an unimpeachable epic hero.[9] However, the revisers subsequently responsible for the development of the poem have disrupted the simple diptych suggested by this scheme, so that Willame's evocation of spiritual harmony now looks like nostalgic self-satisfaction, as his ineffectual sorties to l'Archamp have to be made good by a combination of Guiburc (supplier of warriors) and Gui, whose uncompromising attitude to the wounded Deramé recalls in a less sublime mode the dedication of Vivien as representative of the *militia nova*. The undermining of Willame is continued in *G2* (which may have inherited it separately from the Rainouart tradition) as the young scullion rescues not only Willame but the whole Narbonnais clan from annihilation by a series of pagan monsters. The final scenes of the poem also appear to parody the earlier scene of religious and marital harmony (ll. 938–40) by having Willame and Guiburc idly indulge in kissing and cuddling at the gates of Orange, while Reneward massacres the messengers sent to bring him back to the feast from which he had been excluded (ll. 3445–46).

This care to maintain the structural unity of the poem through its various revisions is seen most clearly in the echoes established, particularly in regard to eating and drinking, across the whole text (Frappier, 1955, p.197). The drunkenness of Tedbalt and Esturmi is recalled in the accusation of drunken debauchery with the pair of cowards that Willame hurls at his sister in Laon. Similarly the deflection of Lowis from his duty by his queen is mirrored at the end of the poem by Guiburc's re-establishing Willame's role as the good overlord, a role threatened by his earlier forgetfulness in excluding Reneward from the victory celebrations. Feasting, not only in the final meal which is the prelude to Reneward's formal baptism, also

---

[9] The implicit undermining of Willame's reputation in the passage in which Vivien recounts the victories in which he rescued his uncle from disaster is probably an interpolation by the redactor to whom we owe the 'Gui' episode. This may be deduced since it is only in Vivien's speech (*laisse* 55), in Girart's verbatim account of Vivien's message (*laisse* 82) and in l. 1439, in the 'Gui' episode, that he and Vivien are referred to as brothers.

provides unity here, since in contrast to Willame's rejection of his ragged saviour, Lowis invites the destitute Willame to his table and waits deferentially for him to finish eating before questioning him.

On a more symbolic level the drunkenness of the opening scene is contrasted with Vivien's thirst and its Christological overtones. These are accentuated by the vomiting which the hero's drinking from the salt water induces, so that his whole death can be seen as a progress from Gethsemane to Calvary. The motif returns in Gui's collapsing with hunger and thirst during the third battle, although his eating (too little) and drinking (too much) from the food abandoned by the pagans and so stimulating his heroic prowess may be less a parody of Vivien's passion than a whimsical inversion of the ineffectual inebriation of Tedbalt. Reneward suffers similar pangs of hunger in this poem (and it is significant that the motif is absent from *Aliscans*), but far from seeking to assuage his hunger he vows to make the pagans pay for it, and his evocation of it is a prelude to his rescuing the prisoners.

Reneward's journey to the ships none the less makes a link with Gui's visit to the site of the Saracens' 'picnic', which, like the feast indulged in by the ravenously hungry Girart (once, in Barcelona) and Willame (twice — once in Barcelona, once in Orange) unifies the song, and by constantly bringing the audience back to the same point (albeit with different characters present) eliminates linear, historical or narrative time and reinstitutes a cyclic time akin to the atemporality of lyric or traditional epic. A further counterpoint is established by the repeated 'heroic' feasting of Christian warriors, defined as mighty men of valour by the quantities of food they consume, who sink deeper and deeper into defeat, and the elegant, neo-pastoral of the victorious pagans' meals. The contrast is heightened by the increasing gloom of the feasts at Willame's capital, signalled by his refusal to eat at his own high table, and by the emptiness of the hall on the last occasion. The stalemate is broken by the arrival of Reneward, who, despite his association with the kitchen is not seen to eat until the final celebratory meal preceding his baptism. Indeed, on two occasions (ll. 2658–63 and 2674–83) he denies his affinity for the kitchen, and

brutally kills the head cook who has tarred him with that brush. If
he shares this element of asceticism with Vivien, he shares the motif
of drunkenness both with Gui and with Tedbalt and Esturmi.
Nostalgically evoking dinner-times accompanied by a good drink,
he immediately transforms that dream, as he does everything else,
into the obsessive need to destroy the pagans. When he is actually
drunk in the poem (ll. 2697–700 and 2856–58) it is against his will
and leads to the punishment of the malefactors who have demeaned
him. For all the brutal humour these scenes may contain they
foreshadow the joyous carnage of his role as heathen-slayer.[10]

The complexities of *La Chançun de Willame* in its final form
are thus not accidental, even though they are undoubtedly the work
of several hands.

4. *The Edition of the Text*

The text of the poem offered in this edition is a conservative one
based closely on the sole manuscript (British Library, Additional
38663). Since it is clear that the poem as it exists cannot in its
totality have existed in a Continental form (Bennett, 1987) there is
no question of repeating the extensively erudite, but ultimately
misguided reconstruction of Jeanne Wathelet-Willem (1975). Since
it is also impossible to divide some of the composite *laisses* of the
manuscript into individual uniformly mono-assonanced units, which
also appear in composite form in the edition by François Suard
(1991), the present edition reverts to Duncan McMillan's
presentation (1949–50), abolishing the subdivisions into 'a', 'b'
etc., which are a legacy of Wathelet-Willem's reconstruction.

Because the text shows every sign of having been reworked by
an Anglo-Norman redactor, and not merely 'degraded' by Anglo-
Norman scribes, I have not corrected any lines on the basis of
metrics alone. The manuscript's readings have been rejected only

---

[10] The notion of joyous carnage is propounded in the context of *Aliscans* by Nelly
Andrieux-Reix (1993, pp.9–30), but it applies even more accurately to the *Willame*, in
the later parts of *G1* as well as in *G2*, where feasting is more completely integrated into
the battle scenes.

where blatantly faulty syntax or vocabulary, or a similar copying error, have rendered the text meaningless. Even then every effort has been made to avoid corrections that are arbitrary or merely conjectural. Where it has been felt necessary to correct the manuscript, rejected readings are placed at the foot of the page, with the corrected text marked by a superscript '§'.

Abbreviations have been resolved following the normal conventions, and nasal consonants used following the practice of the scribe when words are written in full. The only diacritics used are the cedilla under 'c' before a back vowel and the acute accent to mark stressed 'e' in word final position, or when followed by an 's'. Contrary to the commonest practice I have extended this to monosyllables to distinguish homonyms from each other. However, I have nowhere used the diaeresis, since, in the current state of the text with the probable adoption of an accentual rather than a syllabic metre by the poem's Anglo-Norman revisor(s) (Bennett, 1987), it is impossible to tell with certainty or consistency where a hiatus is maintained and where it is resolved. Nevertheless, it is still possible to read most of the poem's lines as reasonably regular decasyllabics (albeit with a frequently irregular caesura), if the normal conventions on elision in French are applied in reading the text despite its insular orthography, and it is likely that the medieval reader would have made such adjustments of hiatus and elision as part of the 'realisation' of the text.

The other way in which I have broken with tradition in the presentation of the text is in resolving the abbreviation for the co-ordinating conjunction as 'et' rather than 'e', since the latter is wilfully archaising in its orthography, as the conventional sign used by the scribe consistently includes the bar indicating the presence of the 't'. Similarly, because, on the only two occasions on which it is written in full in the manuscript, the hero's name appears as 'Willame', that form is used throughout, although it clearly rhymes in 'è'. Since it is impossible now to say how any thirteenth-century reader of the poem would have realised phonetically the abbreviation 'Wille', I have left the name in the only form in which the manuscript gives it to us.

5. *The Translation of the Text*

The translation into modern English prose follows the text line by line. Its aim is to present a version comprehensible in itself, which reflects the stylistic mixture of the original (including the typical Old French inconsistency of tense usage), while enabling the reader who is not expert in Old French, but who wishes to follow the original, to equate the elements of the two versions. The aim is also to be reasonably idiomatic, avoiding undue modernism and undue archaism. Archaism is inevitable in dealing with terms referring to arms, armour, warfare, social custom and other points of civilisation of the twelfth and thirteenth centuries. A less 'archaeological' approach has been taken in rendering direct speech, which on many occasions breaks with the convention of stylised archaism inherent in the epic to descend to racy obscenity. This has posed a particular problem for rendering the oaths and curses which abound in the poem. Religious references have, on the whole been maintained, although it is no longer the custom of English speakers to swear by saints, or the faith. On the other hand reasonable modern equivalents have been sought for the ubiquitous 'lecchere' and 'glut' which are heaped with the monotonous regularity of thoughtless swearing, and with an intent ranging from the highly aggressive to the playful, on the heads of all and sundry.

Personal names have been left strictly as they are in the text, while geographic and ethnic names have been translated. The mixture of legend (or even myth) bordering at one extreme on fiction and on chronicled history at the other, with all the ideological prejudices which this implies, is, I feel, not far removed from the impact which the original would have had on medieval audiences, as cultural heroes from a misty past no longer dissociable from the poems celebrating them deal decisively with the bogeymen of twelfth- and thirteenth-century Western Europeans.

Bibliography of Works Cited

Adler, 1969: Alfred Adler, 'Guillaume, Vivien, et Rainouart: le souillé et le pur', *Romania*, 90, 1–13.

Andrieux-Reix, 1993: Nelly Andrieux-Reix, '*Grant fu l'estor, grant fu la joie*: formes et formules de la fête épique — le cas d'*Aliscans*', in *Mourir aux Aliscans: 'Aliscans' et la légende de Guillaume d'Orange*, ed. J. Dufournet (Paris, Champion), pp.9–30.

Bennett, 1977: P. E. Bennett, 'Further Reflections on the Luminosity of the *Chanson de Roland*', *Olifant*, 4, 3, 191–204.

——, 1984: Philip Bennett, 'The Storming of the Other World, the Enamoured Muslim Princess and the Evolution of the Legend of Guillaume d'Orange', in *Guillaume d'Orange and the chanson de geste*, ed. Wolfgang van Emden and Philip E. Bennett (Reading, Société Rencesvals British Branch), pp.1–14.

——, 1987: Philip E. Bennett, 'La *Chanson de Guillaume*, poème anglo-normand?', in *Au carrefour des routes d'Europe: la chanson de geste*, X^e congrès international de la Société Rencesvals pour l'étude des épopées romanes: Strasbourg 1985, Senefiance, 21 (Aix-en-Provence), pp.259–81.

Combarieu du Grès, 1993: Micheline de Combarieu du Grès, 'Les "nouveaux" chrétiens: Guibourc et Rainouart dans *Aliscans*', in *Mourir aux Aliscans: 'Aliscans' et la légende de Guillaume d'Orange*, ed. J. Dufournet (Paris, Champion), pp.55–78.

Ewert, 1967: *The Romance of Tristran by Beroul*, ed. A. Ewert (Oxford, Blackwell).

Fassò, 1995: *La Canzone di Guglielmo*, introduction, translation and notes by Andrea Fassò (Turin, Pratiche Editrice) [contains a reprint of the McMillan text].

Frappier, 1955: Jean Frappier, *Les Chansons de geste du cycle de Guillaume d'Orange, I: La Chanson de Guillaume, Aliscans, La Chevalerie Vivien* (Paris, SEDES).

――, 1968: Jean Frappier, 'Le thème de la lumière de la *Chanson de Roland* au *Roman de la Rose*', *Cahiers de l'Association Internationale des Etudes Françaises*, 20, 101–24.

Fritz, 1992: Chrétien de Troyes, *Erec et Enide*, ed. Jean-Marie Fritz, Lettres Gothiques (Paris, LGF).

Godefroy, 1937–38: *Dictionnaire de l'ancienne langue française...*, par Frédéric Godefroy, nouveau tirage (Paris, Librairie des Sciences et des Arts).

Jacques, 1979: *Aiquin, ou la conquête de la Bretagne par le roi Charlemagne*, ed. Francis Jacques (avec la collaboration de Madeleine Tyssens), Senefiance, 8 (Aix-en-Provence).

Kennedy, 1970: Elspeth Kennedy, 'The Scribe as Editor', in *Mélanges de langue et de littérature du Moyen Age et de la Renaissance offerts à Jean Frappier* (Geneva, Droz), pp.523–31.

Lepage, 1978: *Les Rédactions en vers du Couronnement de Louis*, ed. Yvan G. Lepage, TLF, 261 (Geneva, Droz).

Lejeune, 1960: Rita Lejeune, 'Le camouflage des détails essentiels dans la *Chanson de Guillaume*', *Cahiers de civilisation médiévale*, 3, 42–58.

McMillan, 1949–50: *La Chanson de Guillaume*, ed. Duncan McMillan, SATF (Paris, Picard).

――, 1978: *Le Charroi de Nîmes*, ed. Duncan McMillan (Paris, Klincksieck).

Pope, 1934: M. K. Pope, *From Latin to Modern French with Especial Consideration of Anglo-Norman* (Manchester University Press).

Price, 1975: *William, Count of Orange: Four Old French Epics*, ed. Glanville Price, Everyman's University Library (London, Dent).

Régnier, 1990: *Aliscans*, ed. Claude Régnier, CFMA, 110–111 (Paris, Champion).

Robertson, 1965: *La Chanson de Willame, a Critical Study* (Chapel Hill, University of North Carolina Press).

Suard, 1991: *La Chanson de Guillaume*, ed. François Suard , Classiques Garnier (Paris, Bordas).

——, 1993: François Suard, *La Chanson de geste*, Que sais-je?, 2808 (Paris, PUF).

Suchier, 1911: *La Chançun de Guillelme*, ed. Hermann Suchier (Halle, Niemeyer).

Wathelet-Willem, 1952: Jeanne Wathelet-Willem, '*La Chançun de Willame*. Le problème de l'unité du MS British Museum Add. 38663', *Le Moyen Age*, 58, 363–77.

——, 1967: Jeanne Wathelet-Willem, 'Quelle est l'origine du tinel de Rainouart?', *Boletín de la Real Academia de Buenas Letras de Barcelona*, 31, 355–64.

——, 1975: Jeanne Wathelet-Willem, *Recherches sur la Chanson de Guillaume, études accompagnées d'une édition* (Paris, Belles Lettres).

Zumthor, 1991: Paul Zumthor, *Toward a Medieval Poetics*, trans. Philip E. Bennett (Minneapolis, University of Minnesota Press).

1

(1a)   Plaist vus oir...*
de granz batailles et de forz esturs,   (1a)
de Deramed, uns reis sarazinurs,
cum il prist guere vers Lowis, nostre empereur,
mais dan Willame la prist vers lui forçur,
tant qu'il l'ocist§ en l'Archamp§ par grant onur?   5
Mais sovent se combati a la gent paienur,
si perdi de ses homes les meillurs
et sun nevou, dan Vivien le preuz,
pur qui il out tut tens al quor grant dolur.
Lunesdi al vespre: 10
oimas comence la chançun de Willame§ .

2

Reis Deramed il est issu de Cordres,
en halte mer en ad mise la flote;
a Munt Girunde§ en est venu par force:*
[en la tere] entred que si mal descunorted.   15
Les marchez gaste; les alués comence a prendre.

Will you hear...* about great battles and fierce struggles, about Deramed, a Saracen
king, how he went to war against Lowis, our emperor, but Lord Willame waged a fiercer
one against him, until he killed him at l'Archamp achieving great honour? Yet he fought
often against the pagan folk, and lost the best of his men and his nephew, Lord Vivien the
worthy, for whom he ever after had great sorrow in his heart. Monday at vespertide:
Straightway begins the Song of Willame.

King Deramed has sailed from Cordoba, he has set his fleet on the high seas; he has
launched an attack on Gerona:* he has moved inland causing great damage. He lays
waste the marches; he captures the freeholdings.

---

§ 5 quil ocist
§ 5 el larchamp
§ 11 d'Willame (the sign between *d* and *W* resembles a modern apostrophe with a tail
rising to the right)
§ 14 Amund girunde

Les vers corseinz porte par force del regne;
les bons chevalers en meine en chaenes.
Et en l'Archamp est hui fait cest damages.
Un chevaler est estoers de ces paens homes.   20
Cil le nuncie a Tedbalt de Burges.
Iloeques ert Tedbald a iceles hures;
li messagers le trovad veirement a Burges,
et Esturmi, sis niés, et dan Vivien, le cunte,
od els .vii. cent chevalers, de joefnes homes.   25
N'i out cil qui n'out halberc et broine.
Es vus le més, qui les noveles cunte.

3

Tedbald le cunte reperout de vespres,
et sun nevou, Esturmi, qui l'adestre;
et Vivien i fu, li bon niés Willame,   30
et od lui .vii.c. chevalers de sa tere.
Tedbald iert si ivre que plus n'i poet estre,
et Esturmi, sun nevou, que par le poig l'adestre.
Es vus le més§ qui cunte les noveles:
"Deu salt Tedbalt al repeirer de vespres!   35
De Deramed vus di dures noveles:
En l'Archamp est un mult dolente guere.

He strips the kingdom of its true holy relics; the brave knights he leads off in chains. This destruction is wrought today in l'Archamp. A knight has escaped from these pagan men. He brings news to Tedbalt of Bourges. Tedbalt was there at that time; the messenger truly found him in Bourges, and Esturmi, his nephew, and Lord Vivien, the count, in company of seven hundred knights, all young men. Not one was without a halberk or mail shirt Here is the messenger recounting his news.

Count Tedbald was returning from vespers, with his nephew, Esturmi, at his right hand; and Vivien was there too, Willame's good nephew, in his company seven hundred knights from his land. Tedbald was so drunk he could never be more so, and Esturmi, his nephew, who holds his right hand. Here is the messenger recounting his news: "God save Tedbalt as he returns from vespers! I have harsh news to tell you of Deramed: there is a very grievous war at l'Archamp.

---

§ 34 les mes

4

"Reis Deramed est issu de Cordres;
(1b) en halte mer en ad mise sa flote.
A Munt Girunde en est venu par force;   40
en vostre tere est, que si mal desconorted§.
Les marchez guaste et les aluez vait prendre;
les veirs cors seinz trait par force del regne;
tes chevalers en meine en chaenes.
Pense, Tebalt, que paens nes ameinent!"   45

5

"Franche meisné," dist Tebalt, "que feruns?"
Dist li messages: "Ja§ nus i combatuns!"
Tedbalt demande: "Que feruns, sire Vivien?"
Dist li bers: "Nus ne frum el que ben!
Sire Tedbalt," dist Vivien li ber,   50
"vus estes cunte, et si estes mult honuré
des meillurs§ homes de rivage de mer.
Si m'en creez, ne serras ja blamé.
Pren tes messages, fai tes amis mander;
n'obliez mie Willame al cur niés,   55
sages hom est mult en bataille champel;

"King Deramed has sailed from Cordoba; he has set his fleet on the high seas. He has
launched an attack on Gerona; he is in your land, which he is destroying. He is laying
waste the marches and capturing the freeholdings; he is stripping the kingdom of its true
holy relics; he is leading off your knights in chains. Take thought, Tebalt, lest the pagans
take them away!"

"Noble household," said Tebalt, "what shall we do?" Said the messenger: "We are
already fighting out there!" Tedbalt asks: "What shall we do, Lord Vivien?" Said the
noble warrior: "We shall do only what is right! Lord Tedbalt," said Vivien the brave,
"you are a count, and indeed greatly honoured by the best men on the seacoast. If you
take my advice, you will never be criticised. Take your messengers, send for your kin and
allies; do not forget Willame Hooknose, he has great experience of battlefields;

---

§ 41 desonorted
§ 47 ias
§ 52 del meillurs

il la set ben maintenir et garder.
S'il vient, nus veintrums Deramed."

6

"Nel te penser, Tedbalt," ço dist Esturmi.
"En ceste terre, al regne Lowys,   60
u que arivent paen u Arabit*   (60a)
si mandent Willame le marchis.
Si de tes homes i meines tu§ vint mil,
vienge Willame, et des suens n'i ait que cinc,
treis u quatre, que vienge a eschari,
tu te combates et venques Arabiz,   65
si dist hom ço, que dan Willame le fist.
Qui ques prenge, suens est tote voie le pris!
Cumbatum, sire, sis veintrum; jo te plevis.
Al pris Willame te poez faire tenir!"
"Franche meisné," dist Vivien, "merci!   70
Od poi compaignie ne veintrum pas Arabiz.
Mandum nus, seignurs, pur Willame le marchis.
Sages hom est pur bataille tenir.
S'il i vient, nus veintrum Arabiz."
Et dist Esturmi: "Malveis conseil ad ici!   75
Estrange gent tant le loent tut dis,
et noz homes fait tuz tenir a vils!"

he knows well how to stand and fight. If he comes, we shall conquer Deramed."

"Don't even think of it, Tedbalt," said Esturmi. "In this land, Lowys's kingdom,
wherever pagans or Arabs arrive,* people send for Willame the Marquis. If you lead
twenty thousand of your men to the field, should Willame come with only five of his, or
three or four, let him come alone, and should you fight and conquer the Arabs, men will
still say that Lord Willame did it. Whoever defeats them, he invariably gets the glory! Let
us fight, my lord, and we shall conquer them; that I promise. You can have your
reputation held equal to Willame's!" "Noble household," said Vivien, "for pity's sake!
With our small band we shall not conquer the Arabs. Let us send, my lords, for Willame
the Marquis. He is experienced in fighting battles. If he comes we shall conquer the
Arabs." Said Esturmi: "This is bad advice! Foreigners are always praising him and he
causes our men all to be held worthless!"

---

§ 62 meinent

Respunt Tedbalt: "Unques pur el nel dist;
mais a la bataille§ n'ose il pas venir!"

7

Dist Vivien: "Ore avez vus mesdit!   80
(1c) Car il nen est nez, ne de sa mere vis,
de ça la mer, ne de la la Rin,
n'en la crestienté, n'en terre§ Arabiz,
mielz de mei ose grant bataille tenir,
fors sul Willame al curt niés le marchis.*   85
Il est mis uncles; vers li ne m'en atis."
Lunsdi al vespre:
"Jo ne met mie mon pris al pris Willame§!"

8

Dunt dist Tedbalt: "Aportez mei le vin!
Si me donez; si beverai a Esturmi!   90
Ainz demain prime requerrum Arrabiz;
de set liwes en orrat l'em les criz,
hanstes freindre et forz escuz croissir!"
Li botillers lur aporta le vin;
but ent Tedbalt, sin donad a Esturmi.   95
Et Vivien s'en alad a sun ostel dormir.

Tedbalt replies: "He said it for only one reason: he does not dare to come to battle!"

Said Vivien: "That was slander!" The man has not been born or come alive out of his mother, this side of the sea or beyond the Rhine, in Christendom or Arab lands, more daring than I on a battlefield, excepting only Willame Hooknose the Marquis.* He is my uncle; I don't compare myself with him." Monday at verspertide: "I do not set my worth at Willame's worth!"

Then said Tedbalt: "Bring me wine! Give me some; I'll drink with Esturmi! Before prime tomorrow we shall attack the Arabs; From that meeting you will hear the shouts go up seven leagues round, spear shafts breaking, stout shields clashing!" The butler brought them wine; Tedbalt drank and gave some to Esturmi. And Vivien went to his lodging to sleep.

§ 79 batataille
§ 85 nentre
§ 88 Jo ne met mie a pris Wlle

9

Dunc s'asemblerent les homes de lur terre;
quant vint a l'albe, dis mil sunt od helmes.
Par mein levad Tedbalt a unes estres,
devers§ le vent ovrit une fenestre.   100
Mirat le ciel; ne pot mirer la terre,
vit la coverte de broines et de helmes.
....§ *
"Deus," dist Tedbalt, "iço que pot estre!

10

"Seignurs, frans homes, merci, pur amur Dé!   105
Dis et uit anz ad ja, et si sunt tuz passez
que primes oi a bailler ceste cunté,
unc puis ne vi tanz chevalers armez,
que ne seussent quele part turner.
Assaldrez vus ne chastel ne cité?   110
Dolent poent estre que vus avez defié
et dolentes lé marchez que vus devez gaster!"
Dist Vivien: "Cest plaid soi jo assez!
Tedbalt fu ivre erseir de sun vin cler;
or est tut sage, quant ad dormi assez.   115
Ore atendrum nus Willame al curb niés!"

Then the men from their lands gathered; when dawn came, they were ten thousand equipped with helmets. In the morning Tedbalt arose in his apartments; he opened a window to windward. He looked at the sky; he could not look at the ground. He saw it was covered with mail shirts and helmets. ... * "God," said Tedbalt, "what can this be!

"My lords, noble men, mercy, for love of God! Eighteen years are already gone and passed since I first took charge of this county, never since that day have I seen under arms so many knights, that they did not know which way to turn! Will you attack either a castle or a citadel? Whoever you have challenged may well grieve, and grievous the state of the marches you are sent to lay waste!" Said Vivien: "I've heard talk like this before! Last evening Tedbalt was drunk on his bright wine; now that he's had a good sleep, he's sobered up. Now we shall wait for Willame Hooknose!"

---

§ 100 de deuers
§ 103 et de sarazins la pute gent adverse

Dunc out cil hunte, qui al seir out parlez,
et cil greignur qui se furent vanté.

11

Ço dist Vivien, le chevaler oneste:
"Cest plaid soi jo. Erseir, par ma teste, 120
Tedbalt ert ivre al repeirer de vespres.
(1d) Ore ad assez dormi: nus atendrum Willames."
Este vus errant Esturmi par la presse;
vint a Tebalt, sil prist par la main destre:
"Ber, ne te membre del repeirer de vespres, 125
de Deramed, et de la dure novele?"
Respunt Tedbalt: "Ai jo mandé Willame?"
"Nenil, bels sire, car il ne puet a tens estre.

12

"Par mi le col t'en oras herseir dehé
si tu mandoues Willame al curb niés." 130
Respunt Tedbalt: "Ore leissum dunc ester!"
Armes demande; l'em li vait aporter.
Dunc li vestent une broine mult bele et cler,
et un vert healme li lacent en la teste.
Dunc ceint s'espee, le brant burni vers terre, 135

Then he was ashamed, who had spoken out the night before, and those even more ashamed who had uttered boasts.

Said Vivien, the honourable knight: "I've heard this before. Last night, by my head, Tedbalt was drunk when he came out of vespers. Now he's had a good sleep, we shall wait for Willame." Here comes Esturmi through the crowd; he came up to Tedbalt and took him by the right hand: "Noble man, do you not remember about coming back from vespers, about Deramed and the harsh news?" Tedbalt replies: "Did I send for Willame?" "Certainly not, my lord, since he couldn't be here in time.

"Last night you would have had God's curse on your neck rather than send for Willame Hooknose." Tedbalt replies: "Let him be then!" He asks for arms; they are brought to him. Then they put on him a most beautiful mail shirt, and lace a green helmet on his head. Then he straps on his sword, its burnished blade pointing to earth,

et une grant targe tint par la manuele[§] ;
espé tranchant out en sa main destre,
et blanche enseigne, li lange[§] tresque a terre.
Dunc li ameinent un cheval de Chastele;
dunc munte Tidbalt par sun estriu senestre,   140
si en est issu par une des posternes;
al dos le siwent .x.m. homes od helmes:
en l'Archamp vont rei Deramed requere.
Dunc s'en issid Tedbalt de sa bone cité,
al dos le siwent .x.m. homes armez: 145
en l'Archamp requistrent le paien Deramed;
malveis seignur orent a els guier[§].
Lunsdi al vespre;
En l'Archamp vindrent desur mer a destre.

13

Tedbalt garde es haltes eigues,   150
de vint mil niefs i ad veu les vernes.
Ço dist Tedbalt: "Or vei jo lur herberges."
Dist Vivien: "No sunt, car ne poent estre;
navries* est qui aprisme vers terre.
Se cil sunt fors, il purprendrunt herberge."   155

and he took hold of a great round shield by its straps; in his right hand he had a sharp spear, and a white banner, its fine white streamers draping to the ground. Then they bring him a Castilian horse; Tedbalt mounts from the left stirrup and rides out through one of the postern gates; ten thousand men equipped with helmets follow behind him: they go to give battle to King Deramed at l'Archamp. Then Tedbalt left his good citadel, ten thousand armed men follow behind him; they gave battle to the pagan Deramed at l'Archamp; they had an evil lord to guide them. Monday at verspertide: They came to l'Archamp by the sea with the field on their right.

Tedbalt looks out to the open waters; he saw the spars of twenty thousand ships. Said Tedbalt: "Now I can see their camp." Said Vivien: "No it's not; those things can't be a camp; it's a fleet approaching land.* After disembarking they'll pitch camp."

[§] 136 par manuele
[§] 138 li lancent
[§] 147 les out a Guier

Dunc vint avant si choisid les festes,
de cinc cent triefs les pignuns et les verges§ .
Dist Vivien: "Ço poent il ben estre!"
Dist Tedbalt, de Berri li maistres:
"Vivien, ber, car muntez en cele tertre,   160
si surveez iceste gent adverse,
cumben il unt homes en mer et en terre."
(2a)   Dist Vivien: "Nel me devez ja requere!
Encuntreval dei bas porter mun healme*
desi qu'al champ u fiere od le poig destre,   165
car si m'aprist li miens seignurs Willame.
Ja, si Deu plaist, ne surverrai herberge!

14

"Sire Tedbalt," dist Vivien le ber,
"Tu es cunte, et ço mult honuré,
des meillurs homes de rivage de mer.   170
Munte le tertre; tu deis ben esgarder
cum il unt homes en terre et en mer.
Se tant as homes que tu i puisses fier,
chevalche encuntre, si va od els juster:
ben les veintrum solunc la merci Deu.   175

Then he moved forward and picked out the ridge poles of five hundred tents with their pennants and flagpoles. Said Vivien: "Those could well be it!" Said Tedbalt, master of Berry: "Noble Vivien, just ride up that hill and reconnoitre the enemy, assess their numbers on sea and land." Said Vivien: "You should not ever ask me that! I must keep my helm low in the valley* until on the battlefield I strike with my right hand, that is what my lord Willame taught me. By God's grace I shall never reconnoitre a camp!"

"Lord Tedbalt," said the brave warrior Vivien, "You are a count, and a highly honoured one, among the best men on the seacoast. Ride up the hill; you are the one to look to see how many men they have on land and sea. If you have enough men to trust to their strength, ride against them, and come to grips with them; by God's mercy we shall defeat them.

---

§ 157 les herberges

Et si poi as homes pur bataille champel,
veez ci un val: fai les tuens assembler,
et pren tes messages, fai tes amis mander.
N'oblie§ mie Willame al curb niés,
sages hom est mult en bataille champel,   180
si la seet ben maintenir et gaber.
S'il vient, nus veintrum Deramed."
Respunt Tedbalt: "Gent conseil m'as doné."
Le cheval broche, si ad le tertre munté.
Garde Tedbalt vers la lasse de mer,   185
vit la coverte de barges et de nefs,
et de salandres et granz eschiez ferrez.
Mire le ciel, ne pot terre esgarder;
de la pour s'en est tut oblié,
aval devalad del tertre u il ert munté.   190
Vint as Franceis, si lur ad tut cunté.

15

"Franche meisné, que purrum nus devenir?
Cuntre un des noz i ad§ ben des lur mil!
Ki ore ne s'en fuit, tost purrad mort gisir.
Alum nus ent tost pur noz vies garir.   195

And if you've too few men for a pitched battle, here is a valley; assemble your troops in it, find a messenger, send for your kin and allies. Don't forget Willame Hooknose, he has great experience of battlefields, he knows how to stand and fight and give a warrior's boast. If he comes, we'll defeat Deramed." Tedbalt replies: "That is noble advice." He set spurs to his horse and rode up the hill. Tedbalt looked out to the shoreline, saw it covered with barks and ships, with transports and great iron-bound warships. He looked at the sky, he could not look at the ground; he quite forgot himself in his fear, riding back to the bottom of the hill he had climbed. He came to the French and told them all he had seen.

"Noble household, what will become of us? For every man of ours, they have a good thousand! Anyone who doesn't flee may quickly be lying dead. Let's leave here fast to save our lives.

§ 179 n i oblit
§ 193 Cuntre un des noz: ad (the scribe inserts a colon after *noz*)

16

"Vivien, ber, ten tei lunc ceste roche;
parmi cest val nus cundui nostre force
que ne te veit li sarazine flote,
si enverrai pur Willame, qui combatera s'il ose."
Lunsdi al vespre: 200
"Ja ne combaterai sanz Willame."

17

Dist Vivien: "Malveis conseil ad ci!
Tu les as veuz, et il tei altresi.
(2b) Si tu t'en vas, ço ert tut del fuir:
crestienté en ert tut dis plus vils   205
et paenisme en ert plus esbaldi§.
Combat t'en, ber! Sis veinteruns jol te plevis!
Al pris Willame te deis faire tenir!
Des herseir vespre le cunte en aatis."
Lunsdi al vespre: 210
"Ben te deis faire tenir al pris Willame!"

18

Cent mille furent de la gent Deramed
as esneckes et as dromunz de mer

"Noble Vivien, keep close to this cliff; lead our army into this valley for us so that the
Saracen fleet doesn't see you, and I shall send for Willame, who will fight if he dares."
Monday at verspertide: "I will never fight without Willame."

Said Vivien: "This is evil advice! You have seen them, and equally they have seen you. If
you leave now, you will merely be fleeing: Christendom will be forever debased by it and
pagandom have greater cause to rejoice. Stand and fight, noble baron! We'll defeat them,
I promise! You must rival Willame in reputation! Just yesterday evening you were
comparing yourself to the count." Monday at vespertide: "You must rival Willame in
reputation!"

Deramed's folk numbered a hundred thousand with longships and seagoing warships,

---

§ 206 le plus esbaldi

et Tedbalt virent[§] sus al tertre ester:
il le conurent al grant escu bocler.   215
Dunc sorent ben[§] que el val en out remis
de ses homes mulz et de ses amis.

19

Lunsdi al vespre:
Les Sarazins de Saraguce[§] terre
cent mile furent de la pute geste.   220
Il n'i out celui de blanc halberc ne se veste
et de Saraguce verz healmes en lur testes,
d'or les fruntels et les flurs et les esses,
espees ceintes, les branz burniz vers terre.
Les bons escuz tindrent as manueles   225
espees tranchanz et darz as poinz destres,
chevals coranz d'Arabe suz lur seles.
Cil issirent fors al sablun et en la gravele
si purpristrent defors la certeine terre.
Cil mourent al cunte Tedbalt grant guere;   230
pur ço oirent doleruse novele.

and they saw Tedbalt standing on top of the hill: they knew him by his great buckler.
Then they knew well that he had left in the valley many of his men, his kin and allies.

Monday at verspertide: The Saracens from the land of Saragossa numbered a hundred
thousand of the foul race. Not one but was wearing a white halberk and green Saragossan
helmets on their heads, with frontals, damascening and bands of gold; at their belts were
swords with burnished blades pointing to earth. They held their good shields by the grips,
sharp spears and pointed javelins in their right hands, fast running Arab horses under
their saddles. They disembarked on the gravelly beach and took up forward positions on
the dry land. They launched a mighty war against Count Tedbalt; people heard grim
news about it.

[§] 214 e virent
[§] 216 dunc sorent be
[§] 219 sarag(c)uee - *c* expunctuated

20

Clers fu li jurz et bels li matins;
li soleil raed, si est li jurz esclariz.
Paen devalent parmi un broilled antif:
par unt qu'il passent tote la terre fremist.   235
Des dur healmes qu'il unt a or sartid
tres lur espalles tut li bois en reflambist.
Qui dunc les veist esleisser et saillir
de durs vassals li peust sovenir.
Idunc les mustrat Vivien a Esturmi.   240

21

"Esturmi frere, jo vei paens venant.
Lé lur chevals par sunt si coranz:
pur .xv. liwes tuz jurz aler brochanz,
pur plus cure, ja ne lur batera flanc.
(2c)   Aincui morrunt li cuart en l'Archamp.   245
Ore apresment li fueur de devant;
ja ne garrat li petit pur le grant,
nem pot garir le pere sun enfant.
Fium nus en Deu le tut poant,

The day was bright and the morning fine; the sun shone and the daylight grew brighter. The pagans went down through an ancient thicket: wherever they pass the whole ground shakes. From the hard helmets they wear studded with gold the whole wood blazed with light behind their shoulders. Whoever saw them galloping and prancing was put in mind of tough warriors. Then Vivien pointed them out to Esturmi.

"Esturmi, my brother, I can see pagans approaching. Their horses are extremely fast at the gallop: doing fifteen leagues a day under the spur, even further at the gallop won't make them pant. Today those who are cowards will die on l'Archamp. The scouts are getting very near; the little man will never be saved by the great, the father cannot save his child. Let us trust in God Almighty,

car il est mieldre que tut li mescreant.   250
Cumbatum nus si veintrum ben le champ!"

22

Dunc dist Tedbalt: "Qu'en loez, sire Vivien?"
"De la bataille! Car ore vienge§ ben!"
Aprof demande: "Qu'en loez, Esturmi?"
"Que chascuns penst de sa vie garir!   255
Qui ore ne s'en fuit tost i puet mort gisir:
alum nus ent pur noz vies garir!"
Dist Vivien: "Ore oi parler mastin!"
Respunt Tedbalt: "Ainz est pres de mun lin§,
ne volt enquere dunt mun cors seit honi,   260
ne enginné, ne malement bailli."

23

"Esturmi niés, derump cest gunfanun,
ke en fuiant ne nus conuisse l'um;
car a l'enseigne trarrunt paen felun."
Et dist Esturmi: "A la Deu beneiçun!"   265
Encontremunt li gluz presenta sa hanste
sur sun arçun devant mist la lance,

for He overmatches all these miscreants. Let's stand and fight, and the field will be ours!"

Then said Tedbalt: "What is your advice, Lord Vivien?" "To battle! May it start soon!" Then he asks: "What is your advice, Esturmi?" "That every man looks to save his own life! Anyone not fleeing now may quickly be lying dead: let's leave this place, to save our lives!" Said Vivien: "Now I hear a cur speaking!" Tedbalt replies: "No – he is my close kin, he wouldn't seek to have me shamed, or tricked, or brought to ruin."

"Esturmi, my nephew, tear up this pennant, so that no one can recognise us as we flee; you know these filthy pagans will make for the standard." And Esturmi said: "With God's blessing!" The craven swine turned his spear-shaft skywards, placed the lance-head on the saddle-bow in front of him,

---

§ 253 car ore ia vien ben
§ 259 ainz pres de mun lin

a ses dous poinz derump l'enseigne blanche;
puis la folad enz el fanc a ses pez.

24

Tedbalt le cunte§ teneit un grant espé.   270
Le resteot turnad contremunt vers le ciel,
et mist en le fer sur l'arçun detrés;
runt l'enseigne del hanste de pomer,
puis la fulat enz al fanc a ses pez.
"Mielz voil, enseigne, que flambe te arde del ciel   275
qu'en bataille me reconuissent§ paen."
"Graimes§ noveles!" en dist li quons Vivien.
"En champ nus faillent nostre gunfanuner."

25

"Franche meisné, que purrums devenir?
En champ nus sunt nostre gunfanun failli:*   280
laissé nus unt Tedbalt et Esturmi.
Veez paens, qui mult sunt pres d'ici!
Quant li nostre home i sunt u cinc u dis
et li paen i sunt u cent u mil,
dunc n'avrum nus qui nus puisse tenir,   285

with his two hands he tore away the white standard; then he trampled it in the mire at his feet.

Count Tedbalt was holding a great spear. He turned its hand-guard to the sky, and placed its iron tip behind his saddle-bow; he tears away the standard from the apple-wood shaft, then trampled it into the mire at his feet. "I prefer, my standard, that thunderbolts should burn you than that pagans should recognise me in battle." "Grim news!" retorted Count Vivien. "On the field of battle our standard-bearers desert us."

"Noble household, what shall become of us? On the battlefield our standard-bearers have deserted us:* Tedbalt and Esturmi have abandoned us. You can see the pagans are very close by. For every five or ten of our men the pagans have a hundred or a thousand, and then we've no one to hold us together on the field,

---

§ 270 Tedbalt cunte
§ 276 roconuissent
§ 277 Gaimes

(2d)   ne tel enseigne u puissum revertir.
        Genz sanz seignur sunt malement bailli.
        Alez vus ent, francs chevalers gentilz,
        car jo ne puis endurer ne suffrir
        tant gentil home seient a tort bailli.   290
        Jo me rendrai al dolerus peril,
        N'en turnerai, car a Deu l'ai pramis
        que ja ne fuierai pur pour de morir."
        Franceis respundent – or oez qu'il li unt dit:

26

        "Vivien sire, ja es tu de icel lin: 295
        en grant bataille nus deis ben maintenir.
        Ja fustes fiz Boeve Cornebut al marchis,*
        nez de la fille al bon cunte Aimeris,
        nefs Willame al curb niés le marchis:
        en grant bataille nus deis ben maintenir."   300
        "Veire, seignurs, de Deu cinc cenz merciz!
        Mais d'une chose i ad grant cuntredit:
        Vus n'estes mens, ne jo vostre sire ne devinc.
        Sanz tuz parjures me purrez guerpir."
        Et cil respunent tuz a un cri: 305
        "Tais, ber, nel dire! Ja t'averum plevi
        en cele lei que Deus en terre mist

no proper standard to rally round. People without a lord are in a sorry plight. Go your way, free and noble knights, for I cannot endure or suffer so many noble men to be brought low. I shall go into the grievous peril, I shall not turn back, for I have promised God that I shall never flee for fear of death." The French reply — just hear what they said to him:

"Lord Vivien, now you belong to that clan: you must hold us together in the great battle. Indeed you were Marquis Boeve Hornchest's son*, borne by good Count Aimeri's daughter, nephew of Marquis Willame Hooknose: you must hold us together in the great battle." "Indeed, my lords, five hundred fold thanks in the name of God! But there is one important objection: You're not my vassals, nor did I ever become your overlord. You can leave me here without breaking any oath." With one shout of acclamation they all reply: "Silence, noble warrior, do not say so! We've already promised you, by the Testament God set on earth

a ses apostles quant entr'els descendit,
ne te faudrum tant cum tu serras vifs!"

27

"Et jo rafi vus de Deu le rei fort,   310
et en cel esperit qu'il out en sun cors
pur pecchurs quant il suffri la mort,
ne vus faldrai pur destresce de mun cors."
A icest mot dunc mist s'enseigne fors.
Dunc met sa main en sa chalce vermeille,   315
si traist fors un enseigne de paille.
A treis clous d'or la fermat en la lance;
od le braz destre en ad brandie la hanste,
desi qu'as poinz l'en batirent les langes§.
Point le cheval – il ne pot muer ne saille§ –   320
et fiert un paen sur sa doble targe,
tute li fent de l'un ur desqu'al altre,
et trenchat le braz qui li sist en l'enarme;
colpe le piz et trenchad lui la coraille,
parmi l'eschine sun grant espee li passe: 325
tut estendu l'abat mort en la place.
(3a)   Crie: "Munjoie!" Ço fu l'enseigne Charle.

with his apostles when He came down among them, we shall not fail you as long as you
may live!"

"In turn I vow to you by God, the mighty king, and by the spirit He embodied when He
suffered death for sinners, I shall not fail you however hard-pressed my person." So
saying he set forth his standard. Then he put his hand into his scarlet leggings and drew
out a silken standard. With three gold nails he fixed it to his lance; with his right arm he
brandished the shaft, the pennant's fine streamers flap around his fist. He sets spurs to his
horse (it can't help leaping in the air) and strikes a pagan on his cross-braced round
shield, splits it from rim to rim, and cut off the arm as it sat in the strap; he cuts open his
chest and cuts through his entrails, thrusts his great spear right through his spine: he lays
him out dead on the battle ground. He shouts: "Munjoie!", which was Charles's war cry.

---

§ 319 lances
§ 320 failli

28

Si cum li ors s'esmere fors de l'argent,
si s'en eslistrent tote la bone gent.
Li couart s'en vont od Tedbalt fuiant;   330
od Vivien remistrent tuit li chevaler vaillant.
Al chef devant fierent communalment.
Si cum li ors fors de l'argent s'en turne,
si s'en eslistrent tut li gentil home.
Premerement si ferirent en la pointe   335
communalment ensemble li prodome,
le plus hardi n'i solt l'em conuistre.
As premerains colps li quons Tedbald s'en turne;
vait s'en fuiant a Burges tote la rute,
un grant chemin u quatre veies furchent.   340
Quatre larruns i pendirent bouche a boche.
Bas ert le fest, curtes erent les furches;
li chevals tired, par desuz§ l'emporte ultre.
Li uns des penduz li hurte lunc la boche;
vit le Tedbalt sin out doel et vergoigne,   345
de la pour en ordead sa hulce.
Et cum il senti que conchie fu tote,
dunc leve la quisse si la parbute ultre.
Girard apele quil siwi en la rute:

As in purifying heat gold separates from silver all the worthy folk form a group apart.
The cowards take flight with Tedbalt; with Vivien remain all the valiant knights. The
front lines clash in general battle. As gold will not mix with silver, all the noble men
formed a group apart. First off, where the armies came together all the men of valour
strike with a general will, you could not pick out who was bravest. At the very first blows
Tedbalt leaves the field; he rushes in headlong flight back to Bourges, along a broad road
to where four ways cross. Four thieves were hanging there mouth to mouth. The beam
was low, the gibbet short; his horse pulling hard carried him through it. One of the
hanged men hit him right across the mouth; Tedbalt saw it and felt grief and shame, from
fear he dirtied his saddlecloth. And when he felt that it was covered in shit he lifted his leg
and threw it away. He called out to Girard who was following him in the throng:

---

§ 343 par dedesuz

"Ami Girard, car pernez cele hulce! 350
Or i ad bon, et peres precioses:
cent livres en purrez prendre a Burges."
Et Girard li respundi encontre:
"Et jo que fereie, quant conchie est tote?

29

Ço dist Girard, le vaillant meschin: 355
"Sire Tedbalt, atendez mei un petit;
si dirrez tant al regne de Berri,
jo sui remis§ et tu t'en es fui!
Nen di que ja m'en veies vif,
et jo voil socure Vivien le hardi: 360
mis parenz est, si m'en est petit pris.
Et jo ai tresor parfunt en terre mis,
si vus dirrai u l'aveir serra pris
que aprés ma mort n'en creisse nul estrif."

30

La fist Tedbalt une folie pesme, 365
quant pur Girard retirad andous ses resnes;
quant cil l'ateint del poig al col le dresce,
(3b) de l'altre part le botat de sa sele:
desi qu'as laz l'en ferid le healme en terre.

"Girard, my friend, do take that saddlecloth! It is worked with fine gold and precious stones: You'll get a hundred pounds for it in Bourges." And Girard retorted: "What would I do with it, when it's covered in shit?"

Said Girard, the valiant youth: "Lord Tedbalt, just wait for me; You'll tell them in your land of Berry I stayed behind when you fled! I don't say you'll ever see me alive again, and I want to bring help to Vivien the brave: he's related to me, so that's little to my credit. Anyway, I've a treasure buried deep in the earth, and I'll tell you where the goods will be found so that there'll be1 no squabbles after my death."

Tedbalt committed a grave act of folly, when he drew in both reins at Girard's bidding: when he drew level he grabbed him by the collar and thrust him away from him out of the saddle: his helmet sunk in the ground up to the chin straps.

§ 358 Qui io sui remis

Puis tendit sa main juste la Tedbalt gule   370
si li toli sa grant targe duble.
D'or fu urlé envirun a desmesure;
de l'or de Arabe out en mi le bocle.
Cil Vivien la toli a un Hungre
en la bataille as prez de Girunde   375
quant il ocist le paen Alderufe
et decolad les fiz Burel tuz duze.
Al rei tolid cele grant targe duble,
si la donad a dan Willame, sun uncle,
et il la donad a Tedbalt, le cuard cunte: 380
uncore hui l'averad mult prozdome a la gule.
Le halberc li tolit, qui ert fort et duble,
et la bone espee trenchante jusqu'a la mure.

31

Gerard s'adube des armes al chemin;
le runcin laisset, al bon cheval s'asist.   385
Et Tedbalt se redresce cum home esturdi,
devant li garde, si choisist le runcin,
prent sei a l'estriu, entre les arçuns s'asist;
quant fu munté, menbré fut del fuir.
Devant sei garde§, si vit un grant paleiz,   390

Then he stretched out his hand to Tedbalt's throat and took from him his great cross-braced round shield. Its rim was bound in a massive weight of gold; there was Arab gold at the core of its boss. Now our Vivien took it from a Hungarian in the battle in the meadows of Gerona when he killed the pagan Alderufe and decapitated all twelve of Burel's sons. He took that great cross-braced round shield from the king and gave it to Lord Willame, his uncle, and he gave it to Tedbalt, the coward count: today once more a man of great worth will have it at his throat. He took off his halberk, which was strong and double linked, and his good sword, sharp to the tip.

Gerard equipped himself with these arms in the roadway; he abandoned his packhorse and sat on the war-horse. Tedbalt stood up in a daze, he looked about and saw the packhorse, he gets hold of the stirrup and sits in the saddle; when he was mounted, his first thought was flight. He looked ahead and saw a great fence,

---

§ 390 dedeuant se garde

fort fu la§ reille, qu'il ne pot pel tolir,
et tant fu halt qu'il nel pout tressaillir.
Desuz al val n'osad Tedbalt venchir
pur Sarazins dunt il ad oi les criz;
desus al tertre vit un fuc de brebiz.   395
Parmi la herde l'en avint a fuir:
en sun estriu se fert un motun gris.

32

En sun estriu se fiert un gris motun.
Tant le turnad et les vals et les munz,
quant Tedbalt vint a Burges al punt,   400
n'out a l'estriu quel chef del motun.
Une tel preie ne portad mes gentilz hom.
Lunsdi al vespre:
li povres n'i eust tant a perdre!*

33

Ore vus dirrai de Girard le meschin.   405
Cum il returnad dreitement sun chemin,
devant li garde, si choisist Esturmi.
Sun bon cheval aveit si mesbailli
(3c) ço ne volt§ gent que unques home n'i mist;
grant ignelesce en volt traire Esturmi.   410

the railings were too stout for him to remove a single stake and it was so high that he
could not jump it. Tedbalt did not dare turn down into the valley on account of the
Saracens, whose shouts he heard; on top of the hill he saw a flock of sheep. By chance he
fled through the thick of them: a grey sheep got stuck in his stirrup.

A grey sheep got stuck in his stirrup. He dragged it about so far over hill and valley, that
when Tedbalt came to the bridge at Bourges only the sheep's head was left in his stirrup.
Such booty a noble man never carried off before or since. Monday at vespertide: the poor
man could not afford to lose it!*

Now I shall tell you about the lad, Girard. as he rode straight back down the road he
looked ahead and noticed Esturmi. He had so ruined his fine horse that whatever anyone
did to it made no difference; Esturmi wanted to force it to a gallop.

§ 391a
§ 409 co en uolt

Veit le Girard, si l'ad a raisun mis:
"Ço que pot estre, chevaler Esturmi?"
Icil respunt: "Menbre tei§ del fuir!"
"Turnez arere, pensez del renvair:
si ore ne returnes, tost i purras mort gisir!"   415
"Nu frai ja!" ço li dist Esturmi.
Ço dist Girard: "Vus n'en irrez issi!"
Le cheval broche, vassalment le requist.
L'escu li fruisse et le halberc li rumpi,
et treis des costes en sun cors li malmist;   420
pleine sa hanste del cheval l'abati.
Quant l'out a terre, un curteis mot li ad dit:
"Ultre, lechere! Pris as mortel hunte!
Ne t'avanteras ja a Tedbalt, tun uncle,
si tu t'en fuies, n'i remeint prodome.   425
N'aatiras§ ja Willame le cunte,
ne Vivien sun neveu, ne nul altre prodome."
Lunsdi al vespre:
"N'aatiras§ Vivien ne Willame!"

34

Girard s'en vait cum plus tost pout.   430
Gente out la targe et dedenz et defors;

Girard saw him and spoke to him: "What's up, Sir Esturmi?" He replies: "Just
concentrate on fleeing!" "Turn back, think about attacking: if you don't turn back, you
could quickly be lying dead!" "No I shall not!" said Esturmi. Said Girard: "You won't
get away like that!" He spurred his horse; he closed with him like a true warrior. He
splits his shield and tears open his halberk, and broke three ribs in his body; with the full
force of his lance he unhorses him. When he had him on the ground, he exchanged a
pleasantry with him: "You're done, you ragtag! You're shamed for life! You'll never
boast to your uncle, Tedbalt, that if you flee no man of worth stays on the field. You'll
never compare yourself to Count Willame, nor to Vivien, his nephew, nor to any other
man of worth." Monday at vespertide: "You'll not pretend you're the equal of Vivien or
Willame!"

Girard moves on as quickly as he may. Noble was his shield within and without;

---

§ 413 menbre del fuir
§ 426 Nauras
§ 429 Nauras

tute la guige en fu batue a or,
et les enarmes, et tut li pan defors.
Unc plus gent home ne mist Jhesu en l'ost
que fu Girard quant parti de Tidbalt. 435
Vint a la bataille cum il plus tost pout,
fert un paen sur la broine de sun dos;
parmi l'eschine li mist l'espee tut fors:
enpeint le ben, si l'ad trebuché mort.
Crie: "Munjoie!" Ço est l'enseigne des noz. 440
Puis refert altre sur la duble targe,
tote li freint de l'un ur desqu'a l'altre;
trenchad le braz que li sist en l'enarme,
colpe le piz et trenchad la curaille,
parmi l'eschine sun grant espee li passe, 445
tut estendu l'abat mort en la place.
Crie: "Munjoie!" – l'enseigne Ferebrace.
Lunsdi al vespre:
Cil le choisirent en la dolente presse§ .

35

(3d) Li pruz Vivien ses baruns en apele: 450
"Ferez, seignurs, od voz espees beles!
Ferez, Franceis, desrumpez ceste presse!

its strap was all of beaten gold, and the arm straps, and the whole face of it. Jesus never placed a more noble man in his army than Girard was when he separated from Tedbalt. He came to the battle as quickly as he could, struck a pagan on the mail-shirt on his back; he thrust the spear right through his spine and out the other side: he skewered him well, and knocked him over dead. He shouts: "Munjoie!", the war cry of our people. Then he struck another on his cross-braced round shield, smashed it from one edge to the other; he cut off his arm that sat in its strap, cut open his chest and cut through his entrails, passed his great spear right through his spine, stretched him out dead on the battle ground. He shouts: "Munjoie!", the war cry of Ferebrace. Monday at vespertide: They caught sight of him in the grievous throng.

Worthy Vivien calls to his barons: "Strike, my lords, with your fine swords! Strike out, Frenchmen, break up this throng!

§ 449 prise

Jo ai oi Lowis§ u Willames.
S'il sunt venuz, l'estur ne durra gueres."
Franceis i ferent de lur espees beles;   455
tant unt erré§ par la dolente presse,
que Girard conurent; volunters l'en apelent.

36

Dunc li demande Vivien le ber:
"Cosin Girard, des quant iés chevaler?"
"Sire," dist il, "de novel, nient de vielz!"   460
"Sez tu, Girard, que danz Tedbalt devint?"
Et cil li cunte cum il l'aveit bailli.
Respunt li quons: "Tais, Girard, bels amis.
Par vostre lange ne seit prodome honiz.

37

"Trai ça§, Girard, devers mun destre poig.   465
Alum ensemble, si met tun gunfanun;
si jo ai tei§, ne crem malveis engrun."
Il s'asemblerent, le jur furent barun:
en la bataille dous reals compaignuns.
Paene gent mistrent en grant errur.   470

I've heard Lowis or Willame. If they've come the battle won't last long." The French struck out with their fine swords; they made such progress through the grievous throng that they recognised Girard; they call out to him happily.

Then Vivien, the noble warrior, asks him: "Cousin Girard, how long have you been a knight?" "My lord," he said, "only a short time, not for long!" "Do you know, Girard, what happened to Lord Tedbalt?" And he told him how he had treated him. The count replies: "Silence, Girard, good kinsman. Your tongue should not bring shame on a man of rank.

"Come, Girard, ride at my right hand. Let us go on together; show forth your pennant; if I have you with me, I fear no evil pass." They joined forces, were barons on that day, in the battle two royal comrades-in-arms: they whipped the pagans into a great fury.

---

§ 453 liwes.
§ 456 errre
§ 465 Trai vus ca
§ 467 si io ta

Lunsdi al vespre:
dolent est le champ senz le cunte Willame!

38

Vivien garde parmi une champaigne,
devant ses oilz vit la fere compaigne
des mielz de France pur grant bataille faire.   475
Mult en vit de els gisir a tere,
dunc tort ses mains, tire sun chef et sa barbe,
plure de ses oilz, si li moille sa face.
Forment regrette Willame Ferebrace[§]:
"Eh[§]! ber marchiz, qui n'est en la bataille,   480
de tun gent cors avum hui suffraite!
Ces gentilz homes en unt grant damage.

39

"Franche meisné, pur la vertu nostre seignur,
ne vus esmaez, seignurs, freres baruns!
Ci atendruns Willame, mun seignur,   485
car s'il vient, nus veintrum l'estur."
Lundi al vespre:
Mar fud le champ comencé sanz Willame!

Monday at vespertide: grievous is the field without Count Willame!

Vivien looks across the levels, before him he saw the fierce company of the best men France had to fight a great battle. Many of them he saw lying on the ground, then he wrings his hands, tears his hair and beard, weeps from his eyes till his face is wet. He bitterly laments the absence of Willame Ferebrace: "Oh! noble marquis, who are not in the battle, we feel the want of your noble presence this day! These noble men are paying dearly for it.

"Noble household, by the power of Our Lord, be not dismayed, my lords, brother barons! We shall await Willame, my overlord, for if he comes we shall win the battle." Monday at vespertide: What a disaster to start the battle without Willame!

[§] 479 Willame brace
[§] 480 &

40

Trente corns cornerent al piu une menee:
set .c. homes unt la garde muntee,   490
(4a) n'i ad icelui ne porte sanglante espee
dunt al champ unt feru granz colees.
Et ainz qu'il en turnent i ferunt d'altreteles!
Vivien erre parmi le sum d'un tertre,
tels treis cenz homes vit de sa tere: 495
n'i ad icil n'ait sanglante§ sa resne
et d'entre ses quisses n'ait vermeille sele;
devant as braz sustenent lur bouele
que lur chevals nes desrumpent par tere.
Quant il les vit pluralment les apele: 500
"Freres baruns, que purrai de vus fere?
N'avrez mes mirie pur nul home de terre!

41

"Seignurs baruns, pur amur Deu, merci!
Enz en voz liz, pur quei irrez murir?
A qui prendrunt venjance vostre ami?   505
Si non ad home al regne Lowis,
s'il vus aveit si malement baillid,
qui peis ne treu ne preissent ja voz fiz;

Thirty horns sounded the rally on the peak: seven hundred men mounted guard, not one
but was bearing a bloody sword with which they had struck mighty blows in the field.
Before they depart they will strike as many like them! Vivien wanders over the top of a
hill; he saw some three hundred men from his own lands: not one but is holding bloody
reins and between his thighs a saddle dyed scarlet; they are holding up their bowels in
front of them in their arms so that their horses do not trample them on the ground. When
he sees them he calls out to them severally: "Brother barons, what can I do with you? No
man on earth will find you doctor more!

"Lord barons, mercy, for love of God! Why will you go to die in your beds? Who will
your kinsmen and allies take vengeance on? There is not a man in Lowis's kingdom, if he
had reduced you to this state, to whom your sons would ever grant peace or truce;

---

§ 496 saglante

ja nel garreit§ roche ne plesseiz,
chastel ne tur, ne veil fosse antif,   510
qu'a lur espees ne li estust§ morir!
Vengum nus ent, tant cum nus sumes vif!"
Et cil responent: "A vostre plaisir, sire ber marchis!"
Lur armes pristrent, as chevals sunt sailliz;
vienent aval§, si sunt acoilliz: 515
par grant force recomencent a ferir.

42

Del munt u furent, sunt aval avalé.
Franceis descendent sur le herbe al pré,
virent des lur les morz et les nafrez.
Qui dunc veist les danceals enseignez   520
lier lur plaies et estreindre lur lez,
....*   (521a)
dunc colpat sa hanste, qui al braz fu nafrez,
si la liad, qu'il la pout porter;
dunc but del vin qu'il ad el champ trové.
Qui n'out de tel, si but del duit troblé,   525
et sains homes en donent as nafrez.

never would save him rock or palisade, castle or tower or ancient, antique ditch from inevitable death at the end of their swords! Let us avenge ourselves while we have life!" And they reply: "As you please, noble lord marquis!" They took up their weapons, leapt on their horses, ride down the hill, and are met head on: they start striking stern blows again.

From their hilltop they rode down into the valley. The French dismount on the grassy meadow; they saw their fellows dead and wounded. Whoever saw these skilful young nobles binding their wounds and strapping up their sides, ... * then anyone wounded in the arm cut through his spear shaft and tied it to himself, so that he could wield it; then he drank from the wine that he found on the field. Whoever had none of that drank from the polluted brook, and whole men gave some to the wounded.

---

§ 509 ne ia ne garrreit
§ 511 nes(t) estut (*t* expunctuated)
§ 515 vient aual

Qui n'ad seignur, si done a sun per.
Dunc laissent les vifs, si vont les morz visiter.

43

Tels set .c. homes trovent de lur terre
entre lur pez trainant lur bowele;   530
parmi lur buches issent fors lur cerveles
(4b)   et de lur escuz se covrent sur l'erbe.
Trubles unt les vis et palles les meisseles,
turnez les oilz qui lur sistrent as testes.
Geinent et crient cels qui les almes i perdent.   535
Quant il les veient, volunters les apelent:
"Seignurs baruns, que purrat de vus estre?
N'avrez mes mirie pur nul home§ de terre!

44

"Ahi ore! seignurs, pur amur Deu, merciz!
Ja veez vus les feluns Arrabiz   540
qui vos unt mort voz freres et voz fiz,
et voz nevous et voz charnels amis!
Pes ne demandent, ne triwes nen unt pris!
Vengum les morz, tant cum nus sumes vifs,
car saint Estephne ne les altres martirs   545
ne furent mieldres que serrunt tut icil,

Whoever had no lord to serve gave some to his companion. Then they turned from the living and went to view the dead.

They found some seven hundred men from their lands dragging their bowels between their feet; their brains were coming out their mouths and they were covering themselves with their shields on the grass. Their faces were distorted and their cheeks pale, their sunken eyes turned up in their heads. They groan and cry out as their souls depart. When they see them they freely call to them: "Lord barons, what will become of you? Never more will you have a doctor for any man on earth!

"Come, my lords, mercy, for love of God! There you see the vile Arabs who have killed your brothers and your sons, and your nephews and your kinsmen! They ask no peace and have taken no truce! Let us avenge the dead, while we still have life, for Saint Stephen and the other martyrs were no better than all these will be

§ 538 nule home

qui en l'Archamp serrunt pur Deu ocis."
Et cil respunent: "Ei ore!* ber marchis."
Lur chevals pristrent et sur els sunt sailliz,
venent al cham, si sunt rasailliz.   550
Par vive force comencent a ferir:
des Sarazins lur unt mort .xv. mil.

45

Paens les pristrent a merveilus turment:
de dis mil homes ne li leissent que cent.
Dolent poet estre le vaillant chevaler   555
qui od dis mil homes se combati
et des dis mil n'out ore que cent chevalers,
et de cels sunt nafré tute l'une meité.
Car si poet estre Vivien le guerrer!

46

"Vivien, sire, pur Deu que fruns?"   560
Et il respunt: "Tres ben les veintrums§!
Apelum Deu, qu'il nus enveit socurs,
qu'il me tramet Willame, mun seignur,
u que Lowis i vienge, l'empereur."
Et cil responent: "A la Deu beneiçun!"   565
Vivien fert al chef devant dé lur,

who will be killed for God's sake on l'Archamp." And they reply: "At 'em!* noble
marquis!" They took their horses and leapt onto them; they came to the field and suffered
another attack. They set about them with all their might: they killed fifteen thousand of
the Saracens.

The pagans put them to incredible torment; of ten thousand men they leave him only a
hundred. The valiant knight may well grieve who started a battle with ten thousand men
and of these ten thousand had now only a hundred left, and of those a full half are
wounded. That is how things stand with Vivien the warrior!

"Lord Vivien, for God's sake, what shall we do?" And he replies: "We'll defeat them all
right! Let's call on God to send us help, to send me Willame, my overlord, or let Lowis,
the emperor, come." And they reply: "God bless us!" Vivien strikes out in the foremost
rank,

§ 561 ueiutrums

mil Sarazins en jette mort en l'estur.
Paien le mistrent a merveillus irrur:
des cent n'i leissent que vint baruns,
et cil s'en vunt lez le coin d'un munt.   570

47

"Vivien sire, que feruns, pur Deu?"
"De bataille; ja ne vus aprendrai el,
(4c) car ben les veintruns solunc la merci Deu."
Et cil responent: "Il nus ad tut oblié."
Et li plusur dient qu'il ad le sen desvé,   575
quant od vint homes volt en bataille entrer
a .v.c. mille de paiens tuz armez:
"S'il erent pors, u vers, u sengler
de hui a un meis nes avrium tuez!"
Dist Vivien: "Cest plaid soi jo assez!   580
Ore vus remenbre des vignes et des prez,
et des chastels et des larges citez,
et des moillers qu'a voz maisuns avez:
que de ço menbre ne frad ja barné.
Alez vus ent, seignurs, et tut par mun gré.   585
Jo remaindrai ici al champ aduré:
ja n'en turnerai, car pramis l'ai a Dé
que ja ne fuierai de bataille champel.
Jo les veinterai ben, solunc la merci Dé.

---

killing a thousand Saracens in the mêlée. The pagans cause him incredible anguish: out
of his hundred they leave him only twenty barons, and they slip away round the corner of
a hill.

"Lord Vivien, what shall we do, in God's name?" "Fight on; you'll get no other word
from me, for we shall conquer them by God's mercy." And they reply: "He's quite
forgotten us." And most of them say he has gone mad wanting to go into battle with
twenty men against five hundred thousand fully armed pagans: "If they were pigs, or
domestic or wild boars, we couldn't kill them in a month!" Said Vivien: "I've heard that
talk before! You're remembering your vines and meadows, your castles and spacious
citadels, and the wives you have at home: anyone who remembers such things will never
perform brave deeds. Go, my lords, with my full agreement. I shall stay here on the hard
fought field: I shall never depart, for I have promised God that I shall never flee from a
battlefield. I shall defeat them, by God's mercy.

48

"A! seignurs, pur amur Deu, merci! 590
A quei irrez en voz liz morir?
Ja veez vus les francs chevalers malmis;
tant cum il furent sains et salfs et vifs
ensemble od nus furent al champ tenir.
Asez savez que vus lur aviez pramis: 595
a home mort ne devez pas mentir!
Alez vus ent et jo remaindrai ici.
Ja n'en irrai, car a Deu l'ai pramis
que ne fuierai pur creme de morir."
A icel mot l'unt Franceis§ tuit guerpi, 600
fors sul Girard, que od lui est remis.
Cil remistrent al dolerus peril
od dous escuz la bataille tenir.
Lunsdi al vespre:
od dous escuz suls est as prez remis! 605

49

Franceis s'en turnent parmi le coin d'un tertre,
devant els gardent as pleines qui sunt beles.
En icel liu ne poent choisir terre
ne seit coverte de pute gent adverse:
par tut burnient espees et healmes. 610

"Ah! My lords, for love of God, have pity! To what end will you go to die in your beds? You can see already the free-born knights put to the sword; as long as they were alive and hale and hearty they stood their ground with us on the field. You know well enough what you promised them: to a dead man you must not lie! Go your way and I shall stay here. I shall never leave, for I have promised God I shall never flee for fear of death." At that word all the French abandoned him, except Girard, who alone remained with him. They remained in the grievous peril just the pair of them with their shields to hold the field. Monday at vespertide: just two shields stand alone in the meadows!

The French leave across the corner of a hill, they look and see before them the beautiful plains. In that place they could see no ground that was not covered with the filthy foe: everywhere is the glint of burnished swords and helmets.

---

§ 600 franceit

Quant il ço veient que altre ne purrad estre,
ne ja nen isterunt de la doleruse presse,
vers Vivien returnent tost lur reisnes.
(4d)   Venent al cunte, volonters l'en apelent:
"Vivien sire, sez que te feruns?"   615
Respunt li quons: "Jo orrai voz raisuns."
"Si tu t'en turnes et nus nus en turneruns;
et se tu combatz et nus nus combateruns.
Et que que tu faces, ensenble od tei le feruns."
Respunt Vivien: "Multes merciz, baruns."   620
Puis en regarde Girard, sun compaignun,
en sun romanz l'en ad mis a raisun:

50

"Amis Girard, es tu sein del cors?"
"Oil," dist il, "et dedenz et defors."
"Di dunc, Girard, coment se§ contenent tes armes?"   625
"Par fei, sire, bones sunt et aates
cum a tel home quin ad fait granz batailles,
et, si bosoinz est, qui referat altres!"

51

"Di dunc, Girard, sentes tu alques ta vertu?"
Et cil respunt que unques plus fort ne fu.   630

When they see that there is nothing for it, and they will never get out of the grievous press, they turn their horses back to Vivien. They come up to the count, and freely call out to him: "Lord Vivien, do you know what we'll do for you?" The count replies: "I'll hear you out." "If you leave this place, we'll leave this place; if you fight on, we'll keep fighting. Whatever you do, we'll do it with you." Vivien replies: "Many thanks, good sirs." Then he looks at Girard, his companion-in-arms, addressing him in his own tongue:

"Girard, my kinsman, are you fit and well?" "Yes," he said, "within and without." "Well then, Girard, what state are your arms and armour in?" "On my word, my lord, they are in good sound order as befits a man who's had a hard fight, and who, if need be, will fight again!"

"Well then, Girard, how are your strength and courage holding up?" And he replies that he never felt stronger.

§ 625 te

"Di dunc, Girard, cum se content tun cheval?"
"Tost s'elaissed, et ben se tient et dreit!"
"Amis Girard, si jo te ossasse quere
que par la lune me alasses a Willame?
Va, si me di a Willame, mun uncle, 635
si li remenbre del champ de Saraguce§,
quant il se combati al paen Alderufe;
ja set il ben desconfit l'aveient Hungre.
Jo vinc al tertre§ od treis cent de mes homes,
criai 'Munjoie!' pur la presse derumpre. 640
Cele bataille fis jo veintre a mun uncle:
jo ocis le paien Alderufe
et decolai les fiz Bereal tuz duze!
Al rei toli cele grant targe duble:
Jo la toli le jur a un Hungre, 645
si la donai a Willame mun uncle,
et il la donad a Tedbalt, le cuart cunte.
Mais ore l'ad un mult prodome a la gule.
A sez enseignes qu'il me vienge socure!

52

"Cosin Girard, di li, ne li celer, 650
et li remenbre de Limenes la cité

"Well then, Girard, what state is your horse in?" "Full of running, and standing straight and true!" "Girard, my kinsman, what if I dared to ask you to go by moonlight to Willame for me? Go and tell my uncle Willame for me that he should remember the battle at Saragossa when he fought the pagan Alderufe; he knows well that the Hungarians had discomforted him. I came to the hill with three hundred of my men, I shouted 'Munjoie!' to open a way through the press. I won that battle for my uncle: I killed the pagan Alderufe and beheaded all twelve of Bereal's sons! I took that great cross-braced round shield from the king: that day I took it from a Hungarian, I gave it to my uncle Willame, and he gave it to Tedbalt, the coward count. But now a truly worthy man has it at his throat. By these signs let him come to my aid!

"Cousin Girard, tell him, and don't hide it, that he should remember the citadel of Limenes

---

§ 636 del saraguce
§ 639 en la terre

ne del grant port al rivage de mer,
ne de Fluri, que jo pris par poesté:
aider me vienge en bataille champel!

53

(5a) "Sez que dirras a Willame le fedeil?   655
Se lui remenbre del champ Turlen le rei,
u jo li fis batailles§ trente treis:
cent cinquante et plus li fis aveir
des plus poanz de la sarazine lei,
en une fuie, u Lowis s'en fueit.   660
Jo vinc al tertre od dous cent de mes fedeilz;
criai 'Munjoie!' – le champ li fis aveir.
Cel jur perdi Raher, un mien fedeil:
le jur que m'en menbre, n'ert hure ne m'en peist!
Aider me vienge al dolerus destreit!   665

54

"Sez que dirras a Willame, le bon Franc?
Se lui remenbre de la bataille grant
desuz Orenge, de Tedbalt l'Esturman.
En bataille u venquirent Franc,

and the great port on the sea coast, and Fluri, whom I captured by force of arms: let him
come to help me on the battlefield!

"Do you know what to say to faithful Willame? Let him remember the battle against
King Turlen, where I led the attack thirty-three times for him: I captured for him one
hundred and fifty and more of the most powerful men of the Saracen faith, in a rout
where Lowis fled. I came to the hill with two hundred of my faithful followers; I shouted
'Munjoie!' — I won the day for him. That day I lost Raher, one of my faithful followers:
on any day I remember it I have no hour free from grief! Let him come to my aid in this
dire strait!

"Do you know what to say to Willame the good Frank? Let him also remember the great
battle below the walls of Orange against Tedbalt the Steersman. In the battle won by the
Franks

---

§ 657 bataille

jo vinc al tertre od Bernard de Bruban, 670
cil est mis uncles et barun mult vaillant;
a compaignun oi le cunte Bertram,
qui est uns des meillurs de nostre parenté grant.
Od 'Deu aie!' et l'enseigne as Normanz*
cele bataille li fis jo veintre al champ. 675
Iloec li ocist Tedbalt l'Esturman:
aider me vienge al saluz de l'Archamp,
si me socure al dolerus haan.

55

"Sez que dirras a Guiot, mun petit frere?
De hui a quinze anz ne deust ceindre espee, 680
mais ore la cendrat pur secure le fiz sa mere:
aider me vienge en estrange cuntree.

56

"Sez que dirras dame Guiburc, ma drue?
Si li remenbre de la grant nurreture,
plus de .xv. anz qu'ele ad vers mei eue. 685
Ore gardez, pur Deu, qu'ele ne seit perdue!
Qu'ele m'enveit sun seignur en aie:
s'ele ne m'enveit le cunte, d'altre n'ai jo cure."

I came to the hill with Bernard de Bruban, my uncle and a most valiant baron; I had as
my companion Count Bertram, one of the best of our great clan. With 'Deu aie!' and the
war cry of the Normans* I won that battle for him on the field. There I killed Tedbalt the
Steersman for him: let him come to help me on the martyrs' ground at l'Archamp, and
aid me in the grievous strife.

"Do you know what to say to Guiot, my little brother? He shouldn't strap on a sword for
another fifteen years, but now he shall strap it on to rescue his mother's son: let him come
to help me in this hostile country.

"Do you know what to say to my dear lady Guiburc? She should remember how grandly
she brought me up, having me in her care for more than fifteen years. Now, for God's
sake, let her take care not to waste it! Let her send me her lord to help me: if she doesn't
send me the count, I don't care about anyone else."

57

"Allas!" dist Girard, "cum te larrai enviz!"
"Tais, ber, nel dire! Ja est ço pur mé garir."   690
La desevrerent les dous charnels amis.
Il unt grant duel: ne unt giu ne ris;
tendrement plurent andui des oilz de lur vis.
Lunsdi al vespre:
Deus! Pur quei sevrerent en dolente presse?   695

58

(5b)   Girard s'en turne parmi le coin d'un tertre.
Cinc liwes trove tant enconbree presse
que unc n'alad un sul arpent de terre
qu'il n'abatist Sarazin de sa sele,
et qu'il ne trenchast§ pé u poing u teste.   700
Et quant il issi de la dolente presse
Sun bon cheval li creve suz sa sele.

59

Del dolent champ, quant Girard fu turné
desuz ses alves est sun cheval crevé.
Granz quinze liwes fu li regnés effrei: 705
ne trovad home a qui il sache parler,

"Alas!" said Girard, "how reluctantly I will leave you!" "Silence, noble warrior, don't
say such a thing! You do it to save me." At that the two fond kinsmen separated. They
are full of grief: they see nothing to laugh at; they both weep tenderly from their eyes.
Monday at vespertide: God! Why did they part in the grievous mêlée?

Girard retreats across the corner of a hill. Over five leagues he finds such a thronging
crush that he did not advance one rod without unhorsing a Saracen, and without cutting
off a foot, a fist or a head. And when he got out of the grievous mêlée his horse died
under his saddle.

When Girard had left the grievous field his horse died under his saddle-tree. For fifteen
full leagues the kingdom was in turmoil: he found no man to talk to

---

§ 700 quil ne trenchad

ne cel cheval u il puisse munter.
A pé s'en est del dolerus champ turné.
Grant fu li chaud cum en mai en esté,
et lungs les jurz, si out treis jurz juné,   710
et out tele seif qu'il ne la pout durer.
De quinze liwes n'i out ne dut ne gué,
fors l'eve salee, que ert tres lui a la mer.
Dunc li comencerent ses armes a peser,
et Girard les prist durement a blamer.   715

60

"Ohi! grosse hanste, cume peises al braz!
Nen aidera a Vivien en l'Archamp,*
qui se combat a dolerus ahan."
Dunc la lance Girard enmi le champ.

61

"Ohi! grant targe, cume peises al col!   720
Nen aidera a Vivien§ a la mort!"
El champ la getad, si la tolid de sun dos.

62

"Ohi! bone healme, cum m'estunes la teste!
Nen aiderai a Vivien en la presse,

and no horse to mount. He left the grievous field on foot. The heat was great, as you get in May, in summertime, and the days long, and he had fasted for three days, and was so thirsty that he could scarcely endure it. For fifteen leagues there was neither stream nor ford, only the salt water of the sea beside him. Then his arms began to weigh him down, and Girard began to rail against them.

"Oh! great spear shaft, how you weigh down my arm! You will be of no help to Vivien at l'Archamp,* where he fights in grievous strife." Then Girard threw it down in the field.

"Oh! great round shield, how you weigh down my neck! You will be of no help to Vivien at his death!" He took it from his back and threw it down in the field.

"Oh! fine helmet, how you numb my head! You will be of no help to Vivien in the mêlée,

---

§ 721 uiuie

ki se cumbat en l'Archamp§ sur l'erbe!"   725
Il le lançad et jetad cuntre terre.

63

"Ohi! grant broine, cum me vas apesant!
Nen aiderai a Vivien en l'Archamp,
qui se combat a dolerus ahan!"
Trait l'ad de sun dos, sil getad el champ.   730
Totes ses armes out guerpi li Frans,
fors sul s'espee, dunt d'acer fu li brant,
tote vermeille des le helt en avant,
l'escalberc pleine de foie et de sanc.
Nue la porte, si s'en vait suz puiant   735
(5c)   et la mure vers terre reposant.
La plaine veie vait tote jur errant
et les granz vals mult durement corant,
et les haltes tertres belement muntant;
sa nue espee al destre poig portant,   740
devers la mure si s'en vait apoiant.
Cil nunciad a Willame de l'Archamp
u Vivien se combat a dolerus ahan:
od sul .xx. homes fu remis en l'Archamp.
Vivien lur fiert al chef devant,   745
mil Sarazins lur ad ocis el champ.

where he is fighting on the grass of l'Archamp!" He hurled it from him, throwing it hard against the ground.

"Oh! great shirt of mail, how you are weighing me down! You will be of no help to Vivien on l'Archamp, where he is fighting in grievous strife!" He pulled it from his back and threw it down in the field. The noble Frank abandoned all his arms, except his sword with its steel blade red with blood from hilt to tip, its scabbard full of liver and blood. He carries it drawn and is constantly leaning on its tip which he regularly puts to the ground. He travels the open road for a whole day running painfully down the great valleys and stoutly climbing the high hills, carrying his naked sword in his right hand and leaning heavily on its point. He it was told Willame about l'Archamp where Vivien is fighting in grievous strife: he was left with just twenty men on l'Archamp. Vivien strikes out at their head; he killed a thousand Saracens in the field.

§ 725 el archamp

64

Li quons Vivien de ses vint perdi dis;
les altres li dient: "Que ferum la, amis?"
"De la bataille, seignurs, pur Deu mercis!
Ja veez vus, que jo en ai Girard tramis: 750
aincui vendrat Willame u Lowis.
Li quels que i venge, nus veintrum Arrabiz."
Et cil responent: "Ai ore§, ber marchis!"
Od ses dis homes les revait envair.
Paien le pristrent en merveillus peril: 755
de ses dis homes ne li leissent nul vif.
Od sun escu demeine remist le champ tenir.
Lunsdi al vespre:
od sun escu remist sul en la presse!

65

Puis qu'il fu remis od un sul escu   760
si lur curt sovent sure as turs menuz;
od sul sa lance en ad cent abatuz.
Dient paien: "Ja nel verrum vencu,
tant cum le cheval laissum vif suz lui.
Ja ne veintrum le noble vassal   765
quant desuz lui leissum vif sun cheval."
Idunc le quistrent as puiz et as vals

Of his twenty men Count Vivien lost ten; the rest say to him: "What shall we do, good
friend?" "Fight on, my lords, for God's mercy! You can see I've sent Girard to report:
before the day is out Willame or Lowis will come. Whichever of them comes, we shall
defeat the Arabs." And they reply: "Come on then, gallant marquis!" He returns to the
attack with his ten men. The pagans put him in unbelievable peril: they leave not one of
his men alive. With his lordly shield he stands alone to hold the field. Monday at
vespertide: his the only shield to remain in the throng!

Once he was left the sole shield on the field he charged at them fast and furiously; with
his lance alone he cut down a hundred of them. The pagans say: "We'll never defeat him
as long as we leave his horse alive under him. We shall never defeat the noble vassal,
when we leave his horse alive under him." Then they pursued him over hill and vale

---

§ 753 aioie

cum altre beste salvage de cel aguait.
Une compaignie li vint parmi un champ;
tant li lancerent guivres et trenchanz darz,   770
tant en abatent al cors de sun cheval
de sul les hanstes fust chargé un char.
Un Barbarin vint parmi un val,
entre ses quisses out un ignel cheval,
en sun poig destre portad un trenchant dart.   775
(5d)   Treis feiz l'escust, a la quarte le lançad,
et fiert li en la broine de la senestre part
que trente des mailles l'en abat contre val;
Une grant plaie li fist el cors del dart.
La blanche enseigne li chai del destre braz: 780
ne vint le jur que unc puis le relevast.
Lunsdi al vespre:
ne vint le jur que puis le relevast de terre.

66

Il mist sa main de rere sun dos,
trovad la hanste, trait le dart de sun cors,   785
fert le paien sur la broine de sun dos,
parmi l'eschine li mist le fer tut fors;
od icel colp l'ad trebuché mort.
"Ultre, lecchere, malveis Barbarin!"
Ço li ad dit Vivien le meschin.   790

like any wild beast hunted from a hide. A company of warriors came upon him in the midst of a field; they threw so many javelins and sharp spears at him, and so many land in his horse's body, you could have filled a cart just with the shafts. A Berber came along a valley, between his thighs he had a swift horse, in his right hand he carried a sharp spear. Thrice he brandished it, the fourth time he threw it, and it strikes in the left side of his mail shirt, knocking out thirty links which fall to the ground; the spear gave him a great wound in his body. His white standard fell from his right arm: the day never came when he picked it up. Monday at vespertide: the day never came when he again picked it up from the ground.

He felt behind his back, found the shaft, pulls the javelin from his body, strikes the pagan on the mail shirt covering his back, thrust the blade right out through his spine; with that blow he killed him outright. "Take that, you evil swine of a Berber!" That's what young Vivien said to him.

"Ne repeireras al regne dunt tu venis,
ne ne t'en vanteras ja mais a nul dis,
que mort aiez le barun Lowis!"
Puis traist s'espee et comence a ferir.
Qui qu'il fert sur halberc u sur healme,   795
sun colp§ n'arestet desque jusqu'en terre.
"Sainte Marie, virgine pucele,
tramettez mei, dame, Lowis u Willame!"
Cest oreisun dist Vivien en la presse.

67

"Deus, rei de glorie, qui me fesis né,   800
et de la sainte virgne, sire, fustes né,
en treis persones fud tun cors comandé,
et en sainte croiz pur peccheurs pené.
Cel et terre§ fesis, et tere et mer,
soleil et lune (tut ço as comandé)   805
et Eva et Adam pur le secle restorer.
Si verreiement, sire, cum tu es veirs Deus,
tu me defent, sire, par ta sainte bunté
que al quor ne me puisse unques entrer
que plein pé fuie pur la teste colper.   810

"You'll not return to the kingdom you came from, nor will there ever be a day when you boast that you killed Lowis's baron!" Then he drew his sword and began striking blows. If he strikes anyone on the halberk or the helmet, his blow is not checked until it meets the ground. "Blessed Mary, virgin maiden, send me, my Lady, Lowis or Willame!" This was Vivien's prayer in the mêlée.

"God, King of Glory, who caused my birth, and who was born, Lord, from the Blessed Virgin, You ordained Yourself as three persons, and suffered for sinners on the Holy Cross. You made Heaven and Earth, and land and sea, sun and moon (all that you ordained) and Eve and Adam to establish the world. As truly, Lord, as You are very God defend me, Lord, by your holy goodness that it may never enter my heart to flee one pace to save my head.

---

§ 796 sunt colp
§ 804 cele et terre

Tresqu'a la mort me lais ma fei garder:
Deus, que ne la mente pur tes saintes buntez.

68

"Sainte Marie, mere genitriz,
si verreiement cum Deus portas a fiz,
garisez mei pur ta sainte merci,　　　　　　　　　815
que ne m'ocient cist felon Sarazin!"
　(6a)　Quant l'out dit, li bers se repentid:
"Mult pensai ore que fols et que brixs,
que mun cors quidai de la mort garir,
quant Dampnedeu meismes nel fist,　　　　　　820
que pur nus mort en sainte croiz soffri
pur nus raindre de noz mortels enemis.
Respit de mort, sire, ne te dei jo rover,
car a tei meisme ne la voilsis pardoner.
Tramettez mei, sire, Willame al curb nés,　　825
u Lowis, qui France ad a garder:
par lui veintrum la bataille champel!
Deus, de tant moldes pot hom altre resembler –
jo ne di mie pur Willame al curb niés;
forz sui jo mult, et hardi sui assez;　　　　　830
de vasselage puis ben estre sun per,
mais de plus loinz ad sun pris aquité –
car s'il fust en l'Archamp sur mer
vencu eust la bataille champel.

Let me keep faith unto death: God, for your holy goodness' sake, let me not betray it.

"Blessed Mary, fecund mother, as truly as you bore God as your son, save me, for your blessed mercy's sake, from being killed by these foul Saracens!" When he had said it the noble warrior repented: "That was the thought of a stupid fool, thinking that I could save myself from death, when the Lord God Himself didn't do it, suffering death for us on the Holy Cross to redeem us from our mortal enemies. Respite from death, Lord, I may not pray for, since You would not spare Yourself from it. Send me, Lord, Willame Hooknose, or Lowis, who has France to defend: with his aid we shall win the pitched battle! God, a man may resemble another by many features — I don't say it of Willame Hooknose; I am very strong, and brave enough for anyone; in warrior's skills I may well be his equal, but he has earned his reputation over a longer time — now if he were at l'Archamp by the sea he would have won the pitched battle.

Allas, peccable! n'en puis mais, home gent§!"   835
Lunsdi al vespre:
"Que me demande ceste gent adverse?"

69

Grant fu le chaud cum en mai en esté,
et long le jur, si n'out treis jurz mangé.
Grant est la faim et fort pur deporter,   840
et la seif male: nel poet endurer.
Parmi la boche vait le sanc tut cler,
et par la plaie del senestre costé.
Loinz sunt les eves, qu'il nes solt trover:
de .xv. liwes n'i out funteine ne gué,   845
fors l'eve salee qui ert al flot de la mer.
Mais parmi le champ curt un duit troblé
d'une roche ben prof de la mer;
Sarazins l'orent a lur chevals medlé:
de sanc et de cervele fud tut envolupé.   850
La vint corant Vivien li alosé,
si s'enclinad a l'eve salee del gué,
sin ad beu assez estre sun gré.
Et cil li lancerent lur espees adolés§,
granz colps li donent al graver u il ert.   855

Alas, weak sinner! I can't help myself, noble man!" Monday at vespertide: "What does
this fierce foe want of me?"

The heat was great as in May in summertime, and the days long, and he had not eaten for
three days. Great is his hunger and hard to bear, and his thirst wicked: he cannot endure
it. His bright blood issues from his mouth, and through the wound in his left side. The
waters are distant so that he may not find them: for fifteen leagues around there was no
spring nor ford, only the salt water in the tide of the sea. Yet through the field flows a
dirty stream, coming from a rock right by the sea; Saracens had churned it up with their
horses: it was all stirred up with blood and brains. Vivien the renowned came running
down to it and bent down to the salt water of the ford, and drank some against his will.
And the enemy hurl their sharpened spears at him, giving him hard blows where he stood
on the shore.

---

§ 835 nen puis home gent
§ 854 adube

       forte fu la broine, ne la pourent entamer,
       que li ad gari tut le gros des costez,
(6b)   mais as jambes et as braz et par el
       plus qu'en vint lius unt le cunte nafré.
       Dunc se redresce cum hardi sengler,   860
       si traist s'espee del senestre costé;
       dunc se defent Vivien cum ber,
       Il le demeinent cum chens funt fort sengler.
       L'ewe fu salee qu'il out beu de la mer,
       fors est issue, ne li pot el cors durer: 865
       sailli li est arere de la boche et del niés.
       Grant fu l'anguisse, les oilz li sunt troblez;
       dunc ne sout veie tenir ne esgarder.
       Paien le pristrent durement a haster,
       de plusur parz l'acoillent li guerreier,   870
       lancent li guivres et trenchanz darz d'ascer.
       Tant l'en abatent§ en l'escu de quarters
       que nel pout le cunte a sa teste drescer:
       jus a la terre li chai a ses pez.
       Dunc le comencent paien forment§ a haster   875
       et sun vasselage mult durement a lasser.

His mail shirt was strong, they could not damage it, and it protected the bulk of his sides, but in his arms and legs and elsewhere they wounded the count in more than twenty places. Then he stands up like a bold wild boar, and draws his sword where it hangs at his left side; then Vivien defends himself like a brave warrior, and they harry him as hounds do a strong wild boar. The water he had drunk from the sea was salt, it came back up, he could not keep it down: it came spurting back out of his mouth and nose. His pain was great, his eyes grew dim; then he could not see to keep his way. The pagans began to harry him closely, the warriors attack him from all sides, hurling at him their javelins and sharp steel spears. So many land in his quartered shield that the count could not lift it in front of his face: it fell to the ground at his feet. Then the pagans began to press him closely and to wear down his warrior's courage.

---

§ 872 en labatent
§ 875 formen

70

Lancent a lui guivres et aguz darz;
entur le cunte debatent sun halberc,
le fort acer detrenche le menu fer
que tut le piz covre§ de claveals.   880
Jus a la terre li cheent les boels:
nen est fis que durt longement mes.
Dunc reclaime Deus qu'il merci en ait.

71

Vivien eire a pé parmi le champ;
chet lui sun healme sur le nasel devant,   885
et entre ses pez ses boals trainant:
al braz senestre les vait contretenant.
En sa main destre porte d'ascer un brant,
tut fu vermeil des le helz§ en avant,
l'escalberc pleine de feie et de sanc:*   890
devers la mure s'en vait apuiant.
La sue mort le vait mult destreignant
et il se sustent contreval de sun brant.
Forment reclaime Jhesu le tut poant
qu'il li tramette Willame, le bon Franc,   895
u Lowis, le fort rei combatant.

They hurl javelins and sharp spears at him; all around the count they smash away his halberk, the strong steel cuts through the thin iron covering all his chest with rivets. His entrails fall to the ground: He is not at all sure he can hold out much longer. Then he calls on God to have mercy on him.

Vivien wanders on foot through the field, his helmet tips forward till it rests on its nose guard, and his bowels are dragging between his feet: he keeps gathering them up on his left arm. In his right hand he carries a blade of steel, all stained red from hilt to tip, his scabbard full of liver and blood:* he leans heavily on its point. He is in the throes of his death and he keeps himself up by lowering his sword. Loudly he calls upon Jesus the all powerful to send him Willame, the good Frank, or Lowis, the powerful warrior king.

---

§ 880 courent
§ 889 holz

72

"Deus veirs de glorie, qui mains en trinité,
et en la virgne fustes regeneré,

(6c)   et en treis persones fud tun cors comandé.
En sainte croiz te laissas, sire, pener.   900
Defent mei, pere, par ta sainte bunté,
ne seit pur quei al cors me puisse entrer
que plein pé fuie de bataille champel.
A la mort me lait ma fei garder:
Deus, ne la mente par ta sainte bunté!   905
Tramettez mei, sire, Willame al curb niés:
sages hom est en bataille champel
si la set ben maintenir et garder.

73

"Dampnedeus, pere, glorius et forz,
ne seit unques que cel vienge de fors   910
que ça dedenz me puisse entrer al cors,
que plein pé fuie pur creme de mort!"
Un Barbarin vint parmi un val,
tost esleissant un ignel cheval;
fiert en la teste le noble vassal   915
que la cervele en espant contreval.
Li Barbarins i vint eslaissé,
entre ses quisses out un grant destrer,
en sa main destre un trenchant dart d'ascer.

"Very God of Glory, living Trinity, conceived in the Virgin, your Being ordained as three
Persons. On the Holy Cross You allowed Yourself, Lord, to suffer. Defend me, Father, by
your holy goodness, that for no reason it may occur to me to flee one pace from the
battlefield. Let me keep my faith at my death: God, don't let me betray it, for your holy
goodness' sake! Send me, Lord, Willame Hooknose: he is a man wise in the ways of
battlefields and knows well how to stand and fight. — *This is fulfilled.*

"Lord God, Father, glorious and strong, let nothing ever come upon me from without and
get inside me to suggest that I should flee one pace for fear of death!" A Berber came
down a valley, giving free rein to a fast galloping horse; he struck the noble vassal on the
head spilling his brains all around. The Berber came on at a gallop, between his thighs
was a great charger, in his right hand a sharp steel spear.

Fert en la teste le vaillant chevaler   920
que la cervele sur l'erbe li chet.
Sur les genoilz abat le chevaler:
ço fu damage quant si prodome chet!
Sur li corent de plusurs parz paens:
tut le detrenchent contreval al graver.   925
Od els l'enportent, ne l'en volent laisser.
Suz un arbre le poserent, lez un senter,
car il ne voldreient qu'il fust trové de crestiens.
Des ore mes dirrai de Girard, l'esquier,
cum il alad a Willame nuncier.   930
Lunsdi al vespre:
a Barzelune la le dirrad al cunte Willame.

74

Li quons Willame ert a Barzelune,
si fu repeiré d'une bataille lunge
qu'il aveit fait a Burdele sur Girunde;   935
perdu i aveit grant masse de ses homes.
Este vus Girard qui noveles§ li cunte.

75

Li ber Willame ert repeiré de vespres;
a un soler s'estut a unes estres,*

He strikes the valiant knight on the head so that his brains spill on the grass. He knocks the knight down to his knees: that was a loss when such a worthy man fell! Pagans run upon him from all sides: down on the shore they hack him to pieces. They carry him away with them, will not leave him behind. They put him under a tree beside a path, for they do not want Christians to find him. From now on I will speak of Girard, the squire, telling how he took the message to Willame. Monday at vespertide: in Barcelona he will tell his tale to count Willame.

Count Willame was in Barcelona and just returned from a long battle that he had fought at Bordeaux on the Gironde; there he had lost a great mass of his men. Now, here comes Girard to tell him the news.

Brave Willame had just come from vespers; he was standing in an open loggia on an outer wall*

---

§ 937 noves

(6d) et dame Guiburc estut a sun braz destre.   940
      Dunc gardat par la costere d'un tertre,
      et vit Girard, qui de l'Archamp repeire.
      Sanglante espee portat en sun poig destre,
      devers la mure se puiat contre terre.

76

      "Seor, dulce amie," dist Willame al curb niés,   945
      "bone fud l'ore que jo te pris a per,
      et icele mieldre que eustes crestienté.
      Parmi cel tertre vei un home avaler,
      sanglante espee en sa main porter.
      Si vus dirrai une chose pur verité,   950
      qu'il ad esté en bataille champel,
      si vient a mei pur socurs demander.
      Alun encontre pur noveles escolter."
      Entre Guiburc et Willame al curb niés
      devalerent contreval les degrez.   955
      Quant furent aval, Girard unt encontré.
      Veit le Willame, sil conuit assez.
      Dunc l'apelad, sil prist a demander.

77

      "Avant, Girard, si dirrez de voz noveles."
      Ço dist Girard: "Jo en sai assez de pesmes!   960
      Reis Deramed est eissuz de Cordres;

and Lady Guiburc was standing linking his right arm. Then he looked across the slope of
a hill, and saw Girard, who was returning from l'Archamp. He carried a bloody sword in
his right hand, leaning its point on the ground.

"Sister, my sweet," said Willame Hooknose, "it was a good hour when I took you to
wife, and better still when you became a Christian. I see a man coming down the side of
that hill, carrying a bloody sword in his hand. Now I'll tell you this for a fact: he's been
in a pitched battle, and is coming to ask me for help. Let's go to meet him to hear his
news." Guiburc and Willame Hooknose together went down the stairs. At the bottom
they met him. Willame sees him and recognises him. Then he called out to him and
started to interrogate him.

"Come forward, Girard, and tell your news." Said Girard: "They're as grim as can be!
King Deramé has sailed from Cordoba;

en halte mer en ad mise la flote,
et est en France que si mal desenorte.
Les marchez guaste et les aluez prent,
tote la tere turne a sun talent: 965
u que trove tes chevalers sis prent,
a lur barges les maine coreçus et dolent.
Pense, Willame, de secure ta gent!

78

"Reis Deramé est turné de sun pais
et est en la terre qu'il met tut a exil.   970
Alez i furent Tedbalt et Esturmi,
ensemble od els Vivien le hardi:
li uns se combat; les dous en sunt fuiz!"
"Deus," dist Willame, "ço est Vivien le hardiz!"
Respunt Girard: "Or avez vus veir dit!   975
Il te mande, et jo sui quil te di,
que tu le secures al dolerus peril.

79

"Sez que te mande Vivien, tun fedeil?
Si te remembre del champ de Turleis le rei,
u te fist batailles trente treis.   980
(7a)   Cent cinquante et plus te fist aveir

he has put his fleet on the high seas, and is in France, where he is causing great damage. He is laying waste the marches and capturing the freeholdings, he is working his will on the whole land: wherever he finds your knights, he captures them, taking them heartbroken with grief to their barges. Take thought, Willame, to rescue your folk!

"King Deramé has left his own country and is in the land which he puts to fire and the sword. Tedbalt and Esturmi marched against him, along with them Viven the bold: one stayed to fight; two turned in flight!" "God," said Willame, "that will be Viven the bold!" Girard replies: "Now you have spoken truth! He sends the message to you, and I am telling you, that you must aid him in the grievous peril.

"Do you know what message Vivien, your faithful follower, sends you? Remember the battle against King Turleis, in which he led thirty-three attacks. He captured a hundred and fifty men and more for you

en une fuie, u Lowis s'en fuieit.
Il vint al tertre§ od dous cent Franceis,
criad 'Munjoie!' Le champ te fist aveir.
Cel jur perdi Rahel, un sun fedeil: 985
quant li en membre n'ert hure ne li em peist!
Aider li algez al dolerus destreit.

80

"Sez que te mande Vivien le ber?
Ke te sovenge de Limenes, la cité,
ne de Breher, le grant port sur mer,   990
ne de Flori qu'il prist par poesté!
Aider li vienges en l'Archamp sur mer!

81

"E sez que mande a dame Guiburc, sa drue?
Ke lui remenbre de la grant nurreture
qu'il§ ad od lui plus de .xv. anz eue.   995
Ore gard pur Deu qu'ele ne seit perdue,
qu'ele li enveit sun seignur en aiue§ ,
car si lui n'enveit, d'altres n'ad il cure!

in a rout where Lowis fled. He came to the hill with two hundred Frenchmen, shouted
'Munjoie!' and won the battle for you. That day he lost Rahel, one of his faithful
followers: when he remembers that, no day passes without his grieving for it! You should
go to help him in his grievous plight.

"Do you know what message the brave warrior Vivien sends you? Remember the citadel
of Limenes, and Breher, the great seaport, and Flori whom he captured by force of arms!
You should come to help him at l'Archamp by the sea!

"And do you know what message he sends to his dear lady Guiburc? Let her remember
with what pains she brought him up, and how he spent more than fifteen years with her.
Now let her take heed, for God's sake, that her time is not wasted, and be sure to send her
lord to his aid, for if she doesn't send him, he doesn't care for any others!

---

§ 983 Il vint le tertre
§ 995 qui il
§ 997 aide

82

"E sez que mande a Guiot, sun petit frere?
De hui en quinze anz ne dust ceindre espee,   1000
mais ore la prenge pur le fiz de sa mere!
Aider li vienge en estrange cuntree!"

83

"A! Deus," dist Willame, "purrai le vif trover?"
Respunt Guiburc: "Pur nient en parlez!
Secor le, sire! Ne te chalt a demander: 1005
se tu li perz, n'avras ami fors Deu."
Quant l'ot Willame, sin ad sun chef crollé,
plorad des oilz pitusement et suef,
l'eve li curt chalde juste le niés,
la blanche barbe moille tresqu'al baldré.   1010
Guiburc apele, si li prist a mustrer:
de sun corage l'i volt li bers espermenter
de si cum aime lui et sun parenté.
Quant il parlad, si ad dit que sené:
"Seor, dulce amie, pur amur Dé,   1015
uncore n'en ad que sul treis jurz passez
que jo sui venu de bataille champel,
que ai fait grande a Burdele sur mer,
si ai perdu mun nobile barné.

"And do you know what message he sends to Guiot, his little brother? He shouldn't strap on a sword for fifteen years from today, but now let him take it up for the son of his mother! Let him come to help him in the harsh land!"

"Oh! God," said Willame, "will I be able to find him alive?" Guiburc replies: "You're wasting your breath! Go to his aid, my lord! What a question to ask: if you lose *him*, you'll have no one to count on but God." When Willame heard that he shook his head, wept soft and copious tears, which run hot down the side of his nose, wetting his white beard right down to his baldrick. He spoke to Guiburc, remonstrating with her: the mighty warrior wanted to test her innermost feelings on the matter and her love for himself and his clan. When he spoke, what he said was good sense: "Sister, my sweet, for love of God, it's only just three days since I came back from a pitched battle, a great one that I fought at Bordeaux by the sea, where I lost my noble war band.

Loinz sunt les marches u jo ai a comander: 1020
fort sunt les homes que devreie asembler.*
(7b) Et ensurquetut nel purreie endurrer:
fer et acer i purreit hom user.
Ben se combat Vivien l'alosé.
A iceste feiz nel puis mie regarder;   1025
ceste bataille pot ben sanz mei finer."
Dunc començad Guiburc forment a plorer.
Ele s'abeissad, baisa lui le soller.
Willame apele, si li prist a mustrer:
"Secor le, sire! Ne te chaut a demurer!   1030
Mun nief§, Guischard, te voldrai comander.
Tue merci, ben le m'as adubé.

84

"Sire Willame, jo te chargerai Guiscard.
Il est mis niés mult est prof de ma char.
Tue merci, avant her le m'adubas;   1035
si nel me renz, ne girras mes entre mes braz!"
Il li afia – cher se repentirad –
que vif u mort sis niés li rendrat.
En bataille reneiad Deu Guischard.
Lunsdi al vespre: 1040
en bataille reneiad Deu celestre!

Distant are the marches over which I have command: strong are the men I should gather
about me.* Above all I could not bear the strain: A man could wear out iron and steel in a
place like that. Vivien is renowned and fights well. On this occasion I can't take notice of
him; he can win this battle without me." Then Guiburc began to weep violently. She
bowed herself down and kissed his shoe. She spoke to Willame, remonstrating with him:
"Go to his aid, my lord! What are you waiting for? I shall send my nephew, Guischard,
in your care. You made him a knight for me, and I am grateful.

"Lord Willame, I shall put Guischard under your care, He is my nephew and my closest
kin. You made him a knight for me the other day, and I am grateful; if you don't bring
him back, you'll sleep with me no more!" He gave her his word — dearly will he repent
— to bring her nephew back dead or alive. In battle Guischard renounced God. Monday
at vespertide: in battle he renounced the Heavenly God!

---

§ 1031 niefs (a small "s" added in superscript)

85

Guiburc meismes servi Girard de l'eve,
et en aprés le servit de tuaille.
Puis l'ad assis a une halte table,
si lui aportat d'un sengler un espalle.   1045
Li quons la prist, si la mangat a haste;
ele li aportat un grant pain a tamis
et dunc en aprés sun grant mazelin de vin.
Girard mangat le grant braun porcin,
et a dous traiz ad voidé le mazelin   1050
que unques a Guiburc mie n'en offrit
ne ne radresçat la chere ne sun vis.
Veist le Guiburc, a Willame l'ad dit:
"Par Deu, bel sire, cist est de vostre lin!
Qui si§ mangue un grant braun porcin,   1055
et a dous traiz beit un cester de vin,
ben dure guere deit rendre a sun veisin,
ne ja vilment ne deit de champ fuir§!"
Respunt Willame: "Pur Deu, Guiburc, merci!
Ço que ad mangé, de volenté l'ad pris: 1060
il ne mangat ben ad passé treis dis."
Prest fu li liz, si firent Girard dormir.

Guiburc herself brought the water to Girard, and afterwards presented him with a towel.
Then she sat him at a high table, and brought him a shoulder of boar. The count took it
and ate it straight off the spit; she brought him a great, fine white-loaf and then to follow
a great maser of wine. Girard ate the great pork brawn, and emptied the maser in two
draughts without ever offering a drop to Guiburc and without looking up or raising his
head. Guiburc saw it and said to Willame: "By God, my good lord, he's one of your
family! Anyone who can eat a great brawn of pork and drink a whole gallon of wine in
two draughts will wage a bitter war on his neighbour and never disgrace himself by
fleeing the field!" Willame replies: "For God's sake, Guiburc, have pity on us! He was
ready for a good meal: he hasn't eaten a good three days past." The bed was close by,
they sent Girard to sleep.

---

§ 1055 & si
§ 1058 ne de champ fuir

(7c)   Lunsdi al vespre:
       prest fu li liz, si firent dormir Girard.

86

Girard se dresce et levad del manger.   1065
Prest fu li liz, si s'est alé colcher.
Guiburc la franche le servi volenters;
tant fud od lui qu'il endormi fu,
puis le comande al cors altisme Deu.
Tant dormi Girard qu'il fu avespré,   1070
puis salt del lit cume Francs naturel.
"Munjoie!" escrie, "chevalers, car muntez!"
Armes demande, et l'en li vait aporter:
idunc a primes fu Girard adubé.*

87

Dunc li vestirent une broigne mult bele,   1075
et un vert healme li lacent en la teste;
Willame li ceinst l'espee al costé senestre.
Une grant targe prist par la manuele;
cheval out bon, des meillurs de la terre.
Puis muntad Girard par sun estriu senestre;   1080
dame Guiburc li vait tenir la destre,
si li comande a Deu, le grant paterne.

Monday at vespertide: the bed was close by, they sent Girard to sleep.

Girard stood up and rose from eating. The bed was close by, he went to lie down.
Freeborn Guiburc served him willingly; she stayed with him until he fell asleep, then
commended him to the person of the all high God. Girard slept until evening had come,
then he leapt from bed like a true born Frank. He cries out: "Munjoie! Knights, mount
up!" he asks for arms and they are brought to him: then for the first time was Girard
made a knight.*

Then they put a very fine mail shirt on him, and a green helmet they laced on his head;
Willame straps the sword to his left side. He took a great round shield by the grips; he
had a good horse, one of the best in the land. Then Girard mounted by the left stirrup;
Lady Guiburc holds the right one for him, and commends him to God, the mighty Father.

88

Quant il avesprad a la bone cité,
issu s'en est Willame al curb niés
od trente mile de chevalers armez;   1085
en l'Archamp requistrent le paen Deramé.
A la freidure unt tote nuit erré,
jusqu'al demain que le jur apparut cler.
Si cum il furent en l'Archamp sur mer,
la bataille out vencue Deramé   1090
et out pris l'eschec et les morz desarmez.
Entrez erent Sarazins en lur nefs,
et as salandres et as granz escheis ferrez.
Lur vent demoert, si n'en poent turner,
mais les demeines, les seignurs et les pers   1095
tere certeine alerent esgarder
une grant liwe lez le graver de la mer.
Est vus Willame al conseil assené
od .xxx. mille de chevalers armez;
les quinze mile furent si aprestez   1100
cum a ferir en bataille champel.
Cil crient "Muntjoie!" si vont od els juster,
mais li paien nel poeient endurer,
(7d)   car il n'unt armes pur lur cors garder.
Coillent fuie vers la grant eve de mer,   1105
saillent as salandres, et as barges et as niefs;
pernent lur armes, si sunt conreiez.

When evening fell on the good citadel, Willame Hooknose rode out with thirty thousand armed knights; they went to do battle at l'Archamp with the pagan Deramé. They travelled all night in the cold until next morning when the day came bright and clear. By the time they reached l'Archamp by the sea Deramé had won the battle and had gathered in the booty and stripped the dead of their arms. The Saracens had boarded their ships, their great galleys and iron bound barks. The wind they needed had dropped, they could not put to sea, but their leaders, lords and peers were inspecting the country inland over a league behind the seashore. Here is Willame of the wise counsel with thirty thousand armed knights; fifteen thousand of them were equipped and ready to fight in a pitched battle. They shout "Munjoie!" and close with the enemy, but the pagans were in no state to resist, since they had no arms to protect themselves. They turn in flight towards the open sea, leap into their galleys, barges and ships; take their arms and put them on.

89

Ces Sarazins de Saraguce§ tere,
cent mile furent si apresté de guere.
N'i ad nul qui n'ait halberc et healme,   1110
d'or les fruntels et les esses,
espees ceintes, les branz burniz vers terre.
Les escuz tindrent as manueles,
espez trenchanz eurent en lur poinz destres;
chevals d'Arabe unt corant suz lur seles.   1115
Cil s'en issirent en la sable gravele,
si se pristrent defors a la certeine terre.
Par icels orrez doleruses noveles:
cil murent al cunte Willame grant guere.
Cele bataille durad tut un lundi,   1120
et al demain, et tresqu'a mecresdi,
qu'ele n'alaschat, ne hure ne prist fin
jusqu'al joesdi devant prime un petit,
que li Franceis ne finerent de ferir,
ne cil d'Arabe ne cesserent de ferir.   1125
Des homes Willame ne remist un vif
(joesdi al vespre)
fors treis escuz qu'il out al champ tenir.

These Saracens from the land of Saragossa numbered one hundred thousand fully
equipped for war. Not one but has halberk and helmet with gold frontals and decorative
bands, their swords strapped on, their burnished blades pointing to the ground. They held
their shields by the grips, and had sharp spears in their right hands; they had free-running
horses under their saddles. They rode down onto the sandy foreshore and took their
position forward on the firm ground. These people will be the cause of ill tidings: they
embroiled Willame in fierce fighting. That battle lasted a whole Monday, all the next day
and through to Wednesday without easing up, and it did not stop for one hour until
shortly before prime on Thursday, and all that time the French did not stop striking
blows, and likewise the Arabs struck incessantly. Of Willame's men not one remained
alive — Thursday at vespertide — just him and two more shields with which to hold the
field.

---

§ 1108 segune

90

Od treis escuz remist§ al champ tut sul:
li uns fu Girard, li vaillant ferur,   1130
li altres Guischard, le nevou dame Guiburc.
Plaist vus oir des nobles baruns,
cum il severerent del real compaignun?

91

Plaist vus oir des nobles vassals,
cum il severerent del chevaler real?   1135
Desur senestre s'en est turné Girard;
en un sablun li chai sun cheval,
sur ses espalles sun halberc li colad.
Trente paens descendirent al val,
en trente lius naffrerent le vassal   1140
parmi le cors d'espeiez et de darz.
Crie et husche quant la mort l'aproçad.
Dunc survint Willame icele part
(les dis ocist; les vint fuient del val)
(8a)   et vint a Girard, dulcement l'apelad: 1145

He remained all alone on the field with two other shields: one was Girard, the valiant
swordsman, the other was Guischard, Lady Guiburc's nephew. Would you like to hear
about the noble barons, and how they parted from their royal companion?

Would you like to hear about the noble vassals, and how they parted from the royal
knight? Girard turned to his left; his horse fell into a sand hole, his halberk rucked up
over his shoulders. Thirty pagans came down into the valley, in thirty places they
wounded the noble warrior through the body with their spears and javelins. He yelled and
screamed when death came upon him. Then Willame arrived on the scene (he killed ten
of them; the remaining twenty fled from the valley) and came up to Girard, speaking to
him gently.

---

§ 1129 remis

92

"Amis Girard, qui t'en fereit porter,
et des granz plaies purreit tun cors saner,
dites, ami, garreies§ ent, ber?
Tun escientre, entereies ja en ciel?
Respunt Girard: "Sire, laissez ço ester!   1150
Ja ne querreie que jo en fuisse porté,
Ne des granz plaies que fust mun cors sané,
car ne garrai ja pur nul home mortel.
Mais qui tant me ferreit que jo fuisse munté,
et mun vert healme me fust rafermé,   1155
mesist mei al col mun grant escu bocler,
et en mun poing mun espé adolé,
puis me donast un sul trait de un vin cler
(et qui nen ad vin, me doinst del duit troblé)
ne finereie ja mais, par la fei que dei Dé,   1160
cher lur vendereie les plaies de mes costez
dunt a grant force en est li sancs alez!"
Respunt Willame: "N'i remaindrez!"
Joesdi al vespre:
descendi li quons Willame,   1165
tendi sa main, sil prist par la main destre,
en seant le dresçat sur l'erbe:
troble out le vis, et palle la maissele,

"Girard, my kinsman, if someone could carry you from here, and heal your great
wounds, tell me, kinsman, could you get well, brave friend? Do you believe you might
enter Heaven?" Girard replies: "My lord, enough of that! I would never seek to be
carried from here, nor to have my great wounds healed, for I shall get better for no mortal
man. But if someone could put me on my horse, and settle my green helmet back on my
head, hang my great buckler round my neck, and put my sharp spear in my hand, then
give me just one draught of bright wine (if there's no wine give me a drink from the
muddy stream) I would not stop, by the faith I owe God, until I had sold them dearly the
wounds in my sides from which the blood has gushed!" Willame replies: "You'll not stay
here!" Thursday at vespertide: Count Willame dismounted, reached out and took him by
the right hand, sat him up on the grass: his face was twisted with pain, his cheeks pale,

§ 1148 garreie

turnez les oilz que li sistrent en la teste.
Tut le chef li pendi sur senestre,   1170
sur le mentun l'enbronchat sun healme:
quant l'alme en vait ne pot tenir la teste.
Et dist Willame: "Girard, ne poet altre estre!"
Deus, quel doel quant tels baruns desevererent!
N'en pot que ne l'en plainst Willame.   1175

93

Plaist vus oir del nevou dame Guburc
ki de Willame deseverad le jur?
Od sun cheval chai en un sablun§;
sur ses espalles sun halberc li colad tut.
Trente paiens devalerent d'un munt,   1180
en trente lius nafrerent§ le barun;
crie et husche le "aie" de prodom.*
Atant i vint Willame le barun:
les dis oscist; les vint fuient le munt.
Dunc vint a Guischard, si l'ad mis a raisun: 1185

94

(8b)   "Ami Guischard, qui t'en fereit porter
et des granz plaies fereit tun cors saner,

his sunken eyes were turned up in his head. His head hung right over to the left, his
helmet sagged down on his chin: when his soul departed he could not keep his head up.
And Willame said: "Girard, it could not be otherwise!" God, what grief when such brave
warriors part! Willame could not help but lament over him.

Would you like to hear about Lady Guiburc's nephew, who parted from Willame that
day? He fell into a sand hole with his horse; his halberk rucked right up round his
shoulders. Thirty pagans rode down from a hill, in thirty places they wounded the brave
warrior; he yelled and screamed for help from a man of valour.* At that Willame the
brave warrior arrived: he killed ten of them; the other twenty flee back up the hill. Then
he came to Guischard, and spoke to him:

"Guischard, my kinsman, if someone could carry you from here and heal your body of its
great wounds,

---

§ 1178 en sun cheval chai al sablun
§ 1181 nafrererent

tun escientre entereies§* ja en ciel?"
Respunt Guischard: "Sire, laissez mei ester!
Jo ne querreie§ que ja en fuisse porté,   1190
ne des plaies fust mun cors sanez.
Qui me ferreit tant que jo fuisse munté
ja de voz armes ne querreie nul porter!
Mais donez mei sul§ un trait de vin cler;
si n'as altre, veals de cel duit troblé.   1195
Puis m'en irreie a Cordres u fui né,
nen crerreie meis en vostre Dampnedé,
car ço que jo ne vei, ne puis aorer.
Car, si jo eusse Mahomet merciez,
ja ne veisse les plaies de mes costez   1200
dunt a grant force en est le sanc alez."
Respunt Willame: "Glut, mar fuissez tu nez!
Tant cum aveies creance et buntez
retraisistes a la sainte crestienté.
Ore es ocis et de mort afolé,   1205
n'en poez muer, tant as de lasseté.*
Ja de cest champ ne serrez pur mei porté!
Joesdi al vespre:
si s'abeissat li quons Willame,

do you think you might yet enter* Heaven?" Guischard replies: "My lord, leave me be! I
would not seek ever to be carried from here, nor to have my wounds healed. If someone
could put me on my horse I would never seek to bear any weapon of yours! But give me
just one draught of bright wine; if you've nothing else, at least let me have a drink from
this muddy stream. Then I'd be off to Cordoba, where I was born, no more would I
believe in your Lord God, for what I can't see I can't pray to. For if I'd given thanks to
Mahomet I would not be seeing these wounds in my sides from which the blood has
gushed." Willame replies: "Gut bag, a curse on your birth! As long as you believed and
had your health and strength you held yourself to be part of holy Christendom. Now you
have been killed and wrecked by death, you can't help it: you're such a coward.* You'll
never be carried from this field by me! Thursday at vespertide: Count Willame bent
down,

---

§ 1188 entreis

§ 1190 querrereie

§ 1194 mais dunez sul

tendit sa main, sil prist par le braz destre,   1210
en sun seant le levad detrés sa sele.

95

Un Barbarin vint eslaissant§ le val.
Entre ses quisses out un ignel cheval,
en sa main destre§ porte un trenchant dart,
treis feiz l'escust, a la quarte le lançat,   1215
fert en la loigne de la senestre part,
grant demi pé enz el cors li enbat§ :
detrés le cunte en ad mort Guischart.
Peisit le cors, si turne une part,
et il le redresce od sun senestre braz;   1220
devant li le mis sur le col de sun cheval.
Al poig destre li traist del cors le dart
et fier le paien desur le tuenard;
enpeint le ben, par grant vertu l'abat.
N'en fuit mie Willame, ainz s'en vait,   1225
devant li aporte mort Guischard.

(8c)   Joesdi al vespre:
        N'en fuit mie li bons quons Willame!

reached out and took him by the right arm, and raised him to a sitting position behind his saddle.

A Berber came at full tilt along the valley. Between his thighs he had a fast horse, in his right hand he carries a cutting javelin, thrice he brandishes it, the fourth time he threw it, he hit him in the left side of the lumber, burying a good six inches of it in his body: killing Guischard where he sat behind the count. The corpse was heavy and slumped to one side, and he pulls it upright with his left arm; he placed it before him on his horse's neck. With his right hand he pulls the javelin from the body and strikes the pagan on his shield; he sticks him well, and knocks him over with great force. Willame does not flee, he merely goes away, bearing the dead Guischard before him. Thursday at vespertide: the good Count Willame really did not flee!

makes clear hes going for help God + someone else

§ 1212 Un barbarin eslaissant
§ 1214 deste
§ 1217 enabat

96

Dame Guiburc nel mist mie en oblier.
Ele sout en l'Archamp Willame al curb niés   1230
en la bataille le paien Deramé.
Prist ses messages, ses homes fait mander,
tant qu'ele en out .xxx. mile de tels.
Lé .xv. mille furent si apresté
cum de ferir en bataille champel.   1235
Tuz les demeines en ad Guiburc sevrez,
sus al paleis les assist al digner;
chançuns et fables lur fait dire et chanter.
Guiburc meimes les sert de vin aporter.
Dunc s'apuiad al marbrin piler,   1240
par une fenestre prist fors a esgarder
et vit Willame par une tertre avaler
un home mort devant li aporter.
Dunc li sovint de Vivien l'alosé;
si anceis ert lie, dunc comence a plorer: 1245
"Par Deu, seignurs, a faire ai asez!
Parmi cel tertre vei mun seignur avaler,
un home mort devant li aporter;
en gisant l'ad sur sun arçun turné.
Ço est Vivien; jol sai ben assez."   1250
"Tais, ma dame, ja sur li nel turnez!"
Ço li dient les baruns del regné.

Lady Guiburc did not put him out of her mind. She knew that Willame Hooknose was on l'Archamp in battle with the pagan Deramé. She called her messengers to her, sent for her men, raising thirty thousand of them. Fifteen thousand of them were equipped and ready to fight in a pitched battle. Guiburc called aside all the great lords and sat them down to dinner in the great hall she had songs and tales told and sung to them. Guiburc herself served them with wine. Then she leant against a marble pillar turned to look out through a window and saw Willame riding down a hill carrying a dead man before him. Then she remembered Vivien the renowned; if she had been happy before, now she began to cry: "By God, my lords, I have a deal to do! I see my lord riding down that hill, carrying a dead man before him; he's got him lying across his saddle bow. It's Vivien, I'm convinced of it." "Hush, my lady, don't lay that at his door!" say all the barons of the kingdom.

97

"Ki serreit il, dunc, pur Deu merci, seignur,
ke ja Willame aportast de l'estur,
se ço n'ere Lowis, sun seignur,   1255
u Vivien le hardi, sun nevou?"
"Taisez, ma dame, sur els nel metum.
Ainz ad mun seignur Willame un jugleur;
en tote France n'ad si bon chantur,
N'en bataille plus hardi fereur,   1260
et de la geste li set dire les chançuns
de Clodoveu, le premer empereur
qu'en duce France creeit en Deu nostre seignur,
(8d)   et de sun fiz, Flovent le poigneur,
ki laissad de dulce France l'onur,   1265
et de tuz les reis qui furent de valur
tresqu'a Pepin, le petit poigneur,
et de Charlemaigne et de Rollant, sun nevou,
de Girart de Viane, et de Oliver qui fu tant prouz:
cil furent si parent et sis ancesur.   1270
Preuz est mult, et pur ço l'aime mun seignur,
et pur sul itant qu'il est si bon chanteur
et en bataille vassal conquereur,
si l'en aporte mun seignur de l'estur.

"Who could he be then, for God's sake, my lords, whom Willame would ever bring back
from a battle, if it weren't Lowis, his overlord, or Vivien the bold, his nephew?" "Hush,
my lady, let's not think it might be them. Rather, my lord Willame has a jongleur; in the
whole of France there's not such a fine singer, nor a bolder swordsman in battle, and he
can recount in song the ancestral legends of Clodoveu, the first emperor in sweet France
to believe in God our Lord, and of his son Flovent the fighter, who abandoned the sweet
land of France, and of all the kings who were of any account down to Pepin, the little
fighter, and Charlemagne and his nephew Rollant, of Girart de Viane and of Oliver who
was so worthy: they were all his family and his ancestors. He's a man of great worth, that
is why my lord loves him, and just because he is a fine singer and in battle a mighty,
victorious warrior, my lord is carrying him home from the fray.

98

"Seignurs frans, frans homes, pur amur Deu,   1275
preer vus voil que congié me donez.
Il est mi sire, jol dei servir aler."
Ele avale contreval les degrez,
vint a la porte, si li ad desfermé;
ensus le ovre, laissad le cunte entrer.   1280
Il la regarde, et prist lui a demander:
"Dame Guiburc, des quant gardas ma porte?"
"Par ma fai, sire, de novel le faz ore.
Sire quons Willame, mult as petite force!"
"Seor, duce amie, des quant iés mun porter?"   1285
"Par ma fei, sire, de novel nient de vielz!
Sire Willame, poi en remeines chevalers!"

99

"Tien, dame Guiburc, ço est tun nevou, Guischard.
Ja Vivien le cunte vif mes ne verras."
La franche femme li tendi ses braz,   1290
et il li colchat desus le mort vassal.
Peise le cors, si li faillirent les braz:
ele fu femme, si out fieble la char;
contre tere en prist le cors un quas,
tote la langue li turnad une part.   1295

"My Frankish lords, noble men all, for love of God, I beg you to excuse me. He is my lord; I must go and wait on him." She went down the stairs, came to the gate, and unbarred it for him; she also opened it and let the count in. He looked at her and shot a question at her: "Lady Guiburc, how long have you kept my gate?" "By my faith, my lord, I've only just started. My lord Count Willame, you've not much of an army!" "Sister, my sweet, how long have you been my gatekeeper?" "By my faith, my lord, only a short time, not for long! Lord Willame, you've few knights left!"

"Here, Lady Guiburc, this is your nephew, Guischard. You will never see Count Vivien alive again." The noble woman stretched out her arms, and he laid the dead vassal on them. The corpse was heavy, and her arms gave way: she was a woman and her flesh was weak; the corpse tumbled in a heap on the ground, its tongue lolled out on one side.

Joesdi al vespre:
Guiburc le guarde jus a la tere:
troble out le vis et pasle la maissele,
turnez les oilz qui li sistrent en la teste,
tote la langue li pendit sur senestre;   1300
(9a)   sur le mentun li enbrunchat sun halme.
Plurad Guiburc, dunc la confortat Willame.

100

"Par Deu, Guiburc, tu as dreit que tu plurs,
kar ja diseient en la cur mun seignur
que eres femme Willame, uns riche hom,   1305
un hardi cunte, un vaillant fereur;
ore estes femme a un malveis fuieur,
un cuart cunte, un malveis tresturnur
qui de bataille n'ameine home un sul!
Des ore serrez vus vostre keu et vostre pestur: 1310
ne serras mie a la fere barnur,
ne ja verras Vivien mun nevou.
Qui k'en peise, remis est ma baldur,
ja mais en tere n'averai mortel honur."
Plurad Willame, dunc lacrimat Guiburc.   1315
La dame entent la plainte sun seignur,
partie ubliad de la sue dolur.
Quant el parlad, si dist par grant amur:

Thursday at vespertide: Guiburc looked down at it on the ground: its face was livid and
its cheeks pale, its sunken eyes were turned up in the head, its whole tongue lolled out to
the left; its helmet slumped on its chin. Guiburc wept, and then Willame comforted her.

"By God, Guiburc, you're right to cry, for they used to say in my lord's court that you
were the wife of Willame, a powerful man, a bold count, a valiant swordsman; now
you're the wife of a sorry runaway, a coward count, a wretch who abandons the field
leading home from the battle not a single man! From now on you'll be your own cook
and baker: you'll sit no more among the proud barons, and will never see my nephew
Vivien. I don't care whom it upsets, my joy is over, While I'm on earth I'll never again
have honour among men." Willame cried, and Guiburc wept. The lady heard her lord's
lament, and forgot some of her own grief. When she spoke, she said very lovingly:

101

"Marchis Willame, merci, pur amur Dé!
Il est grant doel que home deit plorer,   1320
et fort damage k'il se deit dementer[§].
Il fu custume a tun riche parenté,
quant altres terres alerent purchacer
et tuz tens morurent en bataille champel.
Mielz voil que moergez en l'Archamp sur mer   1325
que tun lignage seit par tei avilé,
ne aprés ta mort a tes heirs reprové."
Quant l'ot Willame prist sun chef a croller,
plurad des oilz[§] tendrement et suef;
Guiburc apele, sa amie et sa moiller,   1330
en sun romanz li ad dit et mustré:
"Seor dulce amie, merci, pur amur Dé!
Qui k'en peise, mult ai a plurer.
Treis cenz anz ad et cinquante passez
(9b)   que jo fu primes de ma mere nez;   1335
veil sui et feble, ne puis armes porter,
ço est failli que Deus m'aveit presté:
la grant juvente que ne poet returner.
Si me unt paiens acuilli a tel vilté,
pur mé ne volent fuir ne tresturner.   1340

"Marquis Willame, mercy, for love of God! It's a great pity for a man to cry, and a great shame for him to rage. It was the custom of your powerful family, when they went to acquire other lands, that they always died on the battlefield. I'd rather you died on l'Archamp by the sea than that your line should be debased by you, or that after your death your heirs should be put to scorn." When Willame heard it he began to shake his head, weeping tenderly and sweetly; he addresses Guiburc, his love and his wife, in his own words explaining to her: "Sister, my sweet, pity, for love of God! I don't care who is upset by it, I've a lot to weep for. It's a full three hundred and fifty years since my mother bore me; I'm old and weak, and can't bear arms any more, what God allowed me has been used up: that is my great youthful manhood, which cannot come back. The pagans have developed such scorn for me that they won't flee or abandon the field for me.

---

§ 1321 dementir
§ 1329 del oilz

La bataille ad vencue Deramé
si ad pris l'eschec et les morz desarmez;
entrez s'en sunt paens en lur niefs.
Loinz sunt les marches u ai a comander,
fort sunt les homes que devreie assembler.   1345
Et quant jo vendreie en l'Archamp sur mer,
si serreient li Sarazin turné.
Ki qu'en peise, jo sui tut sul remés§ :
ja mais en terre n'avrai honur mortel."
Plorad Willame, Guiburc l'a conforté: 1350
"Et, marchis sire, merci, pur amur Dé!
Ore me laissez mentir par vostre gré.
Jo en avrai ja trente mille de tels:
les quinze mille par sunt si aprestez
cum a ferir en bataille champel."   1355
"U sunt il, Guiburc? Tu nel me deiz celer.
Seor duce amie, di m'en la verité."
"Sus el paleis sunt assis al digner."
Dunc rist le cunte, si laissad le plorer.
"Ore va, Guiburc; mentez asez par mun gré."   1360
Dunc contremunt muntad les degrez;
anceis plorat, mais dunc prist a chanter.
Cil la regardent, si li unt demandé:
"Dame Guiburc, que avez vus la defors trové?"

Deramé has won the battle and has gathered up the booty and stripped the dead of their arms; the pagans have embarked on their ships. Distant are the marches over which I have command, strong are the men I should gather about me. By the time I got to l'Archamp by the sea the Saracens would all have gone away. I don't care who's upset, I'm left all alone: while I'm on earth I'll never again have honour among men." Willame wept, and Guiburc comforted him: "Hey! My lord marquis, mercy, for love of God! Now let me lie with your approval. I can get together some thirty thousand: fifteen thousand of them are equipped and ready to fight in a pitched battle." "Where are they, Guiburc? You mustn't keep it from me. Sister, my sweet, tell me the truth." "They're sitting at dinner up in the great hall." Then the count laughed and left off crying. "Go, then, Guiburc; lie in your teeth with my blessing." Then she went up the stairs; previously she had been crying, but now she broke into song. The assembly looked at her and asked her: "Lady Guiburc, what did you find out there?"

---

§ 1348 io sui tut remes

"Par Deu, seignurs, mult de ma volenté.   1365
Ja est venu§ Willame al curb niés
tut sains et salfs, solunc la merci Deu.
Si ad vencu la bataille champel
(9c)   et ocis le paien, Deramé,
mais d'une chose ad malement erré: 1370
il ad perdu sun noble barné,
de dulce France la flur et la belté!
Ocis li unt Vivien l'alosé:
en paisnisme n'en la crestienté
mieldre vassal ne pout estre né   1375
pur eshalcer la sainte crestienté,
ne pur lei maintenir ne garder.
Pur Deu vus pri qu'en l'Archamp alez.
Fruissés sunt les barges et trestotes les nefs;
le vent demoert, ne s'en poent turner.   1380
En une roche, lez un regul de mer,
la sunt dis mille de Sarazins entré;
l'or et l'argent en unt§ od els porté,
et pris l'eschec et les morz desarmez.
Suls fud mi sire, n'i pout mes ester.   1385
Ki ore irreit en l'Archamp sur mer

"By God, my lords, much to my liking. Willame Hooknose has just arrived quite safe
and sound, through God's mercy. Moreover he has won the pitched battle and killed the
pagan, Deramé, but there was one thing went wrong for him: he lost his noble war band,
the flower and adornment of sweet France! They've killed Vivien the renowned: neither
in pagan lands nor in holy Christendom could a better and braver warrior be born to exalt
the holy Christian faith or to defend and keep God's law. I beg you for God's sake to go
to l'Archamp. The barges and all the ships are smashed; the wind has fallen; they can't
put to sea. Up a rocky inlet by the sea, that's where ten thousand Saracens have gone;
they've taken the gold and silver with them, and gathered up the booty and stripped the
dead of their arms. My lord was alone, he could not hold his ground longer. Anyone who
now went to l'Archamp by the sea

---

§ 1366 venue
§ 1383 en vn

prendre icés* dunt vus ai ci cunté

....*   (1387a)

et mis sires ad mult larges heritez,
si vus durrad volenters et de gré.

102

"E ki ne volt sanz femme prendre terres,   1390
jo ai uncore cent et seisante puceles –
filles de reis (n'ad suz cel plus beles),
sis ai nurriz suz la merci Willame,
qui mun orfreis ovrent et pailles a flurs a roeles –
venge a mei et choisist la plus bele!   1395
Durrai lui femme, et mun seignur li durrat terre,
si ben i fert que loez poisse estre."
Tel s'aati de choisir la plus bele
qui en l'Archamp perdi puis la teste.
Joesdi al vespre: 1400
Guiburc meisme sert sun seignur de l'ewe.

103

Puis l'ad assis a une basse table,
(9d)   ne pout aler pur doel a la plus halte.
Puis li aportat d'un sengler un espalle;
li bers la prist, si la mangat en haste: 1405

to take what I have told you about*. . . * and my lord has inherited very extensive lands,
and will freely and willingly give them to you.

"And if there is anyone who will not take lands without a wife, I still have about me one
hundred and sixty maidens — kings' daughters (there are none more beautiful under
Heaven) whom I have brought up with Willame's kind permission, who work my cloth
of gold and embroidered silks — let him come to me and choose the most beautiful! I
shall give him a wife, and my lord shall give him land, if he strikes hard blows enough to
earn his praise." Many boasted they would choose the fairest woman who later lost their
heads on l'Archamp. Thursday at vespertide: Guiburc herself serves her lord with water.

Then she sat him at a low table, he could not go to the highest out of grief. Then she
brought him a shoulder of wild boar; the noble warrior took it and ate it straight from the
spit;

il le§ fist tant cum ele fust mult ate.*
Ele li aportad un grant pain a tamis,
et desur cel dous granz gastels rostiz;
si li aportad un grant poun rosti.
Puis li aportad un grant mazelin de vin: 1410
od ses dous braz i out asez a sustenir!
Mangat Willame le pain a tamis
et en aprés les dous gasteals rostiz;
trestuit mangat le grant braun porcin
et a dous traiz but un sester de vin 1415
et tut mangad les dous gasteals rostiz,
et si que a Guiburc une mie n'en offrid!
Ne redresçad la chere ne le vis!
Veist le Guiburc: crollad sun chef si rist;
pur quant plurat d'amedous des oilz del vis. 1420
Willame apele en sun romanz, si li dist:*
"Par Deu de glorie, qui convertir me fist,
a qui renderai l'alme de ceste peccheriz,
quant ert le terme al jur de grant juis,
qui mangue un grant pain a tamis 1425
et pur ço ne laisse les dous gasteals rostiz
et tut mangue un grant braun porcin
et en aproef un grant poun rosti

he ate it while it was piping hot.* She brought him a great, fine white-loaf, topped off with two roast pasties: she also brought him a great roast peacock. Then she brought him a great maser of wine: she had a job to hold it in both hands! Willame ate the manchet loaf and followed it by the two roast pasties; he ate the whole of the great pork brawn and drank a gallon of wine at two draughts as well as eating the two roast pasties, and all that without offering Guiburc a crumb! He never even looked up or raised his head! Guiburc saw it: she shook her head and laughed; yet she still cried from both eyes. She addressed Willame in her own tongue, and said:* "By the God of Glory, who caused my conversion, to whom I shall deliver my sinner's soul, when the time comes on the great Judgement Day, anyone who can eat a great, fine white-loaf, and not leave because of that his two roast pasties and eats up a whole great pork brawn, and after that a great roast peacock,

---

§ 1406 la

et a dous traiz beit un sester de vin,
ben dure guere deit rendre a sun veisin!   1430
Ja trop vilment ne deit de champ fuir,
ne sun lignage par lui estre plus vil!"
"Seor dulce amie," dist Willame, "merci!
Si jo murreie, qui tendreit mun pais?
Jo n'ai§ tel eir, qui la peusse tenir."   1435
Del feu se dresce un suen nevou, dan Gui.
(10a) Cil fud fiz Boeve Cornebut le marchis,
neez de la fille al prouz cunte Æmeris,*
nevou Willame al bon cunte marchis,
et fud frere Vivien le hardiz.   1440
N'out uncore .xv. anz, asez esteit petiz;
n'out point de barbe, ne sur li peil vif,
fors icel de sun chef, dunt il nasqui.
Sur pez se dresce, devant sun uncle en vint,
si apelad, cum ja purrez oir.   1445
"A la fei, uncle," ço dist li emfes Gui,
"si tu murreies, jo tendreie tun pais!
Guiburc, ma dame, voldreie ben servir;
ja n'averad mal, dunt la puisse garir,
pur ço qu'ele m'ad tant suef nurri."   1450
Quant l'ot Willame, vers l'enfant se grundi.
Dunc li respunt Willame, mult laidement li dist:

and drinks a gallon of wine at two draughts, will wage harsh war on his neighbours! He'll not flee cravenly from the field, or bring shame on his family!" "Sister, my sweet," said Willame, "have pity! If I were to die, who would hold my land? I have no heir who could take it." From the fireside arose a nephew of his, Lord Gui. He was the son of Boeve Hornchest, the marquis, born of the daughter of worthy Count Æmeris,* nephew of Willame, the stout marcher count, and he was brother of Vivien the bold. He was not yet fifteen, and was quite small; he had no beard, nor was he growing any hair, except that on his head, which he was born with. He rose to his feet and came before his uncle, and addressed him as you shall now hear. "In faith, uncle," said the youngster, Gui, "if you were to die, I should hold your land! I would willingly serve my lady Guiburc; she would suffer no harm that I could keep her from, because she has brought me up so carefully." When Willame heard it he lost his temper with the lad. Then Willame answered him very rudely, saying:

§ 1435 Jo na

"Mielz vus vient, glut, en cendres a gisir,
que tei ne fait mun conté a tenir!

104

"Mielz vus vient, gluz, en cendres a reposer,   1455
ke ne te fait a tenir ma cunté!
Guiburc, ma femme, n'avras tu ja a garder!"
Quant l'oi Gui, dunc respunt cum sené:
"A la fei, sire uncle, unques més n'oi tel!"
Respunt Willame: "Glut, de quei m'en culpez?"   1460
"Jo vus dirrai, mais jo m'en voil purpenser
Cum celui qui n'est parfund sené
a sun talent se lait demesurer!
Pur petitesce que m'avez a blasmer?
Ja n'est nul si grant que petit ne fust né!   1465
Et, par la croiz de cel altisme Dé,
ja nen ad home en la crestienté,
men escientre, ne en la bataille Dé,
s'enprof ta mort perneit tes heritez,
puis que mort est Vivien l'alosé,   1470
ne l'ocesisse en bataille champel,
puis saisereie totes voz heritez:
Guiburc, ma dame, fereie mult ben garder!"
(10b) Quant l'ot Willame, prist le chef a croller,

"You, you useless brat, are more suited to lying in the ashes than to having charge of my county!

"You, you useless brat, are more suited to resting in the ashes than to having charge of my county! You'll never have responsibility for guarding Guiburc, my wife!" When Gui heard this he gave a measured answer: "In faith, lord uncle, I never heard the like!" Willame replies: "Brat, what are you accusing me of?" "I'll tell you, but I have it in mind that anyone who isn't deeply reflective gives rein to his feelings and loses control! What have you got to criticise in my being small? No man however big wasn't born small! And, by the Cross of the most high God, there is not this day living any man in Christendom, to my knowledge, nor in God's battalions, if after your death he took your inheritance, since Vivien the renowned is dead, whom I would not kill in pitched battle, after which I would seize all your inheritance: my lady, Guiburc, I would guard very well!" When Willame heard it he began to shake his head,

plurad des oilz tendrement et suef;   1475
l'enfant apele, sil prist a acoler.
Treis feiz le beise, et puis li ad mustré:
"A la fei, niés, sagement as parlé.
Cors as d'enfant, et si as raisun de ber:
aprés ma mort te seit mun fee doné.   1480
Pren le, Guiburc; meine le en ta chimené."
Joesdi al vespre:
n'ad que .xv. anz, si li donad grant terre.

105

Li quons Willame est del manger levé;
prest fu li liz, s'i est culcher alé.   1485
Guiburc la franche l'i tastunad suef.
Il n'i out tele femme en la crestienté
pur sun seignur servir et honorer,
ne pur eshalcer sainte crestienté,
ne pur lei maintenir et garder.   1490
Tant fu od lui qu'il s'endormi suef,
puis comandad sun cors a l'altisme Deu;
dunc vait en la sale as chevalers parler.
Tant dort Willame qu'il fu avespré;
puis salt del lit cum hardi sengler,   1495
criad: "Munjoie! Frans chevalers, muntez!"
Armes demande, et l'em li vait aporter.

he wept tender, sweet tears from his eyes; he spoke to the lad and threw his arms round
his neck. He kissed him three times, and then set out his views: "In faith, nephew, you
have spoken wisely. You have a child's body, but a grown man's judgement: after my
death my fief will be given to you. Take him, Guiburc; lead him to your heated
chamber." Thursday at vespertide: he was only fifteen, but he gave him great lands.

Count Willame got up from eating; the bed was close by, and he went to lie down. Noble
Guiburc gave him a gentle massage. The was no woman like her in Christendom for
serving and honouring her lord, or for exalting the holy Christian faith or for maintaining
and keeping God's law. She stayed with him until he was fast asleep, then commended
his person to the most high God; then she went into the hall to speak to the knights.
Willame slept so long that evening was come: then he leapt from his bed like a brave wild
boar, shouted: "Munjoie! Noble knights, mount up!" He asks for arms, and they are
brought to him.

106

Dunc li vestirent une broine mult bele,
et un vert healme li lacent en la teste;
sa espee out ceinte, le brant burni vers terre;   1500
une grant targe i tint par manevele,
espé trenchante out en sun poig destre.*
. . . .*   (1502a)
Puis li baisad le pié, si l'enclinad vers terre,
sil comandad al glorius rei celestre.

107

Quant il avesprad en la bone cité,   1505
issuz s'en est Willame al curb niés
od .xxx. mille de chevalers armez;
(10c) en l'Archamp requistrent le paien Deramé.
Dunc remist sule Guburc en la bone cité.
En un soler en a§ Guiot mené;   1510
tant cum il virent Willame al curb neis,
Gui et Guiburc sil comanderent a Deu.
Quant plus nel virent, dunc prent Gui a plurer;
veit le Guiburc, prist lui a demander:
"Ami Guiot, que avez a plurer?"   1515
"Par ma fei, dame, a faire l'ai assez!

Then they put on him a very fine mail shirt, and laced a green helmet on his head; his sword strapped on, its burnished blade points to the ground; he held a great round shield by its grips, he had a cutting spear in his right hand.* ...* Then she kissed his foot and bowed down to the ground, and commended him to the glorious King of Heaven.

When evening fell over the good citadel, Willame Hooknose rode out with thirty thousand armed knights; they went to do battle at l'Archamp with the pagan Deramé. Then Guiburc remained alone in the good citadel. She led Gui up to an open loggia; for as long as they could see Willame Hooknose Gui and Guiburc both commended him to God. When they could no longer see him, Gui began to cry; Guiburc saw it, and started asking him: "Guiot, my kinsman, what have you to cry about?" "By my faith, my lady, I've reason enough!

---

§ 1510 unt

N'ai que .xv. anz, si sui en tel vilté
retenu sui de bataille champel.
Qui me durreit ne fee ne heritez,
quant nel deserf od espee de lez? 1520
Parmi cel tertre vei mun seignur aler;
vilment chevalche a bataille champel:
od lui n'ameine nul sun ami charnel,
fors Deu de glorie qui le mund ad a salver!"
Respunt Guiburc: "Merci, Guiot, pur Deu! 1525
Trop par es enfes et de petit eé,
si ne purreies ne travailler ne pener,
la nuit veiller ne le jur juner,
la grant bataille suffrir n'endurer.
Si t'ad le cunte ci a mei comandé; 1530
par nul engin ne te larrai aler,
car jo creim perdre sa amisté et sun gred."
Respunt Guiot: "Unc mais nen oi tel!
Jo sai mentir, si li voldrai cunter
que jo vus sui tut par force eschapé. 1535
Sil te plevis et de Deu et de mei,
se jo n'i vois, en l'Archam sur mer,
ja ne verras Willame od le curb niés.
Et si jo vois, voldrai l'en amener."
Respunt Guiburc: "Dunc te larrai aler." 1540

I'm only fifteen, so they shame me by keeping me from the battlefield. Who would ever give me a fief or inheritance if I didn't earn it with the sword by my side? I saw my lord ride across that hill; he is riding shamefully to the battlefield: he's not taking a single kinsman with him, except the God of Glory, Saviour of the world!" Guiburc replies: "Have pity, Guiot, for God's sake! You really are a child and very young, and couldn't take the pain and effort, keep watch all night and fast all day, and put up with conditions in the great battle. Anyway, the count put you in my care here; for no trick of yours will I let you go, for I fear to lose his love and good will." Guiot replies: "I never heard the like! I know how to lie, and will tell him that I escaped from you entirely by force. And I promise you in God's name and mine, if I don't go to l'Archam by the sea, you'll never see Willame Hooknose again. And if I go I'll be sure to bring him back." Guiburc replies: "Then I'll let you go."

108

Dunc li vestent une petite broine,
(10d) et une petite healme li lacent desure;
petite espee[§] li ceinstrent, mais mult fu bone;
al col li pendirent une petite targe duble.
Puis li aportat une glaive petite,   1545
bon fu li fers, et redde en fu la hanste;
deci qu'as poinz li batid l'enseigne.
El li[§] ameine Balzan, sun sambuer;
bone est la sele, mais curt sunt li estriver –
unc Guiburc nel prestad a chevaler.   1550
Dunc muntat Guiot et Guiburc li tint l'estriu;
puis li comandat al criatur del ciel.

109

Petit est Gui, et li cheval est grant,
n'est que pé et demi desus les arçuns parant,
et sul trei deie suz le feltre brochant: 1555
mielz portad armes que uns hom de trente anz.
Guiot point Balçan, si li laissad la reisne.
Pé et demi out le cors sur la sele;
a sul trei deie brochad desuz le feltre.

Then they put a small mail shirt on him, and laced a little helmet over it; they strapped a little sword on him, but it was a very good one; round his neck they hung a little, cross-braced, round shield. Then they brought him a little spear, its blade was good and its shaft was stiff; its standard hung down to his hands. She brought him Balzan, her palfrey; its saddle was good, but the stirrup straps were short — Guiburc never lent it to a knight. Then Guiot mounted and Guiburc held the stirrup for him; then she commended him to the Creator of Heaven.

Small is Gui, and the horse is big, he shows only a foot and a half above the saddlebow, and his spurs strike just three hands below the saddlecloth: he bore his arms better than a thirty year-old man. Guiot spurred on Balçan, and gave him full rein. His body rose a foot and a half above the saddle; his spurs struck just three hands below the saddlecloth.

[§] 1543 petite espec
[§] 1548 eli li ameine

Et ele le comandat a Deu, le grant Dé paterne. 1560
As esquiers se mist Guiot en la grant presse.

110

Tote nuit ad od esquiers erré
jusqu'al demain que li jur apparut cler.
Si cum il vindrent en l'Archamp desur mer,
as chevalers vait Willame parler. 1565
Les baruns en ad par sei sevrez;
a un conseil une part en sunt alé,
en sun romanz lur ad dit et mustré:
"Seignurs baruns, mei devez vus aier.
Jo ne vus toil voz vealtrez ne voz chens, 1570
si voliez ainz vus durrai des miens,
ne nen voil prendre ostur ne espervier,
ne nul semblant faire de nul enplaider.
Si le pere fu morz, jo en oi le fiz si cher
que unc la mere nel laissai corescer. 1575
(11a) Ne ja mais sergant ne fis sun aveir chacer,
ainz en nurri les fiz mult volenters,
sis gardai tant que jo en fis chevalers.
Tote la terre li rendi sanz relef;
s'il fu petit, jo l'acru del mien. 1580
Fel seit Willame, s'il unques en out dener!
Ore socurrez hui vostre gunfanuner!"

And she commends him to God, the Heavenly Father. Guiot mingled with the squires in the great throng.

He travelled all night with the squires until the next morning when the day came bright and clear. As soon as they arrived at l'Archamp by the sea Willame went to speak to the knights. He took the barons to one side with himself; they went on one side and formed a council, in his own tongue he said to them, explaining: "My lord barons, you must give me aid. I take neither your hounds nor your dogs from you, if you wanted, I had sooner give you my own, and I have no desire to take goshawk or sparrow hawk, or to give the impression of being litigious. If the father died, I held his son so dear that I never gave the mother cause for distress. And I never had a common man-at-arms's goods driven off, but rather willingly brought up his sons, and looked after them until I could make them knights. I returned all his land to the heir without relief; if his fief was small I enlarged it from my own property. May Willame be branded a thief if he ever got a penny out of it! The time has come today to give aid to your standard bearer!"

Et cil respunent: "Sire, mult volenters!
Ne vus faldrum tant cum serrum sur pez."
Lunsdi al vespre: 1585
de tel seignur deit l'um tenir terre,
et, si bosoinz est, morir en la presse.

111

Dunc laist les demeines quant l'orent afié;
as vavassurs en vait dan Willame parler,
a un conseil les ad tuz amenez.   1590
En sun romanz lur ad dit et mustrez:
"Seignurs baruns, vavasurs onurez,
en ceste terre nus ad requis Deramé.
Le sun orguil ne deit gueres durer,
et hom nel deit§ mie soffrir ne esgarder.   1595
Pur ço vus di, frans chevalers provez,
tel home m'unt ocis dunt mult me deit peser,
car il m'unt mort Vivien l'alosé.
Deça la Rin ne de dela la mer,
en paenisme n'en la crestienté   1600
ne pout l'om unques mieldre vassal trover
pur eshalcer§ sainte crestienté,
ne pur lei meintenir et garder.

And they reply: "My lord, most willingly! We'll not fail you as long as we stand on our feet." Monday at vespertide: from such a lord should a man hold his land, and, at need, die for him in the mêlée.

Then he leaves the great lords, when they have sworn fealty to him. Lord Willame went next to speak to the vavassours, taking them all aside into a council. In his own tongue he spoke to them, explaining: "My lord barons, honoured vavassours, Deramé has come to give battle to us in this land. His pride must not last long, and a man should not put up with him or take account of him. I am telling you this, freeborn, proven knights, because they have killed such a man of mine that it must cause me great grief, for they have killed Vivien the renowned. Neither this side of the Rhine nor beyond the sea, in pagan lands nor in Christendom could you ever find a better vassal to exalt the holy Christian faith or to defend and keep God's law.

§ 1595 hom ne deit
§ 1602 esahlcer

Pur ço vus di, francs chevalers menbrez,
il nen ad home en la crestienté   1605
tant vavasurs peusse de tels asembler
fors Lowis, qui France ad a garder
cum dreit seignur, li noble onuré.
Encontre lui ne me dei pas vanter.

112

(11b) "Ore entendez, frans chevalers provez: 1610
ja n'ert ben faite grant bataille champel,
se vavassurs ne la funt endurer
et ne la meintenent les legers bachelers,
les forz, les vigrus, les hardiz, les menbrez!"
Dunc gardat entr'els, si vit Guiot ester.   1615
Il lur demande: "Qui est cel petit armé
sur cel cheval, qui entre vus vei ester?
Bosoing out de homes qui ça l'ad amené!"
Cil respundent: "Pur quei nus demandez?
Guiot, vostre neveu, deussez conuistre assez!"   1620
Quant l'ot Willame, prist le chef a croller;
dunc plurad des oilz tendrement et suef.
Dunc comence Guiburc forment a blasmer:
"Mal gré en ait hui de Deu ma moiller!
Ore i pert, nés, que ne li apartenez!"   1625
Quant l'oi Gui, dunc respunt que senez:

I am telling you this, freeborn, sturdy knights, because there is no man in Christendom
who could assemble so many vavassours like you except Lowis, who has France to
defend as rightful lord, the honoured, noble man. I must not set myself up to equal him.

"Now listen, freeborn, proven knights: a pitched battle will never be fought properly, if
the vavassours do not stand firm and if the fit, young knights do not keep up the pressure,
being strong, vigorous, bold and sturdy!" Then he looked them over and saw Guiot
standing among them. He asked them: "Who's this little fellow under arms on that horse,
whom I see standing among you? Whoever brought him along was short of men!" They
reply: "Why are you asking us? You ought to recognise your nephew, Guiot, well
enough!" When Willame heard it he started shaking his head; then he wept tender, sweet
tears from his eyes. Then he began to criticise Guiburc roundly: "God's curse on my wife
today! It's quite clear, nephew, that she has no control over you!" When Gui heard that
he gave a measured reply:

"A ma fei, sire, a grant tort la blamez!
A une femme me comandas a garder,
et jo li sui tut par force eschapé."
"Glut," dit le cunte, "vus de quei me colpez?"   1630
"Jo vus dirrai, mais un petit m'atendez.
Veez paiens§ as barges et as niés:
tel home unt mort dunt§ mult vus deit peser.
Il unt ocis Vivien l'alosé:
sur els devon nus vostre maltalent torner."   1635
"Par ma fei, nés, sagement as parlé;
cors as d'enfant, et raisun as de ber:
aprof ma mort tei seit mun fé doné.
Mais d'une chose me pot forment peser:
trop par es joefne et de petit eed,   1640
si ne purras travailler ne pener,
les nuiz veiller et les jurz juner,
la grant bataille suffrir ne endurer.
(11c) Mais jo te ferai sur cel munt mener;
a vint de mes homes te ferai iloec garder.   1645
Itant i perdirai, et si ne gaignerai el;
icil m'aidassent en bataille champel."
Respunt dan Guiot: "Unc mais n'oi itel!"
"Niés," dist Willame, "de quei m'aculpez?"

"By my faith, my lord, you're very wrong to criticise her! You commended me to the
care of a woman, and I escaped from her by pure force." "Brat," said the count, "what are
you accusing me of?" "I'll tell you, but just hang on a minute. You can see there the
pagans at their barges and ships: they have killed such a man as must cause you great
grief. They have killed Vivien the renowned: we should turn our anger on them." "By my
faith, nephew, you have spoken wisely; you have a child's body, and the judgement of a
grown man: after my death let my fief be given to you. But here's one thing upsets me
greatly: you are extremely young and of few years, you will not be able to stand the effort
or the pain, keep watch all night and fast all day, or stand up to the hardships of the great
battle. I'll just have you led up onto that hill; I'll have twenty of my men guard you there.
I'll lose that much by it which I won't make up elsewhere; those men would have
supported me on the battlefield." Replies Lord Guiot: "I never heard the like!"
"Nephew," said Willame, "what are you accusing me of?"

---

§ 1632 paies
§ 1633 dut

"Jol vus dirrai, quant tu le m'as demandé.   1650
Quidez vus dunc que Deus seit si oblié,
qui les granz homes pot tenir et garder,
qu'il ne face des petiz altretel?
Ja n'est nul granz que petit ne fud né.
Uncore hui ferrai de l'espee de mun lez,   1655
si purrai ben mun hardement prover,
si en mei ert salve l'onur et le herité."
Respunt Willame: "Sagement t'oi parler.
Poig dunc avant, fai cel cheval errer:
ore voil veer cum poez armes porter."   1660
Gui point Balçan, si li laschad les reisnes.
Pé et demi ad le cors sur la sele;
a sul trei deie broche desuz la feltre.
Brandist la hanste desur le braz senestre,
tote l'enseigne fait venir tresk'en terre;   1665
il la redresce, et le vent la ventele.
Balçan retient en quatre pez de terre,
si que la cue li trainad sur l'erbe§;
dreit a sun seignur dresçat sa reisne.
Ço dist Willame: "Ben deis chevaler estre: 1670
si fut tis pere et ti altre§ ancestre."

"I'll tell you, since you've asked. Do you think God is so out of reckoning, if He can
protect and keep the big men, that He can't do the same for the small? There is no big
man who wasn't born small. This very day I'll strike blows with the sword by my side,
and I'll thoroughly prove my hardihood, and your office and inheritance will be safe with
me." Willame replies: "I hear you speak wisely. Spur on, get that horse moving: now I
want to see how you bear your arms." Gui put spurs to Balçan, and gave him full rein.
His body came a foot and a half above the saddle; the spurs strike just three hands below
the saddlecloth. He brandished his lance across his left arm, making the whole standard
sweep down to the ground; he lifted it high, and the wind made it flap. He reined Balçan
to a halt in just four paces, so that his tail dragged on the grass: he turned his rein to face
his lord. Said Willame: "You just have to be a knight: just like your father and the rest of
your ancestors."

---

§ 1668 lerbes
§ 1671 tis altres

113

"Ça traez, niés Gui, vers mun destre poig;
od le mien ensemble porte tun gunfanun:
si jo t'ai, ne crem malveis engrun."
Il s'asemblerent; le jur furent baruns,   1675
en la bataille dous reals conpaignuns.
Paene gent mistrent a grant dolur.
Lunsdi al vespre:
(11d) si n'i alast Gui, ne revenist Willame!

114

La bataille out vencue Deramé   1680
a l'altre feiz que Willame i fu al curb niés,
si out pris l'eschec et les morz desarmez.
Entrez erent Sarazins en lur nefs;
lur vent demoert, ne s'en poent turner.
Mais les seignurs des paens et les pers[§],   1685
ben tresqu'a vint mile de la gent Deramé,
terre certeine alerent regarder
une grant liue loinz del graver sur la mer.
Ensemble od els unt lur manger aporté:
en renc esteient assis a un digner.   1690
Es vus Willame al manger asené
od .xxx. mile de chevalers armez,

"Come over here, nephew Gui, by my right hand; carry your pennant alongside mine: if I have you by me I fear no evil pass." They stood together; that day they were both barons, in the battle they were two royal companions. They caused great grief to the pagan folk. Monday at vespertide: if Gui had not gone, Willame would not have returned!

Deramé had won the battle the previous time when Willame Hooknose was there, and had gathered up the booty and stripped the dead of their arms. The Saracens had entered their ships; the wind they needed had dropped, they could not put to sea. But the pagan lords and peers, a good twenty thousand of Deramé's people, had gone to inspect the country inland, a good league distant from the seashore. They had taken their food with them: they were sitting in a row eating dinner. Here comes Willame bent on dinner with twenty thousand armed knights,

[§] 1685 perers

qui un freit més lur ad aporté.
Crient: "Muntjoie!" si vont od els juster.
Paien escrient: "Francs chevalers, muntez!" 1695
Dunc saillent des tables a l'estur communel.
Iço i remist, que ne s'en pout turner:
pain et vin et char i ad remis assez,
vaissele d'or et tapiz et dossels.
Mais li paien nen purent endurer, 1700
acuillent fuie vers la halte eve de mer,
si entrent es barges et es nefs.
Pernent lur armes pur lur cors conreier,
a terre certeine lur vint estur doner.

115*

Li quons Willame l'eust dunc ben fait, 1705
a grant honur l'eust Dampnedeu atrait,
quant Deramé li salt d'un agait,
od lui .xv. reis que jo nomer vus sai:
Encas de Egipte et li reis Ostramai,
Butifer li prouz et li forz Garmais, 1710
Turlen de Dosturges et sis nief Alfais,
Nubles de Inde et Ander li Persans,
Aristragot, Cabuel et Morans,
(12a) Clamador et Salvains et Varians
et li reis de Nubie et li guerreres Tornas. 1715

bringing them a cold dish. They shout "Muntjoie!" and close with them. The pagans shout out: "Freeborn knights, mount up!" Then they leap up from the tables into the general mêlée. What could not get away stayed behind : plenty of bread and wine and meat stayed behind, gold plate and carpets and cushions. But the pagans could not withstand the charge, they took flight towards the high seas, and embark on their barges and ships. They take their arms to equip themselves; they came to give battle on the firm ground.

Count Willame would have had great success – the Lord God would have accorded him great honour — when Deramé came suddenly upon him from an ambush, accompanied by fifteen kings whom I can name for you: Encas of Egypt and King Ostramai, Butifer the worthy and the strong Garmais, Turlen of Dosturges and his nephew Alfais, Nuble of India and Ander the Persian, Aristragot, Cabuel and Morans, Clamador and Salvains and Varians and the king of Nubie and the warrior Tornas.

Chascun d'els out mil homes de sa part,
si manguent la gent cum dragun et leppart.
En bataille ferent sanz nul regart;
li uns les meine quant li altre les abat:
huimais irrunt Franceis a dolerus ahan.   1720
La fu pris le nevou Willame, Bertram,
et Guielin et li vaillant quons Guischard,
Galter de Termes et Reiner le combatant.
Estreit les unt liez Sarazins et Persant;
veant le cunte les meinent as chalans   1725
que unques de rien ne lur poet estre garant.
Tuz sunt Franceis pris et morz al champ,
fors sul Willame qui ferement se combat,
et Guiot, sis niés, qui li vait adestrant.

116

Clers fu li jurz et bels fu li matins,   1730
li soleiz raie qui les armes esclargist.
Les raies ferent sur la targe dan Gui,
mult tendrement pluret§ des oilz de sun vis.
Veit le Willame; a demander li prist§ :
"Ço que pot estre, bels niés, sire Gui?"   1735
Respunt li enfes: "Jo vus avrai ja dit.

Each of them had a thousand men in his train, and they eat people like dragons and leopards. In battle they strike without taking heed; one leads off captive those another strikes down: from now on the French will have grievous strife. There were captured Willame's nephew, Bertram, and Guielin and the valiant Count Guischard, Galter of Termes and Reiner the fighter. The Saracens and Persians bound them up tightly; before the eyes of the count they led them to the transports without his being able to offer them any support. All the French were either captured or killed on the field, with the sole exception of Willame, who fought fiercely, and Guiot, his nephew, who rode at his right hand.

Bright was the day and fair the morning, the sun was shining making the arms gleam. Its beams struck Lord Gui's round shield; very tenderly he wept tears from the eyes in his head. Willame saw it; he immediately asked him: "What is the matter, dear nephew, Lord Gui?" The lad replies: "It's soon told.

---

§ 1733 plurent
§ 1734 demander li prist

Mar vi Guiburc, qui suef me norist,
qui me soleit faire disner si matin!
Ore est le terme qu'ele le me soleit offrir;
ore ai tel faim, ja me verras morir. 1740
Ne puis mes armes manier ne sustenir,
brandir ma hanste, ne le Balçan tenir,
ne a mei aider, ne a altre nuisir.
Aincui murrai; ço est duel et peril.
Deus, quele suffraite en avront mi ami, 1745
car tele faim ai, ja m'enragerai vif.
Ore voldreie estre a ma dame servir!
(12b) Moert mei le quor; falt mei mun vasselage.
Ne puis aider a mei, ne nuisir a altre;
porter ne puis, ne justiser mes armes. 1750
Ancui murrai; ço est duel et damage!

117

"Moerent mi, uncle, anduis les oilz de mun chef;
faillent mei les braz, ne me puis prof aider,
car tel faim ai, ja serrai esragé.
Mar vi Guburc, vostre franche moiller, 1755
qui me soleit faire si matin manger!
Aincui murrai a duel et a pecché:
Deus, quele suffreite en avreient chevaler!
Uncore vivereie, si aveie a manger."

To my cost did I ever know Guiburc, who brought me up so tenderly, who was in the habit of giving me such an early dinner! This is the time when she used to offer it to me; now I'm so hungry, you're about to see me die. I can't handle or hold up my weapons, brandish my lance or keep control of Balçan, or help myself, or harm others. This very day I shall die; it's a shame and a real danger. God, how my kinfolk will miss me, because I'm so hungry I'll go running mad. How I would love to be serving my lady just now! My heart is dying in me; my warrior's strength is giving out. I can't help myself or harm others; I can neither carry nor control my weapons. I shall die this very day; it's a crying shame!

"Uncle, both my eyes are dying in my head; my arms are growing weak, they are of no use to me, for I'm so hungry I shall soon go mad. To my cost did I get to know Guiburc, your noble wife, who regularly made me eat so early in the morning! This very day I shall die in grief and shame: God, how the company of knights will miss me! I could yet live, if I had anything to eat."

"Deus, u le prendrai?" Willame li respundi.   1760
Lunsdi al vespre:
Deus, que ore n'ad pain et vin Willame!

117a*

"Uncle Willame, que purrai devenir?
Falt mei le quor, par fei le vus plevis.
Ne puis mes armes manier ne tenir,   1765
ne mun cheval poindre ne retenir.
Se jo moerc, ço ert doels et perilz!
Dunc ne remaindrat gueres de mun lin."
"Niés," dist Willame, "mult en sui entrepris.
Savriez vus aler al meisnel   1770
u nus trovames lunsdi les Sarazins?
La u il esteient a lur manger asis,
ço i remist que ne s'en pout fuir."
"Que fu ço, uncle?" "Pain et char et vin.
Alez i, niés," ço li dist li marchis.   1775
"Mangez del pain; petit bevez del vin,
puis si me socurez al dolerus peril.
Ne me ublier: mult sui en tei fis."
Iloec desevrerent entre Willame et Gui.

118

Lores fu mecresdi.   1780
Quant s'en turnad Gui li enfes

"God, where will I find anything?" Willame replied. Monday at vespertide: God, why hasn't Willame got bread and wine!

"Uncle Willame, what will become of me? My heart is failing, I give you my word on it. I can neither handle nor lift my weapons, nor spur on nor rein in my horse. If I die it will be a shame and a danger! Then will hardly any of my kin be left." "Nephew," said Willame, "I can't think what to do. Do you think you could make it to the farmstead where we found the Saracens on Monday? In the place where they were sitting eating, what couldn't flee stayed behind." "What was that, uncle?" "Bread and meat and wine. Go there, nephew," said the marquis, "eat some of the bread; drink a little of the wine, then come and help me in the grievous peril. Don't forget me: I'm putting a lot of trust in you." With that Willame and Gui parted from each other.

Then it was Wednesday. When young Gui went away

(12c) par la terre al meisnel pur la viande quere, *
       paien l'acuillent as chevals de la terre.
       Mult lur ert loinz, quant fu hors de la terre.
       Quant paien veient que ne l'ateindrunt en fin,   1785
       lessent le aler; de Mahomet l'unt maldit:
       "Cist nus querrat ço que Girard nus quist,
       quant il Willame nus amenat ici.
       Cist vait en France pur le rei Lowis.
       Turnum arere al dolerus peril: 1790
       Cil qui de la est ne returnerat ja vif!"
       Dunc corurent sur Willame le marchiz.
       Et Guiot vait tut dreit al meisnil,
       si descendi del cheval u il sist.
       Mangat del pain – mes ço fu petit;   1795
       un grant sester but en haste del vin!
       Puis est munté, si acuilli sun chemin.
       Et paens venent et Turs et Sarazins,
       si acuillent Willame le marchis.
       Li quons Willame, quant il les veit venir,   1800
       crie "Munjoie!" sis vait tuz envair:
       a sul s'espee en ad seisante ocis.
       Si cum paiens li furent de totes parz,
       si li lancent lur guivres et lur darz,
       et lur falsarz et lur espeez trenchanz.   1805
       Entre les quisses li gettent mort Liard.

across the land* to the farmstead to look for the food, the pagans charged down on him,
riding local horses. He was a long way ahead of them when he left the land. When the
pagans saw that they would not finally catch up with him, they let him go; they cursed
him in the name of Mahomet: "This one will bring on us what Girard did, when he
brought Willame here. This one's going to France for King Lowis. Let's get back to the
grievous peril: the man out yonder won't get away alive! Then they charged at Willame
the marquis. And Guiot went straight to the farmstead, and dismounted from his horse.
He ate some of the bread – but just a little; he gulped down a great gallon of the wine!
Then he mounted and got on his way. And pagans come and Turks and Saracens, and
attack Willame the marquis. When Count Willame sees them coming he shouts
"Munjoie!" and charges at them: with just his own spear he has killed sixty of them.
Since the pagans were all around him they threw their javelins and spears at him, and
their falchions and sharp spears. They kill Liard under him.

Es vus a pé le noble vassal!
Il traist s'espee, vassalment§ se combat.

119

Si cum paiens l'unt si acuilliz,
lancent li lances et lur trenchanz espeez.   1810
Tant en abatent en sun escu§ a quarters
qu'envers sa teste nel pout§ mie drescer.
Encontre terre mistrent le chevaler:
tote la forme repert al graver!
Granz colps li donent de lances et d'espees;   1815
(12d) forte est la broine, quant ne la poent desmailler.
Parmi la gule li funt§ le sanc raier,
dunc huche et crie: "Vien, Gui, bels niés!
Securez mei, si unques fus chevalers!"
Idunques repeirout li enfes qui out mangé;   1820
encontreval l'escri entendi ben.

120

Quant Gui li enfes devalad le tertre,
si oit Willame crier en la presse§.

Behold the noble vassal on foot! He draws his sword, and fights as a warrior should.

When the pagans attacked him they threw lances and sharp spears at him. So many land in his quartered shield that he cannot raise it up to his face. They beat the knight down to the ground: his whole shape appeared in the beach! They rain great blows on him with lances and swords: his mail shirt was strong since they could not loosen its links. They make him bleed copiously from the throat, then he screams and shouts: "Come here, Gui, dear nephew! Rescue me, if ever you were a knight!" Just then the lad, who had finished eating, was coming back; he heard the cry down in the valley all right.

When young Gui came down the hill, he heard Willame shouting in the mêlée

---

§ 1808 vaissalment
§ 1811 a sun en sun escu
§ 1812 ne pout
§ 1817 li fun
§ 1823 la press

Fiert un paien§ sur la duble targe novele;
tote li fent et froisse et encantele,   1825
sun bon halberc li desrunt et deserre,
mort le trebuche del cheval a terre.
Crie: "Munjoie!" Et dist: "Vis, uncles Willame?"
Puis fiert un altre sur la targe novele;
tote li fent et fruisse et escantele,   1830
et sun halberc li runt et desmaele,
colpe le piz suz la large gonele
que mort le trebuche des arçuns de la sele.
Crie: "Munjoie! Vis, uncle Willame?"
Puis fert le terz sur la targe duble;   1835
tote la fent de sus jusqu'a la bocle:
les asteles l'en ferent suz la gule.
Sun grant espee al graver li met ultre
que l'os del col li bruse et esmuille;
tres ses esspalles l'enseigne li mist ultre.   1840
Quant li gluz chai la hanste li estruse.
A icel colp la bon' espee mustre.

121

Gui traist l'espee, dunc fu chevaler;
la mure en ad contremunt dresçé.

He strikes a pagan on his new, cross-braced, round shield; he splits it through and smashes it to splinters, he tears wide open his sturdy halberk, knocks him off his horse and kills him. He shouts: "Munjoie!" and says: "Are you alive, uncle Willame?" Then he strikes another one on his new, round shield: he splits it right through and smashes it to splinters, and tears rows of links from his halberk, cuts open his chest under his broad tunic with the result that he knocks him dead out of his saddle. He shouts: "Munjoie! Are you alive, uncle Willame?" Then he strikes a third on his cross-braced, round shield; He splits it right to the boss: the shards hit him under the throat. He puts his great spear right through him into the beach so that he breaks his neck and the marrow spills from the bone; he thrusts his standard right out through his shoulders. When the swine fell he broke the shaft of the lance. On that stroke he shows forth his fine sword.

Gui drew his sword, and then became a knight; he raised its point on high.

---

§ 1824 paie

Fert un paien sus en le halme de sun chef,   1845
tresque al nasel li trenchad et fendit,
le meistre os li ad colpé del chef.
Grant fud li colps, et Guiot fu irez;
tut le purfent desque enz al baldré,
(13a) colpe la sele et le dos del destrer: 1850
en mi le champ en fist quatre meitez!
De cel colp sunt paien esmaiez,
dist li uns a l'altre: "Ço est fuildre que cheit!
Revescuz est Vivien le guerreier."
Turnent en fuie, si unt le champ laissié.   1855
Dunc se redresçat Willame desur ses pez,
et li quons Willame fud dunc punners.

122

Ço fu grant miracle que nostre Sire fist:
pur un sul home en fuirent vint mil!
Dreit a la mer s'en turnent Sarazin.   1860
Dunc se redresçat Willame le marchiz,
sis enchascerent as espees acerins.

123

Si cum paiens s'en fuient vers la mer,
li ber Willame est sur pez levez,
sis enchascerent as espees des liez.   1865
Gui vit sun uncle el champ a pé errer,

He struck a pagan on the helmet covering his head, the cut split it open down to the nasal, and sheared through his skull. Great was the blow, and Gui was in a fury: he split him open right down to his baldrick, cuts through the charger's saddle and back: in the midst of the field he made four halves of them! The pagans were dismayed by that blow, and said to each other: "It's a thunderbolt falling! Vivien the warrior has come back to life." They turn in flight and abandon the field. Then Willame stood up and Count Willame became an infantryman.

Our Lord performed a great miracle: for a single man twenty thousand flee! The Saracens headed straight for the sea. Then Willame the marquis stood up, and they pursued them with their steel swords.

As the pagans fled towards the sea, brave Willame stood up, and they pursued them with the swords at their sides. Gui saw his uncle walking through the field,

le cheval broche, si li est encontre alé.
"Sire," dist il, "sur cest cheval muntez.
Guiburc, ma dame, le me prestad de sun gré."
Gui descent, et Willame i est munté.   1870
Quant il fu sus, començad a parler:
"Par ma fei, niés, tu m'as§ pur fol mené!
L'altrer me diseies que li eres eschapé;
ore me dis que sun cheval t'ad presté.
Qui te comandat ma muiller encuser?"   1875
Ço respunt Gui: "Unc mais n'oi tel!
Poignez avant, dreitement a la mer:
ja s'en serrunt li Sarazin alé!"
A cel colp ad sa bone espee mustré§ .*

124

Li bers Willame chevalche par le champ,   1880
sa espee traite, sun healme va enclinant.
Les pez li pendent desuz les estrius a l'enfant;
a ses garez li vunt les fers§ batant.
(13b) Et tint sa espee entre le punz et le brant,*
del plat la porte sur sun arçun devant.   1885
Et Balçan li vait mult suef amblant,
Et Gui, sis niés, le vait a pié siuvant,

spurred his horse and went to meet him. "My lord," he said, "mount this horse. My lady,
Guiburc, willingly lent it to me." Gui dismounts and Willame mounts. When he was on
its back he began to speak: "By my faith, nephew, you've treated me like a fool! The
other day you were saying you'd escaped from her; now you're telling me she lent you
the horse. Who told you to make accusations against my wife?" Gui replies: "I never
heard the like! Spur on, straight to the sea: the Saracens will have got away already!"
With that blow he showed forth his fine sword.*

The brave warrior Willame rode through the field, his sword drawn, his helmet tilting.
His feet hang below the young lad's stirrups; the metal stirrups catch him behind the
knees. He held his sword between pommel and blade* with the flat of the blade resting on
his saddle bow. And Balçan ambles on most gently, and Gui, his nephew, follows him on
foot,

§ 1872 tu as
§ 1879 a cel colp sa bone espee mustre
§ 1883 li vint les fers

d'ures en altres desqu'al genoil el sanc.
Reis Deramé giseit enmi le champ
envolupé de sablun et de sanc.   1890
Quant Willame le veit, sil conuit al contenant.
Quidat li reis qu'il eust pris de darz tel haan,
qu'envers nul home ne fust mes defendant.
Ore se purpense de mult grant hardement;
sur piez se dresce, si ad pris sun alferant,   1895
ostad la raisne del destre pé devant,
prist sun espé qui fu bone et trenchant,
de plaine terre sailli sus a l'alferant,
dreit envers els en est alé brochant.

125

Li bers Willame vit le paien venir,   1900
le cors escure, la grant hanste brandir;
et il tint s'espee devant enmi le vis.
Dunc l'en esgarde li reis dé Sarazins;
le cure leist, al petit pas s'est mis.
"A! uncle Willame," dist sun petit nevou Gui,   1905
"ore pri vus, sire, pur la tue merci,
que vus me rendez mun destrer arabi,
si justerai al culvert sarazin.

repeatedly sinking in blood up to his knees. King Deramé was lying in the field
smothered in sand and blood. When Willame saw him he knew his face. The king
thought he had suffered so many javelin wounds that he could no longer defend himself
against anyone. Now he determines on a very brave deed; he rises to his feet, and takes
hold of his grey war-horse, untangles the rein from its right front leg, takes up his fine,
sharp spear, leaps from the ground onto the grey's back, and comes spurring towards
them.

The brave warrior Willame saw the pagan coming at him, his body shaking, brandishing
his great spear; and he held his sword before his face. Then the king of the Saracens
looked at what he was doing; he reins in his horse, and comes forward at a walk. "Oh,
uncle Willame," said his little nephew Gui, "now I beg you, my lord, of your generosity,
to give back my Arab charger, and I shall joust with the Saracen wretch.

126

"Uncle sire, car me faites buntez:
vostre merci, mun cheval me rendez,   1910
si justerai al paien d'ultre mer."
"Niés," dist Willame, "folement as parlé,
quant devant mei osas colp demander:
nel fist mais home qui de mere fu né
puis icel hure que jo soi armes porter!   1915
Iço ne me fereit mie mis sire Lowis le ber.
S'a ma spee li peusse un colp doner,
(13c) vengé serreie del paen d'ultre mer."
Lores fu mecresdi:
le petit pas prist Deramé...*   (1919a)
Willame fiert le paien en le healme,   1920
l'une meité l'en abat sur destre;
del roiste colp s'enclinat vers tere,
et enbraçad del destrer le col et les rednes.
Al trespassant le bon cunte Willame
tute la quisse li trenchad desur la sele,   1925
et de l'altre part chiet li bucs a la terre.
Dunc tendi sa main li bons quons Willame,
si ad pris le corant destrer a la raisne.
Vint a Guiot, sun nevou, si l'apele.

"Lord uncle, do me a favour; of your generosity, give me back my horse, and I shall joust
with the pagan from over seas." "Nephew," said Willame, "you're out of your mind since
you ask to strike a blow before I do: no man born of mother ever did it since the hour I
learnt to bear arms! Not even my lord Lowis the brave would do it to me. If I could give
him a blow with my sword I would be avenged on the pagan from over seas." Then it was
Wednesday: Deramé came on at a walk...* Willame strikes the pagan on the helmet, one
half of it falls over to the right; that mighty blow doubles him up and he holds on round
the horse's neck and reins. As he passed the good Count Willame cut off his thigh above
the saddle, and his trunk fell over away from him. Then the good Count Willame reached
out and took the free-running charger by the reins. He came to his nephew Gui and called
out to him.

127

Li Sarazin se jut enmi le pré,   1930
si vit Willame sun bon cheval mener,
et il le comence tant fort a regretter:
"Ohi! Balçan, que jo vus poei ja tant amer!
Jo te amenai de la rive de mer,
cil§ qui ore te ad ne te seit proz conreier,   1935
ne costier, ne seigner, ne ferrer."
"Glut!" dist Willame, "laissez cest sermun ester,
et pren conseil de ta quisse saner,
et jo penserai del bon cheval garder."
Vint a Gui et si li ad presenté.   1940

128

Li Sarazin out al quor grant rancune:
"Ha! Balçan, bon destrer, tant mar fustes!
Vostre gent cors et voz riches ambleures!
La me portas u ma quisse ai perdue.
Tantes batailles sur vus ai vencues: 1945
meillur cheval n'ad suz ces nues!
Paene gent en avront grant rancune."
"Glut," dit Willame, "de ta raisun n'ai cure!"

The Saracen lay in the middle of the meadow, and saw Willame leading off his fine
horse, and began a loud lament for him: "Ah me, Balçan! How I did love you! I brought
you from the seashore; he who now has you does not know not how to turn you out
properly, how to curry you, bleed you or shoe you." "Gut bag!" said Willame, "just shut
up and get advice on healing your thigh and I'll think to take care of this fine horse." He
came up to Gui and presented it to him.

The Saracen was taking it very badly: "Oh! Balçan, fine charger, how ill-fated you were!
Your noble body and your fine easy walk! You carried me to the place where I lost my
thigh. I have won so many battles mounted on your back: there is not a better horse
beneath these cloudy skies! The pagan folk will be sorely aggrieved by this." "Gut bag,"
said Willame, "I don't give a fig for your speech!"

---

§ 1935 & il

129

Li bers Willame vait parmi le pré;
le bon cheval ad en destre mené.   1950
Gui apele, et si li ad presenté:
(13d) "Bels niés, sur cest cheval muntez.
Si me prestez le vostre par tun gré,
et vus muntez sur cest qui fu Deramé,
kar cest u jo sez m'est mult atalenté."   1955
"Bels sire uncles, fai mei dunc bunté.
Vostre merci, ma sele me rendez,
si pernez cel' del cheval Deramé."
Respunt Willame: "Ço te ferai jo asez."
Dunc descent a terre pur les seles remuer.   1960

130

Tant dementers cum Willame remout les seles,
Gui vit le rei travailler sur l'erbe;
trait ad s'espee, si li colpad la teste.
De cele chose se corozat mult Willame.
"A! glut lecchere, cum fus unc tant osé   1965
que home maigné osas adeser?
En halte curt te serrad reprové."
Ço respunt Guiot: "Unc mes n'oi tel!
S'il n'aveit pez dunt il peust aler,
il aveit oilz dunt il poeit veer,   1970
si aveit coilz pur enfanz engendrer.

The brave warrior Willame rode across the meadow; he led the fine horse in his right hand. He called out to Gui and gave it to him: "Dear nephew, get on this horse. Do me the favour of lending me yours and you can ride the one that belonged to Deramé, because the one I'm sitting on is much to my liking." "Dear lord uncle, you can do me a favour then. If you please, give me back my saddle and take the one on Deramé's horse." Willame replies: "I'll do that for you happily." Then he dismounted to swap the saddles.

While Willame was swapping over the saddles Gui saw the king writhing on the grass; he drew his sword and cut off his head. This made Willame furious. "You bloody brat, how dare you lay hands on a disabled man? You'll be reproached for it in noble courts." Guiot replies: "I never heard the like! If he didn't have feet to walk on he had eyes to see with and balls to breed more children.

En sun pais se fereit uncore porter,
si en istereit eir Deramé
qu'en ceste terre nus querreit malté.
Tut a estrus se deit hom delivrer!"   1975
"Niés," dist Willame, "sagement t'oi parler.
Cors as d'enfant, et raisun as de ber:
aprés ma mort ten tote ma herité."
Lores fu mecresdi:
ore out vencu sa bataille Willame!   1980

131

Li quons Willame chevalche par le champ.
Tut est irez et plein de maltalant,
rumpit les laz de sun healme luisant,
envers la terre li vait mult enbronchant,
sa bone enseigne teinte de vermeil sanc.   1985
(14a) Mult grant damage trove de sa gent;
Guiot le vait de loinz adestrant.
Vivien trove sur un estanc
a la funteine dunt li duit sunt bruiant,
desuz la foille d'un oliver mult grant,   1990
ses blanches mains croisies sur le flanc:
plus suef fleereit que nule espece ne piment.
Parmi le cors out quinze plaies granz,
de la menur fust morz uns amirailz,

He could still have himself carried to his own country from which would issue Deramé's
heirs who would visit evil on us in this land. At all costs a man must spare himself that!"
"Nephew," said Willame, "You're talking sense. You've the body of a child, but the
wisdom of a grown warrior; after my death my inheritance is yours." Then it was
Wednesday: now Willame had won his battle!

Count Willame rode through the field. He was very distraught and in a foul temper, the
chin straps on his shining helmet were broken, so that it kept tipping over, and his proud
standard was stained red with blood. He finds he has lost a lot of his men; Guiot follows
him at a distance on his right. He finds Vivien by a pool at the source of a bubbling
brook, beneath the leafy shade of a very large olive tree, with his white hands crossed on
his side: he smelled sweeter than any spice or mulled wine. Through his body he had
fifteen great wounds, from the least of them an emir would have died,

u reis, u quons, ja ne fust tant poanz.
Puis regrette tant dolerusement:
"Vivien sire, mar fu tun hardement,
tun vasselage, ta prouesce, tun sen!
Quant tu es mort, mes n'ai bon parent:
n'averai mes tel en trestut mun vivant.   2000

132

"Vivien sire, mar fu ta juvente bele,
tis gentil cors et ta teindre meissele!
Jo t'adubbai a mun paleis a Termes;
pur tue amur donai a cent healmes,
et cent espees, et cent targes noveles.   2005
Ci vus vei mort en l'Archamp en la presse,
trenché le cors et les blanches mameles,
et les altres od vus qui morz sunt en la presse:
merci lur face le veir paterne,
qui la sus maint et ça jus nus governe!"   2010

133

A la funtaine dunt li duit sunt mult cler,
desuz la foille d'un grant oliver
ad bers Willame quons Vivien trové.
Parmi le cors out quinze plaies tels,
de la menur fust morz uns amirelz.   2015

or a king or count however powerful. Then he laments him grievously: "Lord Vivien,
how ill-starred were your boldness, your warrior's abilities, your prowess, your
judgement! With you dead I have no more worthy family left: never more in all my life
will I find the likes of you.

"Lord Vivien, how ill-starred were your shining youth, your noble body and your tender
cheek! I made you knight in my palace at Termes: for love of you I gave out a hundred
helmets, a hundred swords and a hundred new round shields. Here I see you dead in the
mêlée at l'Archamp, your body and white breasts cut open, as well as the others who died
with you in the mêlée: may the true Father have mercy on them, Who lives above and
governs us below!"

By the clear running spring, beneath the leafy shade of a great olive tree the noble warrior
Willame found Count Vivien. Through his body he had fifteen wounds so bad an emir
would have died of the least of them.

Dunc le regrette dulcement et suef:
"Vivien sire, mar fustes unques ber!
Tun vasselage que Deus t'aveit doné!
N'ad uncore gueres que tu fus adubé,
(14b) que tu plevis et juras Dampnedeu,   2020
que ne fuereies de bataille champel.
Puis covenant ne volsis mentir Deu;
pur ço iés ore mort, ocis et afolé.
Dites, bel sire, purriez vus parler
et reconuistre le cors altisme Deu?   2025
Si tu ço creez qu'il fu en croiz penez,
en m'almonere ai del pain sacré,
del demeine que de sa main saignat Deus;
se de vus le col en aveit passé
mar crendreies achaisun de malfé."   2030
Al quons revint et sen et volenté,
ovri les oilz, si ad sun uncle esgardé;
de bele boche començat a parler:
"Ohi! bel sire," dist Vivien le ber,
"iço conuis ben, que veirs et vifs est Deu   2035
qui vint en terre pur sun pople salver,
et de la virgne en Belleem fu nez,
et se laissad en sainte croiz pener,
et de la lance Longis fu foré
que sanc et eve corut de sun lé: 2040

Then he laments him sweetly and low: "Lord Vivien, it was your ill fortune to be so brave! How ill fated the warrior's skill God gave you! It was but a short time ago you were made knight, and you pledged and swore to the Lord God that you would not flee from the battle field. After that you did not want to break your word to God; that is why you are now dead, killed and brought low. Tell me, my dear lord, could you speak and recognise the Body of the Most High God? If you believe he suffered on the Cross I have some consecrated bread in my pouch, a portion of the supreme bread that God blessed with his own hand; if you could swallow some you would have no cause to fear the attacks of the devil." Judgement and will returned to the count; he opened his eyes and looked at his uncle; he began to speak nobly: "Oh! my dear lord," said Vivien the noble warrior, I know indeed that God is true and living and that He came to earth to save His people, and was born of the Virgin in Bethlehem, and let Himself suffer on the Holy Cross, and was pierced with Longinus's lance so that blood and water flowed from His side:

a ses oilz terst, sempres fu enluminé;
merci criad, si li pardonad Deus.
Deus, meie colpe§, des l'ore que fu nez,
del mal que ai fait, des pecchez et des lassetez!
Uncle Willame, un petit m'en donez."   2045
"A!" dist le cunte, "a bon hore fui nez!
Qui ço creit, ja nen ert dampnez."
Il curt a l'eve, ses blanches mains a laver;
de s'almosnere ad trait le pain segré,
enz en la boche l'en ad un poi doné.   2050
Tant fist le cunte que le col en ad passé:
l'alme s'en vait; le cors i est remés.
Veit le Willame, comence a plurer.
(14c) Desur le col del balçan l'ad levé
qu'il§ l'en voleit a Orenge porter.   2055
Sur li corent Sarazin et Escler,
tels .xv. reis qui ben vus sai nomer:
reis Mathamar et uns reis d'Aver,
et Bassumet et li reis Defamé,
Soldan d'Alfrike et li forz Eaduel,   2060
et Aelran et sun fiz Aelred,
li reis Sacealme, Alfame et Desturbed,
et Golias et Andafle et Wanibled.
Tuz .xv. le ferent en sun escu boclé;

Longinus rubbed it into his eyes and was immediately enlightened; he called for mercy and God pardoned him. God, *mea culpa*, from the hour I was born for the wrong I have done, for my sins and acts of cowardice! Uncle Willame, give me a little of it." "Ah!" said the count, "I was born in a <u>propitious</u> hour! Anyone who believes that will never be favorable damned." He runs to the water to wash his white hands; he took the sacred bread from his pouch, he gave him a little straight into his mouth. The count managed to swallow it: his Greek / soul departed; his body remained behind. Willame sees it and begins to cry. He lifted him mass onto the back of the bay horse to carry him off to Orange. Saracens and Slavs rush at him, fifteen kings such as I can name for you: King Mathamar and a king of Aver, and Bassumet and King Defamé, Soldan of Africa and the strong Eaduel, and Aelran and his son Aelred, King Sacealme, Alfame and Desturbet, and Golias and Andafle and Wanibled. All fifteen struck him on his buckler;

---

§ 2043 mei colpe
§ 2055 qui len uoleit

pur un petit ne l'unt acraventé.   2065
Quant veit Willame que ne la purrad endurer,
colché l'en ad a tere, sil comandad a Deu;
mult vassalment s'est vers els turné.
Et ces .xv. l'unt del ferir ben hasté,
que par vife force unt fait desevrer   2070
l'uncle del nevou qu'il poeit tant amer.
Puis unt Sarazins Guiot environé,
et sun cheval suz li unt mort geté§,
et li enfes est a tere acraventé.
A! Deus, quel duel quant li vassal chet!   2075
Sur li corent treis cent a espees,
si unt l'enfant pris et estreit liez
veant Willame, qui mult l'ad regretté:
"E! Deus," fait il, "qui mains en trinité§,
et governes terre et ciel esteillé,   2080
cum se vait declinant ma grant nobilité
et cum est destruit tut mun riche parenté!
Gui amis, ore es enprisoné:
cil vus delivre qui se laissa pener
al jur de vendresdi pur crestiens salver!"   2085
Par devant le cunte l'unt mené as niefs.
Et li quons Willame s'est mult adolusez;
(14d) turne as Sarazins cum hom qui est irrez:

---

they almost smashed it to pieces. Since Willame saw that he could not hold out, he laid
him on the ground and commended him to God; as a very brave warrior should he turned
to face them. And those fifteen hastened to strike him, so that by main force they parted
the uncle from his beloved nephew. The Saracens encircled Guiot, and killed his horse
under him, and the lad came crashing to the ground. Oh, God, what grief when the brave
vassal falls! Three hundred bearing swords run at him and captured him and bound him
tightly before Willame's eyes, and he lamented him sorely: "Oh, God!" he said, "Living
Trinity, who govern Earth and the starry heavens, how my great nobility goes into decline
and how my powerful family is all being destroyed! Gui, my kinsman, now you are
imprisoned: may He deliver you who let Himself suffer on Friday to save Christians!" In
full view of the count they took him to the ships. And Count Willame was very grief
stricken; he turned on the Saracens like a man in wrath:

---

§ 2073 suz li li unt mort get
§ 2079 &deus fait qui mains en trinite

quinze en ad morz et .lx. nafrez,
si que nuls ne pout ester sur ses piez. 2090

134

Lunsdi al vespre:
morz sunt Franceis et pris a males pertes:
ne remaint cheval ne home en sele.
Enz en l'Archamp remist tuz suls Willame,
fors Dampnedeu, de tuz les homes de terre, 2095
quant Alderufe li vint brochant sur destre.
Vint lui devant, enmi le vis l'enfeste:
"Vus n'estes mie Bertram ne Willames,
ne Guielin, ne dan Walter de Termes,
ne Guischard§, ne Girard quis cadele; 2100
ne parez mie d'icele fere geste!"
"Par ma fei," dist li quons, "un de cels devoie estre!"
Dist Alderufe: "Ne m'en cheut, par ma destre!
Qui qu'en seez, ancui perdras la teste:
ne te garreit tut li ors de Palerne!" 2105
"Ço ert en Deus," dist li marchis Willame.

135

"Sarazin frere, quant tu te vols combatre,
kar me dites ore de quele chose me blames.
Si t'ai fait tort, prest sui que dreit t'en face:
sil vols receivre, jo t'en doins mun gage." 2110

he killed fifteen of them and wounded sixty so badly that none of them could stand.

Monday at vespertide: the French are dead and captured to their grievous loss: no horse remains, nor man in the saddle. Willame remained in the heart of l'Archamp all alone, bereft, except for the Lord, of all his fellows, when Alderufe came up on his right spurring on his horse. He came up in front of him, staring him straight in the eyes: "You are not Bertram or Willame, or Guielin, or Lord Walter of Termes, or Guischard, or Girard the Captain; you don't look as though you belong to that fierce clan!" "By my faith," said the count, "I must be one of them!" Said Alderufe: "By my right hand, I don't care! Whichever of them you are, you'll lose your head today: all the gold in Palermo wouldn't save you!" "As God wills," said Marquis Willame.

"Brother Saracen, if you wish to fight, tell me what you are accusing me of. If I have wronged you, I am ready to make amends: if you'll take it, I'll give you my gage for it."

---

§2100 Gisschard (both letters "s" expunctuated)

Dist Alderufe: "Sez dunt t'ared, Willame?
Que home et femme crestien ne deivent estre;
nule baptisterie ne deit aver en terre:
a tort le prent qui le receit sur la teste.
Cele baptisterie ne valt mie une nife!*   2115
Deus est el ciel et Mahomet en terre:
quant Deus fait chaud et Mahomet yverne,
et quant Deus plut, Mahomet fait creistre l'erbe.
Qui vivre volt, congié nus en deit quere,
et a Mahomet qui le secle governe."   2120
"Ne sez que diz," dist li quons Willame.
(15a) "Culvert paien, mult avez dit grant blame!
Ço escondi jo, que issi ne deit estre.
Meillur est Deu que nule rien terrestre."
Point Alderufe; dunt broche Willame.   2125
Si s'entreferent sur les targes noveles,
d'un ur en altre les freignent et deserrent,
et lur halbercs desrumpent et desmaillent.
Jambes levees chet li marchis Willame.
et Alderufe trebuche sur l'erbe.   2130
Ne pout tenir ne cengle ne seele,
tut le nasel ne l'en fierge en terre:
les plantes turnent cuntre curt celestre§.

Said Alderufe: "Do you know what I arraign you for, Willame? Because no Christian man or woman should exist; there should be no baptising on Earth: he is wrong to take it who receives the mark on his head. This baptising isn't worth a fig!* God is in Heaven and Mahomet on earth: when God makes it hot, Mahomet brings winter, when God makes it rain, Mahomet makes the grass grow. Anyone wanting to live must ask our leave, and Mahomet's, since he governs the world." "You don't know what you're saying," said Count Willame. "Pagan wretch, what you've said is scandalous! I refute it, for it's indefensible. God is better than any earthly creature." Alderufe spurs on; then Willame clapped spurs to his horse. They struck each other so firmly on their new round shields that they smashed them and split them apart from rim to rim, and tore rows of links out of their halberks. Marquis Willame fell head over heels, and Alderufe fell on the grass. Neither girth nor saddle could prevent his whole nose guard from sinking in the ground and the soles of his feet from facing the course of the stars.

§ 2133 cunte curt celestre

136

Li Sarazin, Alderufe, fu hardiz et prouz:
chevaler bon, si out fere vertuz. 2135
Mais Deu nen out, par tant est il tut perdu;
ainz creit le glut Pilate et Belzebu,
et Antecrist, Bagot et Tartarin,
et d'enfern le veil Astarut.
Tut premereins sur ses pez salt sus 2140
li quons Willame, si est sure coruz;
trait ad Joiuse qui a Charlemaigne fu.
Li Sarazin fu grant et corporuz,
halte out la teste, si out mult long le bu;
n'i pout ateindre, par desuz ad feru, 2145
tote la quisse li deseverad del bu.
De desur l'erbe est li pié chau,
et de l'altre part est trebuché le bu.
"Frere," dist Willame, "qu'en ferreie jo plus?
Escacher es: n'est mais joie de ta vertu!" 2150
A Florescele est al estriu venu.
Quant saisi ad l'arçun li bers, si muntad sus,
si l'ad broché des esperuns aguz,
et il li salt par force et de vertu.
"A!" dist Willame, "mult ben m'ad mun Deu veu; 2155
(15b) sun champiun deit estre maintenu.
Qui ben le creit, ja nen ert confundu!

Alderufe the Saracen was brave and worthy: he was a good knight, fierce and resolute. But he knew not God, for that he was totally lost; the gut bag believed rather in Pilate and Beelzebub, and Antichrist, Bagot and Tartarin, and old Astarot from Hell. The first to jump to his feet was Count Willame, who charged at him; he drew Joiuse, which had been Charlemaigne's sword. The Saracen was tall and well built, his head was high and he was very long in the body; he could not reach his head, so he struck him low down, and cut his thigh off his body. The foot fell on the grass, the trunk fell over the other way. "Brother," said Willame, "what else should I do? You're a pegleg; you'll get no more joy from your prowess!" He came up to Florescele and put a foot in the stirrup. When the brave warrior had taken hold of the saddle bow, he mounted and spurred it on with his sharp spurs, and it leapt with strength and vigour. "Ah!" said Willame, "God has looked very kindly on me; it is right that His champion should be upheld. Whoever believes firmly in Him will never be confounded!

Cest cheval n'ert hui mais, ço quid, rendu."
Lunsdi al vespre:
"Ben m'ad veu mun Deu," ço dist Willame.   2160
Cist valt tut l'or al sire de Palerne."
Et vint a Balçan, lores li trencha la teste.
Quant il l'out mort, gentilment le regrette:

137

"Ohi! Balçan, a quel tort t'ai ocis!
Si Deu m'ait, unc nel forfesis,   2165
en nule guise, ne par nuit ne par di,
mais pur ço l'ai fait, que n'i munte Sarazin;
franc chevaler par vus ne seit honi!"
Muat sa veie, et changat sun latin;
salamoneis parlat, tieis et barbarin,   2170
grezeis, alemandeis, aleis, hermin*
et les langages que li bers out ainz apris.
Culverz paiens, Mahun vus seit failli!
Li bers Willame mult en i ad ocis:
ainz qu'il s'en turt, lur getat morz set vinz.   2175

138

Li quons Willame chevalche par grant ferté,
cum prouz quons de grant nobilité;
et Alderufe se jut enmi le pré.

Nevermore, as I think, will this horse be returned." Monday at vespertide: "My God has
looked kindly on me," said Willame. "This horse is worth all the gold of the lord of
Palermo." He came up to Balçan and then cut his head off. When he had killed him he
lamented him nobly:

"Oh, woe! Balçan, how wrong I was to kill you! so help me God, you did nothing to
deserve it, in any way, night or day, but I did it so that no Saracen could mount you; a
noble knight should not be put to shame by you!" He turned into a different path and
switched to a new language: he spoke Hebrew, German and Berber, Greek, Alemannic,
Welsh*, Armenian and all the languages that the noble warrior had ever learnt. Pagan
wretches, may Mahomet fail you! The noble warrior Willame killed many of them:
before he left the field he overthrew one hundred and forty of them.

Count Willame rode with fierce pride, like a worthy count of great nobility; and Alderufe
lay in the midst of the meadow.

Sun balçan ad puis regardé:
"Ohi! Florecele, bon destrer honured, 2180
mieldre de vus ne poei unques trover!
Ja fustes vus al fort rei Deramé;
jo te menai en l'Archamp sur mer
pur gent colp ferir et pur mun cors aloser.
Willame t'ameine, si ad mun quer vergundé. 2185
A ses diables le peusse jo comander!
Ahi! Willame, quel cheval en menez!
(15c) Fuissez home quil seussez garder,
Il n'en ad si bon en la crestienté,
n'en paesnisme nel purreit l'en recovrer. 2190
Rend le mei, sire, par la tue bunté;
par quatre feiz le ferai d'or peser
del plus fin d'Arabie et del plus cler."
Quant l'ot Willame, rit s'en suz sun nasel:
"Pense, fols reis, de ta quisse saner, 2195
de faire escache cum tu puisses aler
et le crochet et le moinun ferrer!
Jo penserai del cheval conreier,
cum li home qui le covine en set.
Jo en ai eu maint bon, la merci Deu!" 2200

Then he looked at his bay horse: "Oh woe! Florecele, fine, honoured charger, I could never find a better than you! You used to belong to the powerful King Deramé; I brought you to l'Archamp by the sea to strike noble blows and acquire fame. Willame is leading you off, and has brought shame to my heart. Well might I commend him to his devils! Ah! Willame, what a horse you're leading off! Were you the man to look after him there's none so good in Christendom, nor to be found in pagan lands. Give him back to me, my lord, out of the goodness of your heart I'll weigh out four times his weight in gold, the finest gold in Arabia and the brightest." When Willame heard this he laughed under his nasal: "Foolish king, just worry about healing your thigh, making a wooden leg to help you walk, and getting a ferule on the end of the stump! I'll worry about turning out the horse, since I'm the man to know the way it's done. I've had plenty of good horses, thank God!"

139

"Ohi! Florescele, bon cheval de nature!
Unc de destrer ne vi tele criature:
itant ne curt vent cum tu vas l'ambleure,
ne oisel ne se tient volure!
La m'as porté u ma quisse ai perdue;   2205
Willame te meine et jo ai la hunte eue."

140

Lunsdi al vespre:
a ces paroles est turné Willame,
vint al paien, lors li trenchat la teste.
Dunc se parcurent li paien de Palerne,   2210
et de Nichodeme, d'Alfrike et de Superbe.
Dreit a Orenge les paiens de la terre
vont chasçant le bon marchis Willame.
Vint a la porte, mais nel trovat mie overte.
Serrement le porter en va apeler: 2215
"Ohi, porter frere, lai me lainz entrer!"
"Qui estes vus?" "Ço est Willame al curb niés!"
Dist le porter: "Certes, vus n'i enterez.
Ainceis l'averai a ma dame cuntez."
(15d) "Va dunc, frere! Gard ne demorez."   2220
Et il munte les marbrins degrez.
"Ahi! Guiburc franche, par la fei que dei Deu,

"Oh woe, Florescele, fine thoroughbred horse! I never saw your like among chargers: the
wind is not as swift as you at a walk, nor flying bird! You carried me to where I lost my
thigh; Willame is leading you away and I have had the shame."

Monday at vespertide: at these words Willame turned round, he came up to the pagan and
cut off his head. Then the pagans from Palermo arrived at the charge, and those from
Nichodeme, from Africa and from Superbe. All the way to Orange the pagans of the land
are pursuing the good Marquis Willame. He came to the gate but did not find it open.
Without delay he calls out to the gatekeeper: "Hey! Brother porter, let me in!" "Who are
you?" "It's Willame Hooknose!" Said the gatekeeper: "You shall certainly not come in.
I'll go and report it to my lady first." "Go then, brother! Mind you don't delay." And he
went up the marble steps. "Ah! noble Guiburc, by the faith I owe to God,

a cele porte ad un chevaler tel
mult par est granz et corsuz et mollez;
tant par est fer ne l'osai esgarder.   2225
Si dist qu'il est Willame al curb niés,
mais ne li voil la porte desfermer,
car il est sul – od lui n'ad home né –
si chevalche un alferant tel,
il n'ad si bon en la crestienté,   2230
n'en paenissme nel poet hom recovrer.
Paenes armes li pendent al costez."
Ço dist la dame: "Jol conuistrai assez.
S'il est iço, sil larrum entrer."
Ele meisme devalat les degrez   2235
et vint al cunte, si l'ad araisonez:
"Ki estes vus, qui a la porte clamez?"
"Dame," dist il, "ja me conuissiez asez!
Ja est ço Willame, le marchis al curb niés."
Ço dist Guiburc: "Vus nus mentez!   2240
"Culvert paien, mult savez controver.
Par tels enseignes çaenz nen enterez,
car jo sui sole: od mei n'ad home nez.
Si vus fuissez Willame al curb niés,
od vus venissent set mile homes armez   2245
des Frans de France, des baruns naturels;
tut entur vus chantassent ces juglers,
rotes et harpes i oist hom soner."

at the gate there's this knight who's big and well built and sturdy; he's so fierce I didn't dare look at him. He says he's Willame Hooknose, but I'm not prepared to open the gate for him, since he's alone — not a living man with him — and he's riding a grey warhorse. There's none so good in Christendom, or as could be found in pagan lands. Pagan weapons are hanging at his side." The lady said: "I'll recognise him all right. If he's who he says, we'll let him in." She went herself down the steps and came to the count and spoke to him: "Who are you, shouting at the gate?" "Lady," he said, "You know me well enough! It's Willame, the hook nosed marquis." Said Guiburc: "You're lying to us! Pagan wretch, you know a trick or two. You won't get in that way, for I'm alone: there's not a single man with me. If you were Willame Hooknose seven thousand armed men would come with you, true Franks from France, high born barons; all around you jongleurs would be singing, we'd hear the sound of viols and harps."

"Allas, pecchable!" dist Willame al curb niés,
"a itele joie soleie jo ja aler.   2250
Dame," dist il, "jal savez§ vus assez,
tant cum Deus volt ad home richeté,
et quant li ne plaist si rad poverté.
(16a) Ja repair jo de l'Archamp sur mer,
u ai perdu Vivien l'alosé;   2255
mun niefs Bertram i est enprisoné,
le fiz Bernard de Bruban la cité,
et Guielin, et Guischard l'alosé."
Guiburc regarde tut un chemin ferré,
si veit venir set mille paiens armez.   2260
De dulce France repeirent de preier,
de saint Martur de Turoine gaster:
le maistre cumble en unt acraventé.
Si ameinent cent chaitifs enchainé;
sovent les batent od fustz et od tinels,   2265
a lur escurges et a lur flagulers.
Veit le Guiburc; comence a plurer:
"Se vus fuissez Willame al curb niés,
ja fust escuse sainte crestientez,
et cele preie qu'i meinent cels lecchers."   2270
"A!" dist le cunte, "unc mais n'oi tel!
Tut veirement me volt espermenter.

"Alas, miserable wretch that I am!" said Willame Hooknose, "I used to go around amid such signs of joy. Lady," he said, "you know well enough, as long as it's God's will a man has riches, and when it's not he falls into poverty. I'm just back from l'Archamp by the sea where I lost Vivien the renowned; my nephew Bertram is taken prisoner there, the son of Bernard of fortified Bruban, and Guielin and Guischard the renowned." Guiburc looked along a metalled road and saw seven thousand armed pagans coming. They were returning from a raid on sweet France where they had laid waste St Martin of Touraine: they had smashed down the highest pinnacle. They were leading a hundred prisoners in chains; they often beat them with heavy sticks and clubs, with scourges and flails. Guiburc saw them; she began to cry: "If you were Willame Hooknose holy Christendom would be rescued, as well as the booty those swine are carrying off." "Ha!" said the count, "I never heard the like! She really wants to try me.

§ 2251 ial le sauez

U moer u vive, la m'estoet aler!"
Dunc point et broche le destrer abrivé;
cil curt plus tost que oisel ne pot voler. 2275
Paien le veient; mult lur fu amé.
Dist li uns a l'altre: "Jo vei nostre avoué,
reis Alderufe de Palerne sur mer,
qui a Orenge alad assalt doner.
Bons est li deus, qui l'en ad amené, 2280
quant ne l'ad mort Willame al curb niés.
Des ore devon Mahomet aorer,
et Apolin et Bagot et Macabeu."
Tant dementers qu'il unt aoré,
li quons Willame n'est mie sejurné, 2285
car le premer qu'il ad encuntré
....* (2286a)
en aprés l'altre si fait le chef voler,
(16b) et puis le quart; unc ne passad par el:
quinze en ad mort Willame d'un ester.
Dist li uns a l'altre: "Or est il vif malfez!" 2290
Et dist li altres: "Mult grant tort en avez,
mais mis sires est vers vus adulez§
pur la bataille de l'Archamp sur mer:
nus n'i avom§ ensemble od lui esté."
Et cuillent ent fuie Sarazins et Esclers; 2295

Whether I live or die I must go that way!" Then he clapped spurs to his fiery charger; it galloped more swiftly than a bird could fly. The pagans saw him; he was well received by them. They said to each other: "It's our protector, King Alderufe of Palermo by the sea, who went to mount an assault on Orange. Good is the god who led him here, since Willame Hooknose hasn't killed him. We must praise Mahomet straight away, and Apolin and Bagot and Macabeu." While they were singing praise, Count Willame did not waste time, for the first man he met ...* after which he cut the head off the next, and then the fourth could not avoid his fate: Willame killed fifteen of them at one go. One said to the other: "Now he's the living devil!" And another said: "You're quite wrong, but my lord is very upset with you over the battle at l'Archamp by the sea: we weren't there with him." The Saracens and Slavs took to flight;

§ 2292 aduler
§ 2294 nus auom

tote la preie li unt abandoné.
Veit le Willame, sin ad Deu aoré.
Il la rent tut as chaitifs del regné.

141

Li quons Willame laisse cure sur destre,
si vait ferir Corberan d'Oliferne;   2300
l'escu li freinst, et le halberc li deserre,
pleine sa hanste l'abat mort a tere.
Dame Guburc l'esgarde d'unes dé fenestres;
dunque reparlad, si ad dite parole veire:
"A icest colp resemblez vus Willame.   2305
Venez vus ent, ja ert la porte overte."

142

Li gentil cunte revint a la cité.
"A! Guburc§ dame, me larrez vus entrer?"
"Nenil," dist ele, "par la fei que dei Deu,
se ne me mustrez la bosce sur le nés,   2310
que aveit Willame, le marchis od le curb nés,
de la bataille reis Tedbald l'Escler.
Et plusurs homes se resemblent assez
de vasselage et de nobilitez,

they abandoned all their booty. Willame saw it and gave thanks to God. He gave all the booty to the prisoners of that kingdom.

Count Willame galloped off to the right, and went to strike Corberan of Oliferne; he broke his shield and tore open his halberk, with a full blow of his shaft he knocked him dead to the ground. Lady Guiburc watched him from one of the windows; then she spoke in her turn, and what she said was true: "By that blow you resemble Willame. Come in, the gate will soon be opened."

The noble count came back to the citadel. "Ah! My lady Guiburc, will you let me in?" "Certainly not," she said, "by the faith I owe God, unless you show me the bump on your nose, which Willame the hook nosed marquis got from the battle with King Tedbald the Slav. Besides a good number of men resemble each other in valorous deeds and nobility,

---

§ 2308 & Guiburc

et jo sui sule, od mei n'ad home nez   2315
fors cest porter, que ci ester veez."
Ço dist le cunte: "Unques n'oi tel!
Mult m'avrad hui cest adverser pené."*
Deslace les laz de sun healme gemmé,
tres ses espalles le lait aval culer;   2320
trestui sun vis li ad abandoné.
(16c) Veit le la dame§ , sil conuit assez,
del quor suspire, des oilz prent a plorer:
"Ami, bel frere, la porte li ovrez:
ja est ço Willame, mun seignur naturel."   2325
Lunsdi al vespre:
ovrerent la porte, si recoillent Willame.
Grant piece est qu'il i volsist estre!

143

Li quons Willame al perun descendi;
dame Guiburc reçut sun destrer,   2330
si l'amenat la jus en un celer
et frein et sele li ad osté premer.
Foer et aveine li donat a manger,
puis l'ad covert d'un bon paille pleié.
Puis vait le cunte acoler et baiser,   2335
si l'en apele curteisement et ben.

and I'm alone, there's not a living man with me except the gatekeeper you see standing here." The count said: "I never heard the like! There's the devil to pay today."* He untied the chin straps on his gem encrusted helmet, and let it slide down on his shoulders; he showed her his whole unprotected face. The lady saw it and recognised him clearly, sighed from her heart and wept from her eyes: "Good friend and brother, open the gate to him: it's Willame all right, my high born lord." Monday at vespertide: they opened the gate and welcomed Willame. He'd been wanting to get in for a long time!

Count Willame dismounted at the block; lady Guiburc took his charger from him, and led it down into a cellar and first of all took off its bit and saddle. She gave it hay and oats to eat, then covered it with a fine, pleated, silk cloth. Then she went and threw her arms round the count and kissed him, and spoke to him courteously and well.

§ 2322 veit la dame

"Sire," dist ele, "qu'as tu fait de ta gent,
dunt tu menas quatre mil et .vii. cent?"
"Par ma fei, dame, vencu les unt paens:
bouches sanglantes gisent en l'Archamps."   2340
"Sire," dist ele, "que avez fait de Viviens?"
"Par fei, dame, ja est morz et sanglanz."
Quant Guiburc l'ot, mult out le quer dolent.
"Sire," fait ele, "qu'as tu fait de Bertram,
le fiz Bernard de la cité de Bruban?"   2345
"Seor, bele amie, mult i fu combatanz.
A quinze esturs i fu pleners el champ;
Al seszime l'en donerent tant
suz li oscistrent sun destrer alferant.
Il traist§ s'espee, mist l'escu devant,   2350
si lur trenchad les costez et les flancs.
Iloec le pristrent la pute adverse gent,
si li lierent les piez et les mains.
Mes oilz veanz le mistrent en un chalant:
par mei n'out unques socurs ne garant."   2355
(16d) "Deus," dist la dame, "quel duel de Bertramt!
Pur ço me peise, que jo l'amoue tant.

"My lord," she said, "what have you done with your men, of whom you led away four thousand and seven hundred?" "By my faith, my lady, the pagans have defeated them: with bloody mouths they lie on l'Archamps." "My lord," she said, "what have you done with Vivien?" "In faith, my lady, he's already dead and covered with blood." When Guiburc heard it she grieved deeply in her heart. "My lord," she said, "what have you done with Bertram, the son of Bernard of the citadel of Bruban?" "Sister, my fairest, he fought hard and well. He was in the thick of fifteen attacks in the field; in the sixteenth they hit him so hard they killed his grey charger under him. He drew his sword and put his shield before him, and cut open their sides and flanks. There the filthy enemy took him prisoner and bound him hand and foot. Before my very eyes they put him in a lighter: he got neither aid nor protection from me." "God," said the lady, "that's a crying shame about Bertram! It upsets me so, because I loved him so much."

---

§ 2350 il trais

144

"Sire," dist ele, "qu'as tu fait de Guiotun,
le bel enfant od la gente façun?
Jo li chargai l'enseigne al rei Mabun,   2360
et le destrer Oliver le Gascun,
et le halberc et le healme Tedbalt l'Eclavun."
"Par ma fei, dame, dedenz i fu cum prouz.
En la bataille portad le gunfanun,
si i fu ben desqu'al seszime estur;   2365
idunc le pristrent li Sarazin felun,
si li lierent§ et les piez et les poinz.
Mes oilz veanz le mistrent en un dromunz;
par mei n'out unques aie ne socurs."
"Deus," dist la dame, "quel duel et quel tristur!   2370
pur ço me peise, que jo l'amoue mult.

145

"Sire, qu'as tu fait de Walter,
de Guielin et del cunte Reiner?"
"Par ma fei, dame, vencu les unt paiens.
Enz en lur barges les tenent en liens."   2375
"Deus," dist la dame, "quel duel et quel pecché!
Si cum tu diz, ne repeire un pé.
Leve tes mains, sire, si alez manger;

"My lord," she said, "what have you done with Guiotun, the handsome lad with the noble face? I entrusted him with King Mabun's flag, and the charger of Oliver the Gascon, and the halberk and helmet of Tedbalt the Slav." "By my faith, my lady, he stood his ground like a true man. He bore the standard in the battle, and was right there up to the sixteenth attack; then the filthy Saracens captured him, and bound him hand and foot. Before my very eyes they put him in a transport; he never had aid or succour from me." "God," said the lady, "what grief and sadness! I'm greatly upset, because I loved him so much.

"My lord, what have you done with Walter, with Guielin and Count Reiner?" "By my faith, my lady, the pagans have defeated them. They hold them in bonds in their barges." "God," said the lady, "what grief and misfortune! As you tell it not one returns. Wash your hands, my lord, and go and eat;

§ 2367 sille lierent

des hui matin le t'ai fait apareiller:
aver en poez a quatre mil chevaler,   2380
et as serganz§, et a tuz les esquiers!"
"Allas, pecchable!" dist Willame li bers,
"uncore nen ad mie que dous jurs enters
que jo avei ben pres de .xv. miller,
et ore sui ça enz ne mes que sul mei tierz.   2385
En petit hore ai grant desturbers."

146

Dunc prent s'amie par les mances de paille;
sus munterent les degrez de marbre,
ne trovent home que service lur face.
(17a) Dame Guiburc li curt aporter l'eve,   2390
et aprés li baillad la tuaille.
Puis sunt asis a la plus basse table,
Ne poeint de duel seer a la plus halte.
Il veit les bancs, les formes et les tables,
la u soleit seer sun grant barnage: 2395
il ne vit nul juer par cele sale,
ne deporter od eschés ne od tables.
Puis les regrete cum gentil home deit faire:

I've had it ready for you since this morning: there's enough for four thousand knights, and for the men-at-arms and all their squires!" "Alas, miserable wretch that I am!" said Willame the noble warrior, "It's not yet two full days ago that I had close to fifteen thousand of them, and now I'm in here with just two for company. I've come to grief in a very short time."

Then he took his love by her silken sleeves; they went up the marble steps, they found no one to serve them. Lady Guiburc ran to fetch him water, and afterwards gave him the towel. Then they sat at the lowest table; for grief they could not sit at the highest. He saw the benches, the forms and the tables at which his great war band used to sit: he saw no one having fun in that hall, enjoying themselves at chess or backgammon. Then he lamented them as a noble man should:

---

§ 2381 & ases serganz

147

"Ohi! bone sale, cum estes lung et lee!
De tutes parz vus veit si aurné: 2400
beneit seit la dame qui si t'ad cunreié.
Ohi! haltes tables, cum estes levees!
Napes de lin vei desure getees,
ces escuiles emplies et rasees
de hanches et d'espalles, de niveles et de obleies.   2405
N'i mangerunt les fiz de franches meres,
qui en l'Archamp unt les testes colpees!"
Plure Willame, Guiburc s'est pasmee;
il la redresce, si l'ad confortee:

148

"Guiburc, dame, vus n'avez que plurer,   2410
kar n'avez perdu nul ami charnel.
Jo dei le duel et la tristur demener,
ki ai perdu mun gentil parenté.
Ore m'en fuierai en estrange regné,
a Saint Michel al Peril de la Mer,   2415
u Saint Pere, le bon apostre Deu,
u en un guast, u ja mes ne seie trové:
la devendrai hermites ordené
et, tu, devien noneine, si faz tun chef veler."

"Oh woe, fine hall, how long and wide you are! I see you adorned on all sides: blessed be the lady who has decorated you like this. Oh woe, high tables, how you are raised up! I see linen cloths thrown over you, platters filled to the brim with haunches and shoulders of meat and cakes and sweetmeats. The sons of freeborn mothers will not eat from them, whose heads are cut off on l'Archamp!" Willame wept and Guiburc fainted; he lifted her up and comforted her:

"My lady Guiburc, you have no reason to cry, for you have lost no kin. I should grieve and give vent to my woe, for I have lost my noble family. Now I shall flee into a foreign land, to Saint Michael at Peril of the Sea, or to Saint Peter's, God's good apostle, or into the wilderness where I shall never be found: there I shall be ordained and become a hermit, and you, become a nun and take the veil."

"Sire," dist ele, "ço ferum nus assez,   2420
quant nus avrom nostre siecle mené.

149

"Sire Willame, al Dampnedeu congié,
par main a l'albe munte sur tun destrer;
(17b) dreit a Loun pense de chevalcher,
a l'emperere qui nus solt aver chiers,   2425
qui del socurs nus vienge ça aider.
Et s'il nel fait, si li rendez sun fee:
mar en tendré un jur un demi pee!
Met en provende et tei et ta moiller,
u a sa table nus laist pur Deu manger   2430
a chascun jur de sun pain dous quarters."
Et dit Willame: "Jol ferai mult iree,
mais tun conseil en dei jo creire ben:
en plusurs lius m'ad eu mult grant mesters."
A icele nuit§ s'est Willame colchié;   2435
par main a l'albe muntad le bon destrer.

150

"Seor bele amie, tun conseil ai creu.
Ore m'en irrai a la sale a lui,*
que l'emperere del socurs nus enveit.
Se dunc se sunt paiens aparceuz,   2440
ben tost m'averunt cest bon paleis toluz

"My lord," she said, "we'll do that right enough when we've lived out our lives.

"My lord Willame, by the Lord's leave, at daybreak tomorrow mount your charger; take care to ride straight to Laon, to the emperor who used to hold us so dear, who should bring us help and aid. If he doesn't, hand him back his fief: be cursed if you'll hold half a foot of land from him one more day! You and your wife will become his pensioners, or out of charity he can let us eat at his table just two quarters of a loaf a day." And Willame said: "I'll do it with a heavy heart, but I'm bound to take your advice: on many occasions I've found it very useful." That night Willame went to bed; at dawn next day he mounted his good charger.

"Dearest sister, I have accepted your advice. Now I shall go to him in his own great hall,* to ask the emperor to send us aid. If then the pagans notice they will very quickly take this fine palace from me,

---

§ 2435 icele mut

Amoravinz et Pincenarz et Turs.
Qui me defendrat le terrail et les murs?"
"Sire," dist ele, "Jhesu et ses vertuz,
et set cenz dames§ que ai ça enz et plus!   2445
As dos avront les blancs halbercs vestuz
et en lur chefz verz healmes aguz;
si esterrunt as batailles la sus,
lancerunt lances, peres et pels aguz.
En petit de hure serra ço trescoru;   2450
si Deus le volt si serrad le socurs venu."
"Ahi!" dist Willame, "cel seignur te aiut,
qui la sus maint, et ça jus fait vertuz!"

151

Vait s'en Willame; Guiburc remist plorant.
Un esquier menat, ço fut un enfant;   2455
tant par fu joefnes n'out uncore .xv. anz.
La hanste fu grosse, si li pesad formanz
(17c) et li escuz vers la terre trainant,
d'ures en altres fors des arçuns pendant.
Veit le Willame, merveillus duel l'en prent;   2460
totes les armes ad pris de l'enfant.
Quant il encontre rumi u marchant,
u vient a chastel u a vile errant,

those Almoravids, and Pechenegs and Turks. Who will defend the earthworks and walls for me?" "My lord," she said, "Jesus and his power, and seven hundred ladies and more I have in here with me! They will put the white halberks on their backs and pointed green helmets on their heads; they will stand firm up on the battlements, and throw down lances, stones and sharp stakes. It won't take you long to make the trip; if God wills it, help will surely come." "Ah!" said Willame, "may the Lord help you, who lives above and reveals His power below!"

Willame goes on his way; Guiburc remains behind weeping. He took with him a squire, just a child; he was so young, he was not yet fifteen. The spear was hefty and extremely heavy for him, and the shield which dragged on the ground, frequently hanging below the saddle bow. Willame saw it and was extraordinarily upset;he took all the arms off the child. When they met a pilgrim or a merchant, or came in their travels to a castle or town,

---

§ 2445 set cenz damas

totes ses armes rebaille a l'enfant.
Quant il sunt ultre, a sun col les prent.   2465
Tote jur plure pur sun nevou Bertram,
pur Guilin et pur le quons Vivien.
Si faitement vait sun duel demenant
tresqu'a Loun al perun, u il descent.
....*   (2469a)
De l'or d'Espaigne lur soleit porter largement;   2470
pur la folie i curent ore tanz.
Unques les trente n'i conquistrent tant,
ne les seisante n'i achatent nient,
dunt entr'els tuz eslegassent un gant!

152

Quant veit Willame les legers bagelers,   2475
de l'or d'Espaige li vienent demander,
car il lur soleit les anels doner,
"Seignurs," dist il, "ne me devez blamer§.
Or et argent ai jo uncore assez
en Orenge, ma mirable citez.   2480
Si Deu m'ait, nel poei aporter,
car jo repair de l'Archamp sur mer,
u jo ai perdu Vivien l'alosed;

he gave all his arms back to the child. When they were past he hung them round his own neck. All day long he wept for his nephew Bertram, for Guielin and for Count Vivien. And so he gave vent to his grief until he reached the mounting block at Laon, where he dismounted. ...* He had been in the habit of bringing them plenty of Spanish gold; foolishly expecting more a great crowd rushed up to him. Never did thirty of them acquire so much, nor sixty of them obtain anything at all, that they could buy one glove between them!

When Willame saw the high spirited young knights coming to ask him for Spanish gold, since he had been in the habit of giving them rings, "My lords," he said, "you mustn't criticise me. I've still got plenty of gold and silver in Orange, my wonderful citadel. So help me God, I couldn't bring it, for I am just returned from l'Archamp by the sea where I lost Vivien the renowned;

§ 2478 seignurs ne me deuez blamer

mun nevou Bertram i est enprisoné,
Walter de Termes, et Reiner le sené,   2485
et Guielin et Guischard al vis cler.
Sule est Guiburc en la bone cité;
pur Deu vus mande que vus la§ socurez."
Quant cil oirent del damage parler,
laissent la resne al destrer sojurné;   2490
tote la place li unt abandoné,
(17d) turnent al paleis, asseent al manger.
Ancui saverad Willame al curb nés
cum povres hom pot vers riches parler,
et queles denrees l'um fait de cunsiler.   2495

153

Li reis demande: "U est Willame alé?"
Et cil li dient: "Ja est el perun remés.
Les vis diables le nus unt amené;
si cum il dit, mal li est encuntré."
Et dist li reis: "Laissez le tut ester;   2500
le gentil cunte ne vus chaut a gaber.
Alez i tost, et sil m'amenez."
"Volenters, sire, quant vus le comandez."
Willame munte lé marbrins degrez;
li reis le beise, si l'aset al digner.   2505
Quant ad mangé, sil prist a raisuner:

my nephew Bertram is imprisoned there, Walter of Termes, and Reiner the wise, and Guielin and bright faced Guischard. Guiburc is alone in the good citadel; for God's sake she sends me to ask you to help her." When they heard him speak of his losses, they let go of the reins of his spirited charger; they left him sole master of the field, went back to the palace and sat down to eat. This very day Willame Hooknose will learn how a poor man speaks to a powerful one, and what price is put on counsel.

The king asks: "Where has Willame gone?" And they tell him: "He's stayed out at the mounting block. The living devils have brought him to us; according to him, things have gone badly with him." And the king said: "Enough of that; it's not your place to make fun of the noble count. Go quickly and bring him to me." "Of course, my lord, since you command it." Willame came up the marble steps; the king kisses him and sits him down to dinner. When he had eaten, he spoke to him:

§ 2488 le

"Sire Willame, cum faitement errez?
Ne vus vi mes ben ad set anz passez,
ne sanz bosoig, ço sai, ne me requerez."
"Sire," dist il, "jal savez vus assez.   2510
Jo aveie Espaigne si ben aquitez,
ne cremeie home que de mere fu nez.
Quant me mandat Vivien l'alosé,
que jo menasse de Orenge le barné:
il fu mis niés, nel poeie veier.   2515
Set mile fumes de chevalers armez;
de tuz icels ne m'est un sul remés.
Perdu ai Vivien l'alosed;
mis niés Bertram i est enprisoné,
le fiz Bernard de Brusban§ la cité,   2520
et Guielin et Guischard al vis cler.
Sule est Guiburc en la bone cité;
pur Dé vus mande que vus la socurez."
Unc li reis nel deignad regarder,
mais pur Bertram comence a plurer.   2525

154

(18a) "Lowis sire, mult ai esté pené,
en plusurs esturs ai esté travaillé.
Sole est Guiburc en Orenge le see;

"Lord Willame, how are things going? I haven't seen you for a good seven years, and I
know you wouldn't seek me out unless there was need." "My lord," he said, "you'll hear
all about it. I had so thoroughly liberated Spain I feared no man born of woman. When
Vivien the renowned sent to ask me to lead my war band out of Orange, he was my
nephew, I couldn't refuse. We were seven thousand armed knights; of all those not a
single one remains to me. I have lost Vivien the renowned; my nephew Bertram is
imprisoned, the son of Bernard of the citadel of Bruban, and Guielin and bright faced
Guischard. Guiburc is all alone in the good citadel; for God's sake she sends me to ask
you to help her." The king did not deign to look at him, but he began to weep on
Bertram's account.

"Lord Lowis, I have laboured hard, and been sore pressed in many battles. Guiburc is all
alone in my seat at Orange;

---

§ 2520 le fiz bertram De Brusban

    pur Deu vus mande, que socurs li facez."
Ço dist li reis: "N'en sui ore aisez; 2530
a ceste feiz n'i porterai mes piez."
Dist Willame: "Qui enchet ait cinc cenz dehez!"
Dunc traist sun guant, qui a or fu entaillez,
a l'empereree l'ad geté a ses piez.
"Lowis sire, ci vus rend voz feez! 2535
N'en tendrai mais un demi pé;
qui que te plaist le refai ottrier."
En la sale out tels quinze chevalers,
freres et uncles, parenz, cosins et niés,
ne li faldrunt pur les testes trencher. 2540
De l'altre part fu Rainald de Peiters,
un sun nevou de sa sorur premer.
A halte voiz començat a hucher:
"Nel faites, uncle, pur les vertuz del ciel!
Fiz a barun, retien a tei tun fé! 2545
Si Deu m'ait, qui le pople maintient,
jo ne larrai pur home desuz ciel,
que ne t'ameine quatre mille chevalers
a cleres armes et a alferanz destrers."
"Et Deus," dist Willame, "vus me volez aider. 2550
Fel seit li uncles qui bon nevou n'ad cher!"

for God's sake she sends me to ask you to help her." The king said: "it's not convenient at the moment; on this occasion I shan't get myself there." Willame said: "Five hundred curses on the man who fails in his duty!" Then he took off his glove with the gold open-thread work and threw it at the emperor's feet. "Lord Lowis, I hereby hand back your fiefs! I'll never more hold half a foot of them; grant them anew to anyone you like." In the great hall there were some fifteen knights, brothers and uncles, all his kin, cousins and nephews, who would not fail him at the cost of their heads. Among them was Rainald of Poitiers, his nephew, his sister's eldest son. He began to shout at the top of his voice: "Don't do it, uncle, by all the powers of Heaven! Baron's son, retain your fief for yourself! So help me the God who maintains his people, I won't fail for any man under Heaven to come to help you at the head of four thousand knights with bright arms and grey chargers." "By God," said Willame, "you want to help me. May the uncle who doesn't cherish a good nephew be branded a criminal!"

155

De l'altre part fu Hernald de Girunde,
et Neimeri, sun pere, de Nerbune,
li quons Garin de la cité d'Ansune.
Dist li uns a l'altre: "Ore feriuns grant hunte   2555
de nostre ami, si le laissium confundre."
Dist Neimeri, sun pere, de Nerbune:
"Jo ne larrai pur rei ne pur cunte
que ne l'i meine set mile de mes homes."
(18b) "Et jo quatre mile," fait Garin d'Ansune.   2560

156

Ço dist Boeves, quons de Comarchiz§ :
"Jo sui sun frere, se ne li puis faillir.
Jo ne larrai pur home qui seit vif,
que ne l'i ameine chevalers quatre mil."
"Et jo treis," fait Hernald le flori.   2565
"Et jo dous," fait li enfes Guibelin.
"Seignurs," ço dist de Flandres Baldewin,
"li quons Willame est prodome et gentil,
si ad amé ses pers et ses veisins,
si socurst les, si les vit entrepris.   2570
Jo ne larrai pur home qui seit vis,
que ne l'i amein chevalers mil.

From among them came forward Hernald of Girunde and Neimeri, his father, of Narbonne, and Count Garin of the citadel of Ansune. They said to each other: "We would bring great shame now on our kinsman if we let him be defeated." Said Neimeri, his father, of Narbonne: "I will not fail for any king or count to lead there seven thousand of my men for him." "I'll take four thousand," said Garin of Ansune.

Said Boeves, Count of Comarchiz: "I am his brother, I cannot fail him. I will not fail for any living man to lead four thousand knights there for him." "I'll take three," said white haired Hernald. "And I'll take two," said young Guibelin. "My lords," said Baldewin of Flanders, "Count Willame is an upright and noble man, and he has kept good relations with his peers and neighbours, and helped them if he saw them in difficulties. I shall not fail for any living man to lead a thousand knights there for him.

§ 2561 quons de somarchiz. la cite

Alum al rei, si li crium merci,
que de socure Willame nus aid."

157

Toz ces baruns devant le rei vindrent;   2575
cil Baldewin li començat a dire:
"Forz emperere, pur Deu, le fiz Marie,
veez de Willame, cum plure et suspire!
Teint ad la charn suz le bliant de Sirie:
ço ne fu unques pur nule coardie!   2580
Sule est Guiburc en Orenge la vile.
Ore l'assaillent li paien de Surie,
cil de Palerne et cil de Tabarie.
S'il unt Orenge, puis unt Espaigne quite;
puis passerunt as porz desuz Saint Gille.   2585
S'il unt Paris, puis avront saint Denise:
fel seit li home, qui puis te rendrat servise!"
Ço dist li reis: "Jo irrai mé meisme,
en ma compaignie chevalers trente mille."
"Nu ferez, sire," ço respunt la reine.   2590
"Dame Guiburc fu né en paisnisme,
si set maint art et mainte pute guische.
Ele conuist herbes; ben set temprer mescines:
(18c) tost vus ferreit enherber u oscire.
Willame ert dunc reis et Guiburc reine,   2595

Let us go to the king and beg him to grant us that he will help us take aid to Willame."

These barons all came before the king; the Baldewin I have mentioned began to speak: "Powerful emperor, for the sake of God the Son of Mary, see how Willame weeps and sighs! His skin is discoloured under his damask tunic: that never came about by cowardice! Guiburc is all alone in the town of Orange. From Syria the pagans are attacking her, and from Palermo and Tiberias. If they take Orange, they'll have Spain back in their possession; then they'll come through the passes below Saint-Gilles. If they take Paris, they'll next get possession of Saint-Denis: any man who serves you after that should be branded a criminal!" Said the king: "I'll go in person and take a company of thirty thousand knights." "No you will not, my lord," replied the queen. "The lady Guiburc was born in pagan lands, and knows many arts and many filthy tricks. She knows about herbs; she knows how to mix medicines: she'll quickly have you drugged or killed. Willame will then be king and Guiburc queen,

si remaindreie doleruse et chaitive."
Ot le Willame, a poi n'esraga de ire.
"Qu'as tu dit? Dampnedeu te maldie!
Pute reine, vus fustes anuit ivre!
Il siet assez, unc ne li boisai[§] mie,   2600
tant par sunt veires lé ruistes felonies
enz en l'Archamp, que vus avez oi dire.

158

"Pute reine, pudneise surparlere,
Tedbalt vus fut, le culvert lecchere,
et Esturmi od la malveise chere!   2605
Cil deussent garder l'Archam de la gent paene:
il s'en fuirent; Vivien[§] remist arere!
Plus de cent prestres vus unt ben coillie,
forment vus unt cele clume chargee;
unc n'i volsistes apeler chambrere!   2610
Pute reine, pudneise surparlere,
mielz li venist qu'il t'eust decolee,
quant tote France est par vus avilee!
Quant tu sez as chaudes chiminees,
et tu mangues tes pudcins en pevrees   2615
et beis tun vin as colpes coverclees!

and I'll be left a grief stricken, miserable prisoner." Willame heard what she said and almost went mad with rage. "What did you say? God curse you! Royal whore, you were drunk last night! He knows well enough — I never tricked him — how true are the grave disasters that you've heard about at l'Archamp.

"Royal whore, filthy slanderer, Tedbalt fucks you, that lecherous slave, and Esturmi with his evil face! They should have been protecting l'Archamp from the pagans: they fled; Vivien stayed behind! More than a hundred priests have been up you hammering away lustily at your anvil; you never wanted to call a chamber maid! Royal whore, filthy slanderer, he would have done better to cut your head off since the whole of France is disgraced by you! When you're sitting in your cosy heated rooms you eat puddings and spicy dishes and drink wine from lidded cups!

[§] 2600 baisai
[§] 2607 Viuier

Quant es colché ben es acuvetee,
si te fais futre a la jambe levee!
Ces leccheurs te donent granz colees,
et nus en traium les males matinees, 2620
sin recevon les buz et les colees:
enz en l'Archamp les sanglantes testes!
Si jo trai fors del feore ceste espee,
ja vus avrai cele teste colpee!"
Pé et demi l'ad del feore levee; 2625
devant fu Nemeri de Nerbune, sun pere,
si li unt dit parole menbree:
(18d) "Sire Willame, laissez ceste mellee.
Vostre sorur est; mar fust ele nee."
Et fait li reis: "Ben fait, par Deu le pere, 2630
car ele parole cum femme desvee.
Si jo n'i vois, si serrad m'ost mandee;
vint mile chevalers od nues espees
li chargerai demain a l'ajurnee."
"Vostre merci," fait Willame, "emperere." 2635

159

Nostre emperere fait ses baruns mander,
si fait ses chartres et ses brefs seeler,
sis enveit par trestuit sun regné.
Dedanz les uit jurz furent vint mil armez,

When you're bedded you're well screwed, you get fucked with your legs pulled up high! These debauched swine ride you hard and we live out evil mornings receiving spear thrusts and sword blows: at l'Archamp our heads are bloodied! If I draw this sword from its sheath, I'll soon cut your head off for you!" He raised it a foot and a half from its sheath; Neimeri of Narbonne, his father, stood before him and spoke with measured wisdom: "Lord Willame, leave this quarrel. "She is your sister; it's a pity she was ever born." And the king said: "Well said, by God the Father, for she's talking like a madwoman. If I don't go, my army will still be summoned; I'll put twenty thousand knights with drawn swords under his command tomorrow at daybreak." "Thank you, my emperor," said Willame.

Our emperor had his barons summoned, and had his charters and letters sealed, and sent them out through the whole kingdom. Within the week there were twenty thousand men under arms,

estre la force Willame al curb niés 2640
que li chargerent ses parenz del regné.
Li emperere ad Willame apelé:
"Sire Willame," dist Lowis le ber,
"tut cest empire ai jo pur vus mandé."
"Sire," dist Willame, "Deu vus en sace gré. 2645
Sire emperere, le congié m'en donez."
Suz Munt Leun ad fait tendre sun tref.
De la quisine al rei issit un bacheler,
deschalcez et en langes, n'out point de solders;
granz out les piez et les trameals crevez, 2650
et desur sun col portat un tinel* –
n'est ore nuls hom qui tel peust porter.
Vient a Willame, si l'ad araisuné:
"Sire Willame, jo voil od vus aler
a la bataille de l'Archamp sur mer, 2655
si tuerai Sarazins et Esclers."
Et dist Willame: "Ço serreit ben assez!
Ben semblez home qui tost voille digner,
et par matin n'ad cure de lever."
Et dist Reneward: "De folie parlez! 2660
Si me menez en l'Archamp sur mer
(19a) plus valdrai que .xv. de voz pers,
de tuz les meillurs que i avrez asemblees."
Ço dist Willame: "Ore avez dit que ber.

not counting the forces of Willame Hooknose that his relatives with lands in the kingdom had given him. The emperor called to Willame: "Lord Willame," said noble Lowis, "I have called all this force together on your account." "My lord," said Willame, "may God requite you for it. Lord emperor, I beg leave to go." Below Mount Laon he pitched his tent. From the king's kitchen came forth a young man, without stockings and in rags, and he had no shoes; he had big feet and his leggings were in a bad way, and on his shoulders he was carrying a yoke:* there's no man alive today could carry one like it. He came up to Willame and spoke to him: "Lord Willame, I want to go with you to the battle at l'Archamp by the sea, and kill Saracens and Slavs." And Willame said: "Well, there's a thing! You look like a man who wants an early dinner, and can't be bothered to get up in the morning." And Reneward said: "What rot! If you take me to l'Archamp by the sea I'll be worth more than fifteen of your peers, even of the very best you have gathered here." Said Willame: "Now you've spoken like a brave warrior.

Se tu vols armes, jo te ferai aduber." 2665
Dist Reneward: "Ne place unques Deus,
que ja altre arme i port que mun tinel;
ne sur cheval ne quer jo ja munter."
Dunc vait a sun maistre le cungé demander.
"Maistre," fait il, "jo ai od vus conversé; 2670
ore vient li termes que jo me voil amender.
Li quons Willame me volt od lui mener
en la bataille de l'Archamp sur mer."
Ço dist sun maistre: "Lecchere, nu ferez,
car les granz feims nem purrez endurer, 2675
ne les haans, ne les travals que averez.
Lores vus faldreient les vins et les clarez,
li pains et la char et li grant richitez,
si murriez a doel et a vilté.
Pité en ai: nurri vus ai mult suef." 2680
Dist Reneward: "De folie parlez!
Ne remaindrai pur quanque vus avez,
que jo n'en alge al fort estur champel."
Quant le maistre de lui est alé,
que il le quidat par force returner, 2685
et Reneward le fer si del tinel
tut estendu l'ad al feu acraventé;
ainz qu'il s'en leve, out les gernuns udlez.
Puis li ad dit: "Maistre, ci jus girrez!

If you want arms, I'll have you kitted out." Said Reneward: "God forbid that I should ever take any arms to that battle except my yoke; and I don't ever want to ride a horse." Then he went to ask his master's permission to go. "Master," he said, "I've been with you a long time; now the time has come for me to improve myself. Count Willame wants to take me with him to the Battle of l'Archamp by the sea." Said his master: "You won't go, you spoiled knave, because you couldn't put up with the great hunger, or the trials and tribulations you would have. Down there you'd miss the wines and wine punches, the bread and meat and all the rich living and would die in grief and shame. I feel sorry for you: I've brought you up very carefully." Said Reneward: "What rot! I'll not hesitate for anything you can offer to go to the fierce pitched battle." When his master approached and thought to take him back by force Reneward hit him so hard with his yoke he made him measure his length in the fire; before he got up, his moustaches were burned. Then he said to him: "Master, just lie there!

Des ore en avant l'ostel garderez;   2690
si l'um i pert rien, il vus ert demandez."*
Suz Munt Loun en vint corant as prez
al pavillun Willame al curb niés;
tant le demande que l'om li ad endité.
En la quisine est Reneward entré,   2695
(19b) prent feu a faire et ewe a porter.
Cels li joirent, car il en solt assez,
si li donerent piment, vin et clarez;
tant l'en donerent que tut l'unt enivrez,
et li leccheur li emblent sun tinel.   2700
Quant s'esveillad n'en ad mie trovez;
dunc se clamad chaitif et maleurez:
"Allas, peccable! Tant mar fu unques nez!"
Et li leccheur se pernent a gaber;
Reneward les ad esgardez§:   2705
"Fiz a putein, avez le me vus emblez?"
Les dous premers qu'il ad encuntrez
a ses dous mains les ad si hurtez,
les oilz tuz quatre les fist del chef voler.
Ço dist li tierz: "Jo rendrai le tinel!"   2710
Et dist Reneward: "Or n'en aiez vus grez."
A un fenil l'en unt od els§ mené;

From now on you will keep the house; if anyone loses anything, you'll be called to
account for it."* He came running down into the meadows below Mount Laon to the tent
of Willame Hooknose; he asked the way to it so insistently that it was pointed out to him.
Reneward went into the kitchen and set about making a fire and fetching water. The
people there appreciated what he did, for he did it well; so they gave him spiced wine,
plain wine and wine cup; they gave him so much they got him quite drunk, and the brutes
stole his yoke. When he awoke he could not find it anywhere; then he called himself an
unlucky wretch: "Alas, miserable wretch that I am! What a pity I was ever born!" And
the louts started making fun of him; Reneward looked at them: "You bastards! Did you
steal it from me?" The first two he met he knocked together so violently with his two
hands that he made their four eyes fly out of their heads. The third one said: "I'll give
back the yoke!" And Reneward said: "You'll get no thanks for it." They led him to a
hayloft;

---

§ 2705 esgarderez
§ 2712 unt els

unques les dous nel purent remuer.
Et Renewart prent cele part aler;
a un de ses mains l'ad en sun col levé,   2715
sin manace Sarazins et Esclers:
"N'en guarrad pé, quant jo ai le tinel!"

160

Uillame* leve par matin quant l'albe pert;
un greille fait mult haltement soner,
plus de seisante l'en responent al pré.   2720
Reneward ot la noise del corner,
tut esturdi sailli de sun ostel;
en la quisine obliad sun tinel,
ne li menbrat desque vindrent a un gué.
Devant Franceis començat a tenter;   2725
de l'ewe freide ad sun vis lavé,
dunc començad del vin a desenivrer.
Idunc a primes li menbrat del tinel,
pas avant altre se prent a returner.
(19c) Li quons Willame l'en ad araisoné: 2730
"Reneward frere, vols tu returner
en la quisine a tes hastes garder?
Ainz que moussez le te di jo assez,
ja nel purriez soffrir ne endurer."
"Nenil, bel sire, ne me vint en penser,   2735

the two of them together could not lift it. And Reneward followed along; he raised it to his shoulder with one hand and threatened Saracens and Slavs with it: "Not one will survive since I've got my yoke!"

Willame* arose in the morning when day appeared; he had a very loud call sounded on a trumpet, more than sixty of them replied around the meadow. Reneward heard the noise of the horn-calls, and left his lodging in a complete daze: he left his yoke behind in the kitchen, and did not remember it until they came to a ford. He began to test its depth ahead of the French; he washed his face in the cold water, then began to sober up. Then he remembered his yoke for the first time, and started plodding back to the camp. Count Willame addressed him: "Brother Reneward, do you want to go back to the kitchen to look after your spits? Before we set out I told you clearly enough you would never be able to suffer and bear up.""Oh! no, my dear lord, such a thought never entered my head,

mais§ a l'ostel obliai mun tinel."
"Va, fols lecchere, laissez cel bastun ester!
Enz en cel bois te ferai un colper
a ta mesure, et long et quarré."
Dist Reneward: "Ne place unques Dé!   2740
Suz ciel n'ad bois u il fust recovré.
Ben ad set anz que jo oi le tinel
en la quisine de Loun la cité;
unc nel vi freindre ne desercler."
Ço dist Willame: "Jol frai ja aporter."   2745
Dist Reneward: "Ore avez dit que ber!"
Devant li garde et vit un Flamenc ester;
gent out le cors, eschevi et mollé,
si chevalche un destrer abrivé.
Il li comandat que alt pur le tinel: 2750
"Volenters, sire, quant vus le comandez."
Il point et broche tant qu'il vint enz al pré,
met pé a tere, sil pensa a lever.
A vifs diables ad le fust comandé;
al cheval munte, brochant s'en est turné.   2755
Tresque a Willame ne volt unques finer:
"Dites, bel sire, avez vus le tinel?"
"Nenil veirs, sire, unques nel poai remuer.
Mal ait de la barbe, qui l'i out oblié,

but I left my yoke behind in my lodging." "Come on, you young clot, let that stick be! I'll have one cut for you in that wood over there, the right size for you, long and square." Said Reneward: "God forbid! There's no wood under Heaven where you could get a replacement for it. I've had that yoke a good seven years in the kitchen at the citadel of Laon; I never knew it break or lose its bands." Said Willame: "I'll have it fetched for you." Said Reneward: "That's nobly said!" He looked around and saw a Fleming waiting there; he was nobly built, slim and well muscled, and riding a fiery charger. He ordered him to go for the yoke: "Certainly, my lord, since you command it." He clapped spurs to his horse all the way back to the meadow, dismounted, and thought he would pick it up. He wished the trunk to the living devils; he mounted and, clapping spurs to his horse, returned to the army. He did not stop until he came up with Willame: "Tell me, my dear lord, have you got the yoke?" "Certainly not, my lord, I could never move it. A curse on the beard of whoever left it there,

§ 2736 mas

et de la mere, si unques le poai remuer!" 2760
Dist Reneward: "Mé i covient aler.
Ja ne vendrat pur nul home qui seit nez
se les meins braz ne l'unt aportez."
(19d) Et dist Willame: "Jo n'i voil mes sejurner.
Mei que cheut, si vus en alez? 2765
Mais ainz que nuit seiez vus a l'hostel§ !"
Les menuz salz i prent a returner,
plus tost n'i fust pas un gascoin sojurnez.
De joie rist, quant il vit le tinel;
od un sul poing l'ad sur sun col levé. 2770
Unc Franceis ne se surent tant haster,
ainz qu'il fuissent al pareissir del gué
fu Reneward devant els al pré.
Li quons Willame l'en ad araisoné:
"Dites mei, frere, avez vus le tinel?" 2775
"Oil, bel sire, la verai Deu merci,
sainte Marie le m'ad amené.
Ço comparunt Sarazin et Escler:
ne garrad pé, quant jo l'ai recovré!"
Lunsdi al vespre: 2780
"Car chevalchez, si alum bataille quere!
Quant nus vendrum en l'Archamp en la presse
fuiz s'en serrunt li paien de Palerne,

and on his mother, if I could ever move it!" Said Reneward: "I'll have to go myself. It'll never come for any man alive if my own arms haven't brought it." And Willame said: "I won't wait here any longer. What do I care if you leave us? Just be at the lodging by nightfall!" He skipped away back along the road, faster than a well rested Gascon horse. He laughed for joy when he saw the yoke; with just one hand he raised it to his shoulder. However fast the French went, before they were all clear of the ford Reneward was before them in the meadow. Count Willame addressed him: "Tell me, brother, have you got your yoke?" "Yes, my dear lord, by the grace of the true God, Saint Mary brought it back to me. Saracens and Slavs will pay for it: not one will survive now I've got it back!" Monday at vespertide: "Ride on, we'll go to join battle! When we come to the mêlée at l'Archamp the pagans from Palermo will all have fled,

---

§ 2766 seie a vus al hostel

de Nichodeme, de Alfrike§ et de Superbe!"
Dient Franceis: "Cist lecchere se desve: 2785
bataille quert, et Deus li doinst pesme!"
Car as cowarz tremblout la bouele,
et les vassals s'afichouent es seles
et as destrers abrivez de Chastele.

161

Uillame chevalche les pius et les vals,   2790
et les muntaines que pas ne se targat.
Vint a Orenge que forment desirad;
a un perun descent de sun cheval.
Dame Guiburc les degrez devalad,
par grant amur la franche li baisad,   2795
puis li demande: "Qu'as tu en France fait?"
"Nent el que ben, ma dame, si vus plaist.
(20a) Vint mil homes en amein ben et mais
que l'emperere de France me chargeat,
estre la force de mi parent leal: 2800
quarante mille, la merci Deu, en ai."
"Ne vient il dunc?" "Nun, dame." "Ço m'est laid!"
"Malade gist a sa chapele a Es."*
Et dist Guiburc: "Cest vers avez vus fait!
S'il ore gist, ja ne releve il més!   2805

and those from Nichodeme, from Africa and from Superbe!" The French say: "This
bugger's mad: he's looking for a battle, may God give him a horrible one!" For the
cowards' bowels were trembling, and the hardened warriors were settling into their
saddles and onto their fiery, Castilian chargers.

Willame rode up hill and down dale, and over mountain ranges without breaking his
march. He came to Orange for which he had been yearning; he dismounted at a block.
Lady Guiburc came down the steps, the noble lady kissed him very lovingly, and then
asked him: "What did you do in France?" "I got on very well, if it please my lady. I've
brought down twenty thousand men and more that the Emperor of France entrusted to
me, without the troops of my loyal kinfolk: I've forty thousand all told, by God's grace."
"Isn't he coming?" "No, my lady." "I'm sorry about that." "He's lying ill in his chapel at
Aix."* And Guiburc said: "You made that up! If he's in bed now, may he never get up!

§ 2784 da alfike

Ne voille Deu, qui tote rien ad fait."
Willame munte le marbrin paleis;
a sun tinel Reneward vait aprés.
Cels qui l'esgardent le tienent pur boisnard,
et asquanz le crement, que trestuz les tuast.   2810

162

Uillame munte les marbrins degrez,
et Reneward le siut od sun tinel.
Dame Guburc l'emprist a esgarder,
vint a Willame, conseillad li suef.
"Sire," dist ele, "qui est cest bacheler,   2815
qui en sun col porte cest fust quarré?"
"Dame," dist il, "ja§ est un bageler,
uns joefnes hom que Deus m'ad amené."
"Sire," dist ele, "estuet le nus doter?"
"Nenal, veir, ben i poez parler."   2820
Et ele le traist a un conseil privé.
"Ami," dist ele, "de quele terre es tu né,
et de quel regne, et de quel parenté?"
"Dame," dist il, "d'Espaigne le regné,
si sui fiz al fort rei Deramé   2825
et Oriabel est ma mere de ultre mer."
"Cum avez num?" "Reneward m'apelez."

May the God who created all things not will it!" Willame went up to the marble palace; Reneward followed him, carrying his yoke. The people watching him think he's a fool, and some fear that he will kill them all.

Willame went up the marble steps, and Reneward followed him with his yoke. Lady Guiburc started to look at him, came over to Willame and spoke quietly to him. "My lord," she said, " who is this young man carrying this square beam on his shoulder?" "My lady," he said, "just a youth, a young man whom God brought to me." "My lord," she said, "do we have anything to fear from him?" "Not at all, you can speak to him if you like." And she drew him to one side for a private talk. "My friend," she said, "in which land were you born, in which kingdom, and of which clan?" "My lady," he said, "in the kingdom of Spain, and I am the son of the powerful king Deramé and Oriabel from beyond the sea is my mother." "What is your name?" "Call me Reneward."

§ 2817 ias

Guiburc l'oi, sil reconuit§ assez;
del quor suspire, des oilz comence a plorer.
Et dist la dame: "Cest nun m'est mult privé: 2830
un frere oi jo, que si se fist clamer.
(20b) Pur la sue amur te ferai jo adubber,
cheval et armes te ferai jo doner."
Dist Reneward: "Ne place unques Deu
que ja altre arme i porte que mun tinel,   2835
ne sur cheval ne quer jo ja munter!"

163

"Ami, bel frere, jo vus adoberai;
chevals et armes par matin vus durrai."
"Ne place Deu, dame," dist Reneward,
"Suz ciel n'ad rien, qui tant hace cum cheval."   2840
"Ami," dist ele, "une espee porterez,
coment que avienge de cel vostre tinel,
que s'il veolt fraindre ne esquasser
que al costé i puissez tost recovrer."
"Dame," dist il, "ma espee me donez."   2845

Guiburc heard it and recognised him; she sighed from her heart and wept from her eyes.
And the lady said: "This name is dear to me: I had a brother who was called that. For
love of him I shall make you a knight and have you given horse and arms." Said
Reneward: "God forbid that I should ever bear other arms than my yoke, and I have no
desire to mount a horse!"

"My friend, dear brother, I shall make you a knight; I will give you horses and arms in
the morning." "God forbid, my lady," said Reneward, "Under Heaven there is nothing I
hate as much as a horse." "My friend," she said, "you will carry a sword, in case
anything should happen to your yoke, such as its taking it into its head to split or break,
you could quickly find a replacement at your side." "My lady," he said, "give me my
sword."

---

§ 2828 sil le reconuit

164

Dame Guiburc li aportad l'espee:
d'or fu li punz, d'argent fu neelee;
ele li ceinst et il l'ad mult esgardee.
Il ne sout mie que fuissent sorur ne frere,
ne nel saverad, si ert l'ost devisee,   2850
et la bataille vencue et depanee.

165

Li quons Willame demande le super,
que la meisné seit ben conreié.
En la quisine est Reneward entré;
espee ceinte vait les hastes turner.   2855
Cels l'i joirent§, car il en solt assez,
si li donerent et piment et claré;
tant l'en donerent que tut l'unt enivré.
Dame Guiburc nel mist pas en oblier;
en mi la sale ad fait sun lit parer,   2860
cum ço fust a Willame al curb niés.
Reneward, sun frere, ad cher apelez:
"Amis, frere, en cest lit girrez."
Guiburc s'en vait lez Willame reposer,
et Reneward ad le lit esgardé,   2865

Lady Guiburc brought him the sword: its pommel was of gold; it was damascened with silver; she strapped it on him, and he looked closely at it. He did not know they were sister and brother, and he will not know until the host is destroyed and the battle won with the enemy put to flight.

Count Willame asked for supper, so that his household would be well supplied. Reneward went into the kitchen; he went to turn the spits with his sword strapped on. The people there appreciated what he did, for he did it well; so they gave him spiced wine and wine cup; they gave him so much they got him completely drunk. Lady Guiburc did not forget him; in the centre of the hall she set up a bed for him, just as if it were for Willame Hooknose. She called tenderly to Reneward, her brother: "My friend, brother, you shall lie in this bed." Guiburc went to lie down next to Willame, and Reneward looked at the bed:

---

§ 2856 cels li oirent

(20c) nel preisad mie un dener moneé;
     en la quisine s'en est colcher alé.
     Les lecchurs li unt sun chef uslé
     et tuz ses dras espris et enbrasé.
     Quant s'esveillad le feu sent al costé.   2870
     Il sailli sus cum home desvé;
     a halte voiz comence a crier:
     "Dolent peccable! Qui m'ad eschaldé?
     Cum mar fui fiz al fort rei Deramé,
     Oriabel, ma mere de ultre la mer!   2875
     Car mar vi unques Willame al curb niés,
     qui m'amenad de Loun la cité,
     de la quisine Lowis l'onuré!
     Ses lecchurs me tienent en vilté,
     qui m'unt ma barbe et mes gernuns uslé!"   2880
     Li leccheur se pernent a gaber,
     et Reneward les prent a guarder:
     "Fiz a puteins, avez me vus ullé?
     Mar i entrastes, par la fei que dei a Dé!
     Si jo puis ja vif ne m'estorterez."   2885
     Od sun bastun en ad quatre tuez.
     Un en consivit al eissir del ostel,
     parmi les reins li dona un colp tel
     en dous meitez li ad le cors colpé;
     del pié le boute, le quor li ad crevé.   2890
     En la quisine s'en est colcher alé,

he wouldn't give you tuppence for it; he went to lie down in the kitchen. The loutish
kitchen boys burnt his head and set fire to all his clothes. When he woke up he felt the fire
at his side. He leapt up like a madman; he began shouting at the top of his voice: "What a
miserable wretch I am! Who has burnt me? It was my bad luck to be the son of the
powerful king Deramé, and Oriabel, my mother from beyond the sea! It's a pity I ever
saw Willame Hooknose, who brought me away from the citadel of Laon, from the
kitchen of honoured Lowis! His scullions hold me cheap and have burnt my beard and
moustaches!" The louts began to make fun of him, and Reneward started to look at them:
"You bastards, did you burn me? You'll regret coming in here, by the faith I owe God! If
I can help it, you'll never get away alive." With his stick he killed four of them. He
caught up with one at the entrance to the building, he hit him so hard in the kidneys that
he cut him in half; he kicked him, and his heart gave out. He went to lie down in the
kitchen,

andous les us ad desur li fermé;
un des morz ad a sun chef turné,
desuz les costez ad sun tinel boté:
tiel gist sur cuilte qui ne dort si suef!   2895

166

Reneward leve ainz que l'albe apert;
de la quisine est al paleis turné.
"Munjoie!" escrie, "Frans chevalers, muntez!
Quant nus vendrum en l'Archamp sur mer
(20d) fui serrunt Sarazin et Escler.   2900
Ja puis cel hure n'i purrum recovrer."
Dient Franceis: "Lais nus, lecchere, ester!
Mal seit de l'ore qui li tuen cors fu né –
uncor n'ad li cocs, ço quid, que dous feiz chanté!"
Dist Reneward: "Ja l'ai jo comandé!   2905
Fiz sui a rei, si dei aver ferté.
Par la grant fei que jo plevi a Dé,
a iceste feiz se ore sus ne levez,
jol vus frai cher a tuz comparer!"
Halce le fust, si fert sur un piler   2910
que un estage* en ad parmi colpé;
tote la sale fait sur els trembler,
pur petit ne l'ad tut acraventé.
De la pour qu'il unt sunt Franceis sus levé;

closing both doors behind him; he put one of the corpses under his head; he stuffed his yoke under his sides: there are people lying on feather beds who do not sleep so peacefully!

Reneward got up before dawn broke; he returned to the great hall from the kitchen. "Munjoie!" he shouted, "Noble knights, mount up! When we arrive at l'Archamp by the sea the Saracens and Slavs will have fled. After that we'll never overtake them." The French say: "Let us be, you sod! A curse on the hour you were born — the cock, I think, has only crowed twice yet!" Said Reneward: "I've given you an order! I'm a king's son, and must have my fierce pride. By the great faith I've pledged to God, if you don't get up at once I'll make you all pay dearly for it!" He raised his beam and struck it against a pillar splitting a shaft in two;* the whole hall shook over their heads, he very nearly brought it down on them. The French got up out of fear;

mil en i out qui perdirent lur solders: 2915
lur garnement ne poent recovrer.
Mettent les seles as destrers sejurnez;
granz .xv. liuues sunt de nuit alé;
nuit fu oscure, nent del jur apert,
trestuit maldient Reneward al tinel: 2920
"Maldit seit il des saintes miracles Deu,
cest lecheur, cest paltoner prové!
Qui a tel hure nus fait ici errer
ben granz colees li devreit l'um doner."
Et dist Willame: "Leissez le tut ester!   2925
s'il est fols, nel vus chet a gaber;
n'i ad nul si fier ne si osé
s'il i tent sun dei, ne seit mort u tué."

167

Uillame en ad l'ost de France mené
tresque il vindrent en l'Archamp enz el pré§.   2930
Ço dist quons Boeves de Cormarchiz, sun frere,
et Neemeri de Nerbune, sun pere:
"Francs chevalers de la nostre cuntree,
(21a) bien est de guere qui tost est finee."
Dient Franceis: "Pur l'alme§ a noz peres,   2935

a thousand of them lost their shoes and could not find their kit. They saddled up their well rested horses; they covered fifteen long leagues by night; it was pitch black, with no sign of day, and they all cursed Reneward with the Yoke: "God's miracles smite him, the brute, the confirmed villain! Anyone who gets us travelling at such an hour deserves a good beating." And Willame said: "Leave him alone! If he's a fool, you've no call to mock him; there's none of you so fierce or so daring who, if he just pointed at you, wouldn't fall down dead."

Willame led off the host of France until they came to l'Archamp in the meadow. Said Count Boeves of Cormarchiz, his brother, and Neemeri of Narbonne, his father: "Freeborn knights of our land, it's a good war that's soon finished." The French say: "For the souls of our fathers

---

§ 2930 enz le pre
§ 2935 pur lalmes

tant i ferum de lances et d'espees§,
aprés noz morz en ert France dotee!"
A icel mot fu "Munjoie!" escriee,
l'enseigne Charles, de France l'emperere§.
Beissent les lances, as paiens se justerent.   2940

168

Uillame en ad l'ost de France mené
tresque il vindrent en l'Archamp sur mer,
et qu'il virent les barges et les niés.
"Seignurs baruns," dist Willame al curb niés,
"ore avum tant espleité et alés§,   2945
que nus veum Sarazins et Esclers.
Car lur alum chalenger et mustrer
qui a tort honissent sainte crestienté.
Qui ore me voldrad felonie mustrer
en bataille en l'Archamp sur mer,   2950
congié de Deu et de mei li voil doner,
qu'en dulce France s'en poent returner."
Quant cil l'oirent, si unt Deu merciez;
tuz les cowarz sunt une part turnez:
mult est crevé sa force et sun barné.   2955
En dulce France se voldrunt returner;

we shall strike so hard with our lances and swords that after our deaths France will be feared!" With that "Munjoie!" was shouted, the war cry of Charles, Emperor of France. They lowered their lances and closed with the pagans.

Willame led off the host of France until they came to l'Archamp by the sea, and they saw the barges and ships. "Lord barons," said Willame Hooknose, "now we have achieved so much and travelled so far that we can see the Saracens and Slavs. Let us enter battle with them and show them that they are in the wrong in bringing shame to holy Christendom. To anyone who wants to act dishonourably in the battle at l'Archamp by the sea God and I willingly give leave to go back to sweet France." When they heard that, they gave thanks to God; all the cowards turned back as a group: his strength and his war band were greatly reduced. They want to go back to sweet France;

§ 2936 des espees
§ 2939 lempere
§ 2945 alesz (or: ales& – the *z* is barred)

vont a Willame le cungé demander,
et il lur dune, ne lur deignad veer.
Mais ne qui mie qu'il algent a itiel,
car Reneward les encuntre a un gué,   2960
a un destreit u il deveient passer;
en sun col portat sun grant tinel.
"Seignurs," dist il, "u devez vus aler?"
"Li quons Willame nus ad cungié doné.
Car t'en revien, Reneward al tinel;   2965
vez tanz en i ad Sarazins et Esclers:
ja pé de noz n'en verrez eschaper!"
(21b) Dist Reneward: "Lecchurs, vus i mentez!
Mar i entrastes, par la fei que dei Deu!"
Dunc lur curt sure, si ad le talent mué.   2970
Plus de quatorze en ad al fust tué,
trestuz les fist par force retorner.
Vint a Willame, si l'ad araisuné:
"Sire Willame, un petit m'atendez.
Icés couarz que vus ici veez,   2975
ceste est ma torbe§ , mun pople et mun barnez.
Et mei et els en la pointe metez,
contre les lances aguz des Esclers."
"Si ferai jo," dist Willame li bers.
"Si Deu m'ait, n'i ert§ mes tresturné!"   2980

they approach Willame to ask leave to go, and he gives it to them, not deigning to refuse.
But I do not think they will get away like that, for Reneward meets them at a ford, in a
narrow crossing they had to pass through; he was carrying his great yoke over his
shoulder. "My lords," he said, "where might you be going?" "Count Willame has
dismissed us. Come away, Reneward with the Yoke; See how many Saracens and Slavs
there are: you'll not see one of us escape them!" Said Reneward: "Scum, you're lying!
You'll regret stepping in there, by the faith I owe God!" Then he rushed at them in a
raging fury. He killed more than fourteen of them with his beam, and he forced all the
rest to turn back again. He came up to Willame and spoke to him: "Lord Willame, just
wait a minute. These cowards you see here are my train, my people, my war band. Put
me and them in the very front rank right up against the sharp lances of the Slavs." "I will
indeed," said Willame the noble warrior. "So help me God, that won't be
countermanded!"

---

§ 2976 torche
§ 2980 i nert

Icés cowarz, dunt vus m'oez parler,
puis furent cels en l'Archamp cum bers:
grant mester eurent a Willame al curb nés.

169

Mult i feri ben Willame al curb niés,
quant Deu de glorie enluminad le barné,   2985
et li quons Boeve de Comarchis le ber,
et Naimeris, et Ernard li barbez,
et Reneward qui portad le tinel
al premer chef en ad treis cenz tuez.
Et tute jur durad l'estur mortel,   2990
et tote nuit en ad l'enchalz duré
tresqu'al demain, que li jor aparut cler.
Parmi l'Archamp corut un doit de sanc tel,
ben en peust un grant coissel§ turner.
Reneward ad vers midi gardé,   2995
vit le soleil mult haltement levé:
"Que est ço, diable? Ferum nus ja mais el
que Sarazins ocire et afronter?
Ben en i at, mais treis itantz i pert!
Si jo fusse a Loun la cité,   3000
en la cusine, u jo soleie converser,
(21c) a cest hure me fuisse jo dignez;

These cowards you hear me speak of then acted like brave warriors at l'Archamp: they were very useful to Willame Hooknose.

Willame Hooknose struck mighty blows on that field, when the God of Glory enlightened the warriors, and brave Count Boeve of Comarchiz and Naimeris and bearded Ernard, and Reneward who bore the yoke killed three hundred with it in the first encounter. And the mortal conflict lasted all day, and the pursuit lasted all night until the morning, when the day dawned bright and clear. In the midst of l'Archamp a stream of blood ran so deep you could have driven a great mill wheel with it. Reneward looked to the south and saw that the sun was very high: "What's going on, in the devil's name? Won't we ever do anything but kill and brain Saracens? There are a lot of them, but they seem three times more than they are! If I were in the citadel at Laon, in the kitchen that I used to frequent, I would be having dinner at this hour;

§ 2994 eioissel

del bon vin cler eusse beu assez,
si m'en dormisse juste le feu suef.
Ço comparunt Sarazin et Escler! 3005

170

"Sire Willame, ci vus pri que m'atendez
et jo irai la jus vers cele mer
– la u vei les dromunz aancrer –
sis irrai freindre et bruser ces nés,
car, quant l'estur serrad vencu champel, 3010
enz as niés enterunt Sarazin et Escler.
Si s'en fuirunt as undes de halte mer,
par Deu celestre, puis n'i poum recovrer!"
Dient Franceis: "Mult est Reneward ber:
beneit seit l'ore que le suen cors fu né!" 3015
Pas avant altre i prent a devaler;
devant li garde, si veit un rei errer.
Nez fud de Cordres, si out a nun Ailred,
et chevalchout un destrer abrived.
Et Reneward le feri del tinel; 3020
tut le bruse, mort l'ad acraventé
et le cheval li ad parmi colpé.
Enz en la nef al fort rei Ailré,
iloec trovad set cenz paiens armez:
tuz les ad morz, ocis et agraventez. 3025
Li quons Bertram i ert enprisonez;

I would have drunk a lot of good bright wine, and have fallen soundly asleep by the fire. Saracens and Slavs will pay for this!

"Lord Willame, please wait for me here and I'll just go down to the sea — where I saw the galleys at anchor — and I'll go and split open and break up these ships, for, when we've won the battle on the field, the Saracens and Slavs will enter their ships. If they flee across the waves of the high seas, by the Heavenly God, we'll never catch up with them!" The French say: "Reneward is a very wise warrior: blessed be the hour of his birth!" He strode down to the beach; he looked around and saw a king go by. He was born in Cordoba, and was called Ailred, and rode a fiery charger. And Reneward struck him with his yoke; he crushed him and killed him stone dead and cut the horse in two. In the ship of the powerful king Ailré he found seven hundred armed pagans: he killed and slaughtered them all. Count Bertram was imprisoned there;

quant il le veit, sil prent a esgarder.
"Chevaler sire," ço dist Bertram le ber,
"fiz a barun, qui cest bastun tenez,
beneit seit le hure que vostre cors fu né! 3030
Es tu de paenisme, u de crestienté?"
Dist Reneward: "Je crei tres bien en Dé.
Cum as tu nun? Gard nel me celer!"
"Jo ai nun Bertram, niés Willame al curb neis."
Dist Reneward: "Lui conuis jo assez. 3035
(21d) Il m'amenad ci de Loun la cité,
de la quisine u jo ai conversé."
"Reneward sire, car me desprisonez:
li quons Willame vus en savra bon grez."
Dist Reneward: "Un petit m'atendez. 3040
Quant paiens vei as fonz de celes niefs,
qui suz ces cleies se muscent pur mun tinel,
od mun bastun les irrai afronter."
Pas avant altre comence a devaler;
il les consiut sur le bord de la nef, 3045
a un sul colp ad tuz esrenés.
Puis vint al cunte, si l'ad desprisonez;
les granz seins li ad del col geté,
si l'enporta a la frecche herbe al pré.
Li quons Bertram l'en ad araisoné: 3050
"Reneward sire, tu m'as desprisoné.
Ore vus pri, pur Deu, que des altres pensez."

when he saw him, he had a good look at him. "Lord knight," said Bertram the brave warrior, "baron's son, holding this stick, blessed be the hour of your birth! Do you belong to pagandom or Christendom? Said Reneward: "I firmly believe in God. What's your name? Mind you don't keep it from me!" "I am called Bertram, nephew of Willame Hooknose." Said Reneward: "I know him all right. He brought me from the citadel of Laon, from the kitchen that I frequented." "Lord Reneward, do release me from prison: Count Willame will be grateful." Said Reneward: "Just wait a minute. Since I can see pagans in the bottom of those ships, hiding from my yoke under those cleats, I'll go and brain them with my stick." He strode down to where they were; he caught up with them at the side of the ship, with one blow he broke all their backs. Then he came to the count and released him from prison; he threw the mighty bonds from off his neck, and carried him to the fresh grass in the meadow. Count Bertram addressed him: "Lord Reneward, you have released me from prison. Now I beg you, for God's sake, to think of the others."

"A il dunc mais?" dist Reneward le ber.
"Oil, veirs, quatre, que mult devez amer:
Walter de Termes, et Reiner le sené,   3055
et Guilin, et Guischard al vis cler."
"Bertram sire, sez tu ben governer?"
"Oil, ami§, jo en soi jadis assez.*
Cest dromund peise, nel purrum remuer,
men escient, se set cent i eust asemblez."   3060
Dist Reneward: "Un petit m'atendez:
ja del trop lent ne dirrat hom buntez,
ne de malveisted n'ert ja bon los chantez."
Enz al graver ad sun bastun fichez;
del liu l'enpeint, tote la fait trembler,   3065
pur un petit ne fait le bord voler.
Et Bertram est al governail alé;
paien les veient, ne lur vint pas a gré;
lancent lur lances, et peres et aguez pels.
(22a) Reneward s'est a els acosteiez;   3070
dunc joinst ses pez, si sailli en lur nés;
dunc les acuilt Reneward a sun tinel,
trestuz les ad morz et acraventez:
treis mille saillent de pour en la mer.
Dist Reneward: "Ore est vus mal alé!   3075
Mielz vus venist morir od mun tinel

"Are there more then?" said Reneward the brave warrior. "Oh, yes, four, whom you should love dearly: Walter of Termes, wise Reiner, and Guilin and bright faced Guischard ." "Lord Bertram, do you know how to steer a ship? "Yes, my friend, I used to be an expert.* This galley is heavy, we won't be able move it, to my knowledge, if we get seven hundred men together for the job." Said Reneward: "Just wait a minute: no good will be spoken of the man who's too slow, and an evil deed's praises will not be sung." He stuck his stick in the beach; he got a good purchase, the whole ship shook, he all but sprang the side. And Bertram went to the steering oar; the pagans saw them, and were displeased; they threw lances and stones and sharpened stakes at them. Reneward came alongside them; then, with his feet together, he jumped into their ship; then Reneward attacked them with his yoke, he killed and slaughtered them all: three thousand leapt into the sea through fear. Said Reneward: "Now things have gone wrong for you! It would have been better for you to die under my yoke

§ 3058 oil aini

que si neer as undes de halte mer.
Fiz a puteins, malveis martire avez!"
Puis vint as cuntes, sis ad desprisonez.
Li quons Bertram l'en ad araisoné: 3080
"Reneward sire, vus m'avez desprisoné,
et tuz ces altres, dunt vus sace Deu grez.
Ore vus pri que de chevals pensez,
de bones armes, dunt fuissum adobez,
puis verriez cum nus savum juer." 3085
Dist Reneward: "Vus en avrez asez.
Tant en vei jo as Sarazins mener."
Devant lui garde, si veit un rei errer
et chevalcher§ un destrer sojurné.
Et il li donad al front de sun tinel: 3090
tut le bruse, que mort l'ad acraventé,
et le cheval li ad parmi colpé.
Dist Bertram: "Cest colp est mal alé:
de cest cheval n'erc mes adubé."
Dist Reneward: "Un petit m'atendez." 3095
De l'altre part garde, veit le rei Overter.
Et Reneward le fiert si del tinel
tut le debruse, mort l'ad acraventé,
et le cheval li ad parmi colpé.
"Se si vus vient, jo n'erc huimés adubé! 3100

than to drown like that in the waves of the high seas. You bastards, you've come to a sticky end!" Then he came to the counts and released them from prison. Count Bertram addressed him: "Lord Reneward, you have released me from prison, and all these others, may God requite you for it. Now I beg you, think about some horses, and good arms to equip ourselves with, then you'll see how we can join the sport." Said Reneward: "You shall have plenty of them. I see so many being led along by the Saracens." He looked around and saw a king go by riding a well rested charger. And he hit him on the forehead with his yoke: he smashed him to pulp and killed him stone dead, and cut the horse in two. Said Bertram: "That was an ill judged blow: I'll never be able to use this horse." Said Reneward: "Just wait a minute." He looked the other way and saw King Overter. And Reneward hit him so hard with his yoke he smashed him to pulp and killed him stone dead, and cut the horse in two. "If that's how you go about it, I'll never get any equipment today!

§ 3089 & cheualche

          Issi en poez quatre mil tuer!"
          Dist Reneward: "De folie parlez!
          Cest fust peise, nel puis mie governer.
(22b) Grosse est la brace qui me tient al costé:
          puis que jo l'ai contremunt levé,   3105
          par nul semblant nel puis adominer,
          ne petit colp ne puis jo pas doner."
          Ço dist Bertram: "Altre conseil en pernez."
          "Bels sire, bor fuissez vus nez."

171

          Ço dist Bertram: "Ja ne verrez vus tel,   3110
          ke en botant nel poez tuer?"
          Dist Reneward: "Vus dites verité.
          Mei' fei! ne m'en ere pensé!"
          Devant lui garde, vit le rei Corduel,
          et chevalcholt un destrer abrivé.   3115
          Dunc li curt sure Reneward al tinel,
          bute le al piz, si l'ad tut debrusé;
          par la boche li salt le sanc, et par le niés.
          Plus tost nen est li paiens jus alé,
          et Bertram est a l'alferant munté.   3120
          Et les altres cuntes ad il ben adobez
          de bones armes et de destrers sojurnez.
          Li quons Bertram l'en ad araisonez:
          "Reneward sire, tu nus as desprisonez;

You could kill four thousand of them like that!" Said Reneward: "You're talking rot! This is a heavy beam, I can't control it. I've got huge arms hanging at my side: once I've raised it up there's no way I can restrain it or give a little tap with it." Said Bertram: "Try something else." "Dear lord, you were born in a blessed hour."

Said Bertram: "Can't you see one that you could kill by prodding him?" Said Reneward: "You're quite right. My word, I'd never have thought of it!" He looked around and saw King Corduel riding a fiery charger. Then Reneward with the Yoke rushed at him, prodded him in the chest and smashed him to pulp; his blood gushed out through his mouth and nose. No sooner was the pagan down than Bertram mounted his war horse. And he found good equipment for the other counts: fine arms and well rested chargers. Count Bertram addressed him: "Lord Reneward, you have released us from prison;

pur Deu vus pri, Willame nus mostrez."   3125
Dist Reneward: "Ben vus sai guier.
Sire Bertram, juste mei vus tenez."
Idunc prent si granz colps a doner:
avant ses poinz ne pot nul eschaper.
Par la bataille, dunt vus me oez parler,   3130
feseit tele rute Reneward a sun tinel
ben se peussent quatre char entrecuntrer.

172

Bertram laist cure l'alferant.
Il ne fu unc laner ne couard,
si vait ferir un paien§, Malagant,   3135
l'escu li freinst, et le halberc li estroad:
pleine sa hanste l'abat mort del cheval.
(22c) Ço dist Bertram: "Vus me veistes ja!
Ben vus conuis a la chere et as dras.
En la nef me feistes maint mals."   3140

173

En sum un pui unt Willame trové§;
Bertram l'ad baisé et acolé.
Dunc li demande Willame al curb niés:
"Bels niés Bertram, qui vus ad desprisonez?"

in God's name I beg you, show us Willame." Said Reneward: "I can show you the way.
Lord Bertram, just keep beside me." Then he started dealing great blows: none could
escape his hands. Through the battle, that you hear me telling of, Reneward cut such a
road with his yoke that four carts could easily pass each other on it.

Bertram gave rein to his war horse. He was neither sluggard nor coward, and went to
strike a pagan, Malagant, broke his shield, and split his halberk: with a full thrust of his
lance he knocked him dead from his horse. Said Bertram: "You've seen me before! I
recognise you from your face and your clothes. You often tortured me in the ship."

They found Willame at the top of a hill; Bertram kissed him and threw his arms round his
neck. Then Willame Hooknose asked him: "Dear nephew Bertram, who released you
from prison?"

§ 3135 un paie
§ 3141 un Willame troue

"A nun Deu, uncle," dist il, "un chevaler,   3145
un fort, un fier, un joefne, un alosez:
Bone fud l'ore que le suen cors fud né.
Plus de treis mil lur en ad mort jeté,
et debrusé lur barges et lur nefs."
"Deus," dist Willame, "tant le deusse amer,   3150
se a nul saveir le veisse aturner."
Lunsdi al vespre:
Ore s'entrebaisent Bertram et Willame,
et Guielin et dan Walter de Termes,
et Guischard et Girard fiz cadele.*   3155
Grant est la joie del parenté Willame.

174

Este vus errant Gloriant de Palerne,
un Sarazin felun de pute geste;
crestiens muet a doel et a perte.
Et Reneward le fiert si en le healme   3160
en quatre lius li ad brusé la teste,
de quinze parz li espant la cervele.
Ço dist Willame: "Tu deis ben chevaler estre!
Fel seie jo se jo ne te doins terre,
et moiller gente qui ert de bons ancestres.   3165
Aincui verrum al chef et en la cue
quele est la geste Naimeri de Nerbune!

"In God's name, uncle," he said, "a knight, a strong man, a fierce man, a young man, a man of reputation; he was born in a good hour. He killed more than three thousand of them, and smashed their barges and ships." "God," said Willame, "I should love him so well if I saw him learn a bit of wisdom." Monday at vespertide: Now Bertram and Willame kiss, and Guielin and Lord Walter of Termes, and Guischard and Girard Fitz Captain.* Great was the joy of Willame's clan.

Here is Gloriant of Palermo riding by, an evil Saracen of filthy race; he caused much grief and loss to the Christians. And Reneward struck him on his helmet breaking his head in four places and spilling his brains in fifteen directions. Said Willame: "You really must become a knight! May I be branded a criminal if I don't give you land and a noble wife of good lineage. This very day we'll see first and last what the race of Naimeri of Narbonne is like!

Unc n'i jut un§ en terre ne en crutes,
ainz sunt oscis a gransz batailles dubles."

175

Este vus errant Tabur de Canaloine,   3170
un Sarazin qui Dampnedeu confunde.
(22d) Gros out le cors et l'eschine curbe,
lunges les denz, si est velu cum urse;
ne porte arme for le bec et les ungles.
Veit Guielin, si li est coru sure,   3175
baie la gule, si li quidad tranglutre
tut ensement cum une meure pome.
Et cil le fer de l'espee en la loigne;
ja l'eust mort, quant sa hanste li fruisse.
Ja le socurad Willame, le prouz cunte;   3180
de sun espé le fiert par angoisse,
en treis meitez la hanste li fruisse:
le quir fud dur, ne volt entamer unques.
Il traist s'espee§, et Willame la sue;
fierent et caplent, et cil baie la gule.   3185
Les branz d'ascer mangue et runge
od les denz granz, que Dampnedeu confunde!
Quidad Willame del tut confundre;

Not one ever lay buried in consecrated ground or crypt, rather they died in the most
almighty battles."

Here is Tabur of Canaloine riding by, a Saracen whom the Lord confound. He had a
huge body and curved spine; he had long teeth and was hairy as a bear; he carried no
weapon except his beak and claws. He saw Guielin and rushed at him, gaped with his
mouth and thought to swallow him up just like a ripe apple. And he struck him in the
small of the back with his spear; he would have killed him, but the shaft broke on him. At
once Willame, the worthy count, came to his rescue; he struck him frantically with his
spear, but the shaft broke into three pieces on him: his hide was tough and could never be
damaged. He drew his sword, and Willame his; they rain blows on him, and the pagan
gapes with his mouth. He chews up and eats the steel blades with his great teeth, which
God confound! He thought he would completely undo Willame;

§ 3168 unc ni vit un
§ 3184 sesespee

plus ad dur le quir que healme ne broine.
Ja ne murrad d'arme pur nul home,   3190
si Reneward od le tinel ne l'afronte.
Reneward vint corant parmi une cumbe;
veit le paien, si li est coru sure,
et cil a lui, qui nel meschoisit unques.
Baie la gule, car il le quidad transglutre,   3195
et cil le fiert del tinel enz el sume:
noef colps i feri, et al disme en vait ultre.
Cil huche et brait que quatre liwes lunges
poeit hom oir de celui dunques.
Quant l'unt entendu li paien et li Hungre,   3200
mult lur est laiz, quant Thabur veient confundre.

176

Quant Willame veit chair l'adverser,
ses mains dresce contremunt vers le ciel,
et dist Reneward: "Beneit seit tun chef!
Deus te defende de mort et d'encombrer.   3205
(23a) Ne munte a rien lance ne espé;
mielz valt cest fust que nul arme suz ciel."

177

A icel colp fuissent paiens vencuz,
quant l'amirail de Balan i est venuz.

his hide was tougher than helmet or mail shirt. On account of no man will he die by a weapon unless Reneward brains him with his yoke. Reneward came running up a coomb; he saw the pagan and rushed at him, and the pagan at him, for he did not fail to recognise him. He gaped with his mouth, for he thought to swallow him up, and he struck him with his yoke on the top of his head: he hit him nine times, and on the tenth he passed on. He screams and brays so loud that four long leagues away you could hear him then. When the pagans and Hungarians heard it, they were very upset, when they saw Thabur defeated.

When Willame saw the devil fall, he raised his hands to Heaven, and said to Reneward: "Blessings on your head! May God defend you from death and tribulation. Neither lance nor spear is worth a thing; this beam is better than all the weapons under Heaven."

With that blow the pagans would have been defeated, when the Emir of Balan came up.

Ne porte arme fors un flael de fust;   3210
de quatre quirs de cerf tut envols fu,
caple et caplers dunt le tienent adesus.
Le flael fud d'un grant jarit fenduz;
de noz Franceis fait un caple si durs
plus en oscist que mangonel de fust: 3215
ne set peres* ne oceissent plus.
Quant le veit Huges, unc tant dolent ne fu;
l'auferant broche, qui li curt de vertu,
de sun espé l'ad al piz feru:
en bise roche en peust faire plus!   3220
Cil ad dresçé sun flael cuntre lui,
tut en travers li trenchad sun escu,
sun cheval li ad tué suz lui.
Cil laist l'estur, ne pout mais si s'en fui.
"Allas!" dist il, "le fiz Bertram mar fui,   3225
cosin Willame, le ber, de Munt Loun,
quant un paien m'ad hui el champ vencu."
Franceis escrient: "Finement est venu,
u Antecrist, u Bagot, u Tartarun,
u d'enfern le veillard Belzebun!   3230
Et, Reneward al tinel, u es tu?
Se ore n'i viens, tuz crestiens avum perdu!"
A itant est Reneward avalé d'un piu,

He carried no weapon except a wooden flail; it was bound up in four deer hides held tightly on by hobnails and metal sleeves. The flail was made of a great split holm-oak; it rained so many blows on our Frenchmen that it killed more than a great wooden mangonel: even seven stones* would not have killed more of them. When Huges saw it he was more grief stricken than he had ever been; he clapped spurs to his war horse, which galloped spiritedly for him, and struck him in the chest with his spear: he could have made more impression on grey rock! He raised his flail against him, cut his shield right through and killed his horse under him. He left the battle; he could not help it if he fled. "Alas!" he said, "it's a shame I was Bertram's son, the cousin of Willame, the noble baron from Mount Laon, since a pagan has today conquered me in battle." The French shout out: "The end of the world has come, or Antichrist, or Bagot or Tartarun, or old Beelzebub from Hell! Hey! Reneward with the Yoke, where are you? If you don't come now, we'll lose all the Christian folk!" At that Reneward came down from a hill,

u a dous reis mult forz s'est combatu[§] ,
al rei Mathanar et al rei Feragu,   3235
mais, merci Deu, il les out ben vencu:
sun bon tinel trestut sanglant en fu.
Vit le Willame, unc tant lé ne fu.
"Bel sire, jo vus quidowe aver perdu.
(23b) Veez la bataille, unques tele ne fu.   3240
Un vif diable ad un flael de fust
dunt nus ocist tuz, et defait et destruit.
Dist Reneward: "Baillez mé set escuz."
Et set halbercs ad en sun dos vestuz,
et en sun chef ad mis set healmes aguz;   3245
prent sun tinel, si vait encontre lui.

178

Quant le paien le veit si aproscé,
en sun latin ad raisun comencé:
"Coment, diable, es tu dunc crestien,
qui a tun col portes si fait bastun?   3250
Tels ne portat mais nuls hom desuz ciel!"
Dist Reneward: "Jo sui ben baptizez.
Se Mahomet ne volez reneier
et Appolin et Tervagant le veil,
aincui verrez qui li nostre Deu ert!"   3255

where he had been fighting with two very strong kings, King Mathanar and King Feragu,
but by God's mercy had defeated both of them: his trusty yoke was all bloodstained from
the fight. Willame saw him and had never been so happy in his life. "Dear lord, I thought
we had lost you. Look at the battle, there never was one like it. A living devil has a
wooden flail with which he's killing, defeating and destroying us all. Said Reneward:
"Give me seven shields." And he put seven halberks on his back, and seven pointed
helmets on his head; he picked up his yoke and went out to face him.

When the pagan saw him approaching, he addressed him in his own language: "How, in
the devil's name, do you reckon yourself a Christian carrying a stick like that on your
shoulders? No man under Heaven ever carried the like!" Said Reneward: "I'm baptised
all right. If you won't renounce Mahomet and Appolin and ancient Tervagant you'll see
this very day who our God is!"

[§] 3234 u dous reis mult forz se sunt combatu

Il li curt sure a lei de chevaler,
del bon tinel§ li mist parmi le chef,
enmi le frunt, juste le surciller,
que li brusat ben plus que demi pé.
Mal ait le. . . , que unc nel sent l'adverser§!   3260
Sa grant vertu ne volt afebleier;
sun fer talent unc ne deignad changer,
ainz ad turné sun flael contre lui,
tut en travers li trenchad sis escuz:
des set qu'il porte ne li lait mais un.   3265
Cil salt ariere quinze pez par vertu;
s'il le conseust en char, tut l'eust confundu.

179

Reneward fud mult prouz et sené:
Al tur franceis lores i est turné.
Al haterel detriés li dunad un colp tel   3270
que andous les oilz li fist del chef voler:
mort le trebuche, veant tut le barné.
Este vus poignant un fort rei, Aildré.
(23c) Celui fud uncle Reneward al tinel;
un mail de fer ad en sun col levé.   3275
Quatre cenz Franceis nus ad afronté,

He ran at him like a knight, and brought his trusty yoke down on his head, right in the middle of his forehead, by his eyebrows, giving him a wound a good six inches across. A curse on him... since the devil never felt a thing! His great fighting spirit did not flinch; he did not deign to alter his fierce determination, but turned his flail on him, cutting right through six of his shields: of the seven he was carrying he left him only one intact. He jumped back with a mighty effort, full fifteen feet; had his adversary hit flesh he would have totally defeated him.

Reneward was very worthy and wise: he turned round using the French move. He gave him such a blow on the back of the head that both his eyes flew out of their sockets: He knocked him down dead before the eyes of the assembled warriors. Here comes a powerful king, Aildré, spurring on. He was the uncle of Reneward with the Yoke; he was carrying an iron mace across his shoulders. He had split open the heads of four hundred of our Frenchmen,

---

§ 3257 de bon tinel
§ 3260 mal ait le quant que unc le sent laduerser

avant ses poinz ne puet un eschaper,
si vait querant Willame al curb niés.
Et Reneward s'est a lui acostez.
"Sire," dist il, "a mei vus combatez!"   3280
"Di va, lecchere, car me laissez ester!
A itel glotun n'ai jo soig de parler,
mais mustrez mei Willame al curb niés,
si l'avrai jo od cest mail afrontez."
Dist Reneward: "De folie parlez!   3285
Des hui matin l'unt paiens mort getez.
Veez le la, u il gist en cel pré,
a cel vert healme, a cel escu boclé."
"Fiz a putein, dis me tu dunc verité?
Pur sue amur t'averai mort geté."   3290
Et Reneward est avant passé,
encontremunt en ad levé le tinel;
et l'amurafle en ad le mail levé.
Reneward le fiert sur le chef del tinel;
fort fu le healme u le brun ascer luist cler: 3295
encontremunt s'en surt le tinel.
Dist Reneward: "Ore sui mal vergundé!
Si mielz n'i fert, perdu ai ma bunté."
Dunc se coruce Reneward al tinel;
par grant vertu li fait un colp ferir,   3300
tut le combruse, mort l'ad acraventé,
et le cheval li ad parmi colpé.

none could escape from before his hands, and he was looking for Willame Hooknose. And Reneward accosted him. "My lord," he said, "fight me!" "Get out of my way, you scum! I can't be bothered to talk to a gut bag like you. Just show me Willame Hooknose and I'll brain him with this mace." Said Reneward: "You're talking rubbish! The pagans killed him already this morning. You can see over there: he's lying in the meadow with his green helmet and his buckler." "Are you telling me the truth, you bastard? I'll kill you because of your alliance with him." And Reneward advanced, and raised his yoke on high; and the emir raised his mace. Reneward hit him on the head with his yoke; the helmet gleaming with bright, burnished steel was strong: the yoke bounced back up. Said Reneward: "Now I'm really put to shame! If it doesn't strike better than that my fighting days are over." Then Reneward with the Yoke became angry; he hit him with all his might, smashed him to pulp and knocked him down dead, cutting his horse in two.

Une grant teise en fert le bastun al pré:
en treis meitez est brusé le tinel.
Qui donast a paiens tote crestienté 3305
et paenisme et de long et de lé,
ne fuissent els si joianz, ço poez saver.
(23d) Sure li corent cum chens afamez;
tuz le volent oscire et demenbrer.
Dunc se rebrace Reneward cume ber; 3310
il nen out lance ne espé adubé,
les poinz que ad gros lur prent a presenter.
Quil fiert al dos, sempres li ad esredné,
et qui al piz, le quor li ad crevé,
et qui al chef, les oilz li fait voler. 3315
Dient paiens: "Or i sunt vifs malfez!
Ore est il pire qu'il ne fu al tinel.
A vif diables le puissum comander:
ja n'ert vencu pur nul home qui seit né.
Dunc alasquid le nou de sun baldré, 3320
si ad le punt de l'espee trové,
que li chargeat Guiburc od le vis cler;
traite l'ad de forere, si li vint mult a gré.
Devant lui garde§, si vit le rei Foré;
amunt el healme§ li ad un colp presenté. 3325

The stick sank a good yard and more into the meadow: the yoke split in three. If anyone had given the pagans the whole of Christendom and the whole length and breadth of pagan lands, they would not have been so joyful, I can tell you. They rush at him like famished dogs; they all want to kill him and tear him apart. Then Reneward flexed his arms like a mighty warrior: he was equipped with neither lance nor spear, so he hit out at them with his huge fists. He instantly smashed the kidneys of anyone he hit in the back, and burst open the heart of anyone he hit in the chest, and knocked the eyes out of the sockets of anyone he hit in the head. The pagans say: "Living devils have come among us! Now he's worse than he was with his yoke. Living devils take him: he'll never be defeated on account of any living man. Then he loosened the knot in his baldrick, and found the pommel of the sword that bright faced Guiburc had entrusted to him; he drew it from its scabbard and was pleased with it. He looked around and saw King Foré; he struck him a blow on the top of the helmet.

§ 3324 dedeuant lui garde
§ 3325 Amunt el le healme

Tut le purfent jusqu'al nou del baldré,
et le cheval li ad parmi colpé;
desi qu'al helt fiert le brant enz al pré.
Dist Reneward: "Merveilles vei, par Deu,
de si petit arme que si trenche suef!   3330
Beneit seit l'alme qui le me ceinst al lé.
Chascun franc home deveit quatre porter:
si l'une freinst, qu'il puisse recovrer."

180

Dient paien: "Mult fames grant folie,
ke cest diable nus laissum ci oscire.   3335
Fuium nus ent, en mer en cel abisme,
la u noz barges sunt rengees et mises."
Mais Reneward les ad si departies,
n'i ad une sule entere, sis ad malmises.
Fuient paiens; Reneward ne fine de oscire.   3340
Ainz qu'il s'en turnent, lur ad mort dous mile.
(24a) Cil s'enfuient si que un sul ne remeint mie.

181

Ore unt Franceis l'estur esviguré,
k'il ne trovent Sarazin ne Escler
....*   (3344a)
Grant est l'eschec qu'il unt conquesté: 3345
n'erent mes povres en trestut lur eé.

He split him down to the knot in his baldrick, and cut his horse in two; the blade sank into the meadow up to its hilt. Said Reneward: "I'm witness to a miracle, by God, since such a little weapon cuts so smoothly! Blessed be the soul who strapped it to my side. Every free man should carry four: if one broke, he'd have a spare."

The pagans say: "We're mad if we let this devil kill us here. Let us flee into the abyss of the sea, where our barges and ships are drawn up in rows." But Reneward had smashed them to pieces: there is not one whole; he has destroyed them all. The pagans flee; there is no end to Reneward's killing. Before they left the field he had killed two thousand of them. They all flee and not one remained behind.

Now the French return to the fray with such a will, that they find no Saracen or Slav ... * Great is the booty that they won: they shall never be poor again as long as they live.

Sonent lur greilles, si s'en sunt tresturné
dreit a Orenge, le mirable cité.
Escrient l'eve, asseent al digner;
as esquiers funt la preie garder. 3350
Pur folie i fud Reneward oblié:
a quel que seit, l'estoverad comparer.
Si cum il durent la preie returner,
si se clamad chaitif maleuré:
"Allas, dolent! Cum mar fui unques nee! 3355
Cum mar fu fiz al fort rei Deramé,
et Oriabel, ma mere de ultre la mer!
Jo ne fu unques baptizé ne levé,
n'en muster n'entrai pur preer Dé.
Jo ai vencu la fort estur champel; 3360
li quons Willame me tient en tiel vilté
que a sun manger ne me volt apeler.
Ore m'en irrai en Espaigne le regné,
si irrai Mahomet servir et aorer.
Si jol voil faire, rei serrai coroné: 3365
meie ert la terre tresqu'en Durester,
de Babiloine desqu'a Duraz sur mer.
En sum mun col avrai un grant tinel
(ne pris altre arme un dener moneé)
al pais vendrai devant ceste cité, 3370
si ferai dunc de crestiens altretel
cum ore ai fait de paiens de ultre mer.

They sound their trumpets, and returned directly to Orange, the wonderful citadel. They call for water and sit down to dinner; they have the booty guarded by squires. Reneward was foolishly forgotten: whoever was responsible will have to pay for it. Just as they were about to sort the booty he called himself a miserable wretch: "Alas, miserable man! What a pity I was ever born! What a pity I was son to the powerful King Deramé, and Oriabel, my mother from beyond the sea! I was never baptised nor raised up from the font, nor did I ever enter a church to pray to God. I won the fierce pitched battle; Count Willame holds me so cheap that he refuses to invite me to eat with him. Now I shall go into the kingdom of Spain, and go to serve and worship Mahomet. If I want to, I shall be a crowned king: the land all the way to Durester shall be mine, from Babiloine to Duraz by the sea. I'll have a great yoke on my shoulders (I don't give tuppence for any other weapon) and I'll come into this land, before this citadel, and I'll do to Christians exactly what I've just done to the pagans from beyond the sea.

182

"Seignurs," fait il, "esquiers et bachelers,
a Dampnedeu vus puisse jo comander.
Jo m'en irrai en estrange regné,   3375
(24b) et vus irrez a la bone cité.
Defiez mei Willame al curb niés;
pur Deu vus pri, Guibur me saluez:
suz ciel n'ad rien que jo dei tant amer."
Et cil li responent: "Si cum vus comandez."   3380
Les esquiers sunt a Orenge alez:
"Sire Willame, le marchiz al curb nés,
le fort s'en vait qui ferit del tinel."
"A!" dist Willame, "leccheres, vus me gabez."
"Nu faimes, sire, ainz§ vus dium veritez.   3385
Tresqu'en Espaigne: n'ert mais returnez.
Il ne fud unques baptizez ne levez,
n'en muster n'entrat pur orer Deus.
S'il le volt faire, rei serrad coronez;
sue ert la terre tresqu'en Durester,   3390
de Babiloine tresqu'a Duraz sur mer.
Puis revendrad devant ceste cité
a cent mil homes, sis volt assembler,
et sur sun col avrad un grant tinel,
si ferad de crestiens tut altretel   3395

"My lords," he said, "squires and young knights, I commend you to the Lord. I shall go into a strange kingdom, and you shall go to the good citadel. Defy Willame Hooknose in my name; in God's name I beg you, greet Guiburc for me: there is no creature under Heaven I should love so much." And they reply: "As you command." The squires went to Orange: "Lord Willame, the hook nosed marquis, the big lad who struck out with the yoke is going away." "Hah!" said Willame, "you buggers, you're pulling my leg." "No we're not, my lord, we're telling you the truth. He's off to Spain: he'll never be turned back. He was never baptised nor raised from the font, and he never went into a church to pray to God. If he wants, he'll be a crowned king; all the land as far as Durester will be his, from Babiloine to Duraz by the sea. Then he'll come back before this citadel with a hundred thousand men, if he wants to assemble them, and he'll have a great yoke on his shoulders, and he'll do to Christians exactly

§ 3385 ainz ainz

cum ad fait de paiens de ultre mer."
Ço dist Willame: "Ço fait mult a doter!
Qui le me irreit hucher et apeler,
jo li durreie grantment de mun aver.
Et qui ça le freit a mei returner,   3400
grant partie li durrie de tute me herité.
Seignurs, frans baruns, car i alez!"
"Volenters, sire, quant vus le comandez."
Quatre mile se corent adober
de halbercs et de healmes, et es destrers sunt muntez,   3405
mais Reneward aconsiverent en un pré,
cum il deveit en une vile entrer.
Quant il les veit si faitement errer,
ne solt que faire, ne ne solt que penser.
(24c) Devant li garde, vit un bordel ester;   3410
passad avant, si enraçad les pels,
et totes les furches en ad acraventés.
En sun col en ad le fest levé,
cuntre Franceis est el champ turné.
"Seignurs," dist il, "u devez vus aler?"   3415
"Willame vus mande que vus vus en venez.
De sun tortfait vus ert gage donez,
et del manger dunt vus fuistes obliez."
Dist Reneward: "Unc mais n'oi tel!
Qui en prendrat gage, el col ait il le mal dehé   3420
tresqu'en verrai morir des suens et pasmer."

what he has just done to the pagans from beyond the sea." Said Willame: "That's much
to be feared! If anyone would go and call after him, I'd give him a lot of my wealth. And
if anyone brought him back to me, I'd give him a large share of my inheritance. My
lords, noble barons, please go for him!" "Willingly, my lord, since you command it."
Four thousand ran to put on their halberks and helmets, and to mount their chargers, but
they caught up with Reneward in a meadow, as he was about to enter a town. When he
saw them coming like that, he did not know what to do or think. He looked around and
saw a hut; he stepped forward and pulled up the stakes, and pulled down all the crucks.
He put the ridge pole across his shoulders, and turned to face the French in the field. "My
lords," he said, "where are you supposed to be going?" "Willame sends to tell you to
come back. He will give sureties for the wrong he has done you, and for the meal at
which you were forgotten." Said Reneward: "I never heard the like! God's curse on the
neck of anyone who'd take his pledge until I've seen his men die and swoon for it."

183

Iloec aveit un chevaler felun,
nun out Guinebald, frere Alealme de Clermunt.
A lei de fol començad sa raisun:
"A! Deu, lecchere, nus vus en remerrum   3425
al quons Willame; en la tur vus rendrum.
Vus me oscistes Winebold, mun nevou.
A la cusine vus ullad l'altre jur,
mais, par la fei que dei saint Simeon,
si nen esteit pur ma dame Guiburc§,   3430
jo vus ferreie de ma lance al polmun."
Dist Reneward: "Ore oi parler bricun!
Mar le parlastes, si Deu joie me doinst."
Halce le fust, sure li est coru,
sil fert el chef: altresi brait cume lou.   3435
Les oilz li volent; la cervele li est espandu.

184

Lunsdi al vespre:
dist Reneward: "Receu avez pusteles!
Ne sai des altres, mais vus morst la feste!"
Franceis s'en turnent le pendant d'un tertre;   3440
moerent chevals et lur lances i perdent.

There was an evil knight there, called Guinebald, the brother of Alealme of Clermunt. He spoke to him like a fool: "Oh, God! you scum, we'll take you back to Count Willame; we'll shut you up in his tower. You killed my nephew, Winebold. He burned you in the kitchen the other day, but, by the faith I owe Saint Simeon, if it wasn't for my lady Guiburc, I'd stick my lance through your lungs." Said Reneward: "Now I hear a fool talking! You'll regret saying that, if God gives me joy." He raised his beam, charged at him, and hit him on the head. That man howled like a wolf; his eyes flew from their sockets; his brains spread around.

Monday at vespertide: said Reneward: "You've really had a hammering! I don't know about the others, but my ridge pole has bitten into you!" The French ran away down a hill; their horses died and they lost their lances.

---

§ 3430 si me nesteit pur ma dame dame Guiburc

185

Reneward tent le grant fest de cele bordel.
En halt le porte et en bas le fait avaler:
(24d) Quil consiut en sum, le chef li crote.
Li quons Willame esteit lez une porte,   3445
lui et Guiburc, si se beisent et acolent.
Ço dist Willame: "Jo vei venir li nostre;
men escientre, Reneward les afole."

186

Lunsdi al vespre:
dient Franceis: "Mar i alames, certes,   3450
a vif diable qui porte une feste!
Cent en ad mort sanz confession de prestre."
"Ore i irrai jo," ço dist li quons Willame.
Oveke lui ameine la raine converte
et Guielin et dan Walter de Termes   3455
et Guischard et Girard fiz cadele
et treis cenz Frans, sanz halbercs et sanz healmes;
mais Reneward trovent sur un tertre.
Dame Guiburc premer l'en apele:
"Sire Reneward, pur les oilz de ta teste,   3460
car pren dreit de mun seignur Willame."
"Volenters, dame, par ceste meie destre.

Reneward was holding the great ridge pole from the hut. He raised it high and brought it swinging down: Whoever he catches on the top-knot has his head caved in. Count Willame was standing by a gate with Guiburc, and they were kissing and cuddling. Said Willame: "I can see our men coming; I reckon Reneward is giving them a hard time."

Monday at vespertide: the French said: "It's certainly a pity we went after a living devil carrying a ridge pole! He's killed a hundred men who could not confess to priests." "I'll go then," said Count Willame. He took the royal convert with him and Guielin and Lord Walter of Termes and Guischard and Girard Fitz Captain and three hundred Franks without halberks or helmets; but they found Reneward on a hill. Lady Guiburc addressed him first: "Lord Reneward, by the eyes in your head, do accept justice from my lord Willame." "Willingly, my lady, by my own right hand.

Si nen esteit[§] pur Guiburc la bele,
jol ferreie al chef de ceste feste:
d'anduis parz en charreit la cervele.   3465
Ore vus pardoins la felonie pesme
del manger, dunt vus me obliastes."
Dient Franceis: "Metez dunc jus cele feste."
Et dist Reneward: "Volenters, par ma teste."
Dunc la ruad quatoze arpenz de terre,   3470
a treis cent Franceis par desure lur testes.
Mult sunt joius quant il guerpi la feste:
tels cent en i out, qui la fevre en porterent!

187

Ore sunt Willame et Reneward asemblez,
par grant amur se sunt entre acordez.   3475
Il en alerent a la cité de Orenge.
Poez saver que a manger eurent sempres.
(25a) Et l'ewe li tint le paleim Bertram;
Guiburc li aportad la tualie devant;
Galter de Termes le sert a sun talant.   3480

188

Quant Reneward ad mangé a plenté,
dame Guiburc le prent a parler:

If it were not for the beautiful Guiburc, I'd strike him on the head with this ridge pole: his brains would tumble down both sides. Now I pardon you the foul crime of forgetting to invite me to the meal." The French say: "Put down that ridge pole then." And Reneward said: "Willingly, by my head." Then he threw it fourteen measured rods, over the heads of three hundred Frenchmen. They were overjoyed when he abandoned his ridge pole: a good hundred got the shakes from it!

Now Willame and Reneward have been got together, and have been reconciled in great affection for each other. They went off to the citadel of Orange. I can tell you they sat down to eat at once. Bertram, count of the palace, held the water for them; Guiburc brought the towel; Galter of Termes happily served them.

When Reneward had eaten his fill, lady Guiburc spoke to him:

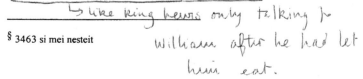

→ like king heros only talking to William after he had let him eat.

[§] 3463 si mei nesteit

"Reneward sire, par sainte charité,
fustes vus unques baptizé ne levé?"
"Nai jo," fait il, "par la fei que dei Dé;   3485
unc en muster n'entrai pur preer Dé."
Ço dist Willame: "Jo te ferai lever,
si te durrai sainte crestienté."
Dist Reneward: "Multes merciz de Dé."
Il le menerent al muster saint Omer;   3490
une grant cuve i unt fait aporter:
ben i puissent quatre vileins baigner.
Willame le tint et Guiburc, sa moiller;
li quons Bertram le tint mult volenters,
de dulce France la flur et le miez.   3495
Poez saveir les duns furent mult chers:
la li donerent mil livres de deners§ ,
et od les mil livres cent muls et cent destrers.
Willame li donad set chastels en fez,
et Ermentrud li dunent a moiller,   3500
et tote la tere Vivien le ber.
Dame Guiburc l'en apelad premer.

189

Dame Guiburc l'en ad primes apelé:
"Reneward sire, pur sainte charité,

"Lord Reneward, by holy charity, were you ever baptised or raised from the font?" "No I wasn't," he said, "by the faith I owe God; I never entered a church to pray to God." Said Willame: "I'll have you baptised, and made a Christian." Said Reneward: "Many thanks, in the name of God." They took him to the church of Saint Omer; they had a great tub brought in: four peasants could easily have bathed in it. Willame supported him, as did Guiburc, his wife; Count Bertram willingly supported him: his sponsors were the flower of France. You can be sure the baptismal gifts were very costly: they gave a thousand pounds in minted coin and with the thousand pounds a hundred mules and war horses. Willame gave him seven castles as fiefs, and he gave him Ermentrud to be his wife, and all the lands of the brave warrior Vivien. Lady Guiburc spoke to him first.

Lady Guiburc was first to speak to him: "Lord Reneward, for holy charity,

---

§ 3497 de de deners

cumfaitement issis de tun regné?"   3505
"Dame," dist il, "or en orrez verité.
Dame," dist il, "jo vus dirrai lealment.
Mun pere ert alé a Meliant,
ensemble od lui l'almaçur de Durant,
si me comandat a mun meistre, Apolicant.   3510
Cil s'en alad parsum l'albe apparisant,
(25b) si me vead que ne meusse niant,
tresque il vendreit de aurer Tervagant.
Jo ne voleie faire pur lui tant ne quant,
ainz m'en turnai tost et ignelemant   3515
solunc la rive ma pelotte culant.
Iloec trovai et nefs et chalant;
en un esnecke entrai par mun boban.
Dunc vint un vent merveillus et bruant,
parmi la mer me menad ignelmant.   3520
Iloec trovai une fule de marchanz,
si hurta ma esnecke a lur chalanz,
si depeçat en peces plus de cenz.
Sempres i neiasse, si ne me fuissent aidanz.
En une barge me traistrent quatre par les mains,   3525
si me menerent en une terre grant,
si me mistrent sur mun chef un raim estant,
si me clamerent chaitif, venal enfant.
Unques n'i out ne Tieis ne Romant,*
Ne Aleman ne Bretun ne Normant,   3530
qui me peust achater a lur talant,

how did you come to leave your kingdom?" "My lady," he said, "now you will hear the truth of it. My father had gone to Meliant, accompanied by the Emir of Durant, and I was put in the care of my tutor, Apolicant. He went off at the crack of dawn, and forbade me to move a muscle until he came back from praying to Tervagant. I didn't want to do anything he told me, but went off as fast as I could rolling my ball along the shore. There I found ships and merchantmen; out of cheek I got into a longship. Then a mighty rushing wind arose, taking me quickly out to sea. There I found a crowd of merchants, and my longship rammed against their vessel, and it broke into more than a hundred pieces. I would have drowned on the spot if they hadn't helped me. Four of them pulled me into a barge by the hands, and they took me to a great land, and put a standing branch on my head, and called me a captive child for sale. There was never a German or Roman,* Swiss or Breton or Norman who could meet their price for me,

quant par la feire vint li reis chevalchant.
Il me esgardeit, si me vit bel enfant,
si me achatad mil livres de besanz;
fist me lever sur un mul amblant, 3535
puis me menad a Paris lealment.
Demandat mei si ere de halte gent,
et jo li dis, ne li celai nient,
que ere fiz Deramé, et ma mere Oriabel.
Quant il oi que jo ere de halte gent, 3540
si suzcrienst mun pere et mes parenz,
si me comandat a sun cu, Jaceram,
et jurad Deu, pere omnipotent,
mieldre mester n'avereie a mun vivant.
En la quisine ai jo esté set anz: 3545
(25c) freit i oi jo, mais unques n'i oi faim,
tant que Willame me menad en l'Archamp.
La li ai mort trente de mes parenz."
Guiburc l'oi, si passad avant.
"Baisez mei, frere: ta soror sui naissant." 3550
Lunsdi al vespre:
"Estes vus dunc mun soruge, Willame?
Se jol seusse en l'Archamp,
bien vus valui, mais plus vus eusse esté aidant!"

when the king came riding through the fair. He looked at me and saw I was a handsome child, and bought me for a thousand pounds in besants; he put me on an easy-riding mule, and took me faithfully to Paris. He asked me if I came from a noble family, and I told him, and hid nothing from him, that I was the son of Deramé, and my mother was Oriabel. When he heard that I was of a noble family, he was much afraid of my father and kinfolk, and handed me over to his cook, Jaceram, and swore to God, the omnipotent Father, that I would have no better trade all my life. I have been seven years in the kitchen: I was cold there, but never hungry until Willame took me to l'Archamp. There I killed thirty of my relatives for him." Guiburc heard him, and stepped forward. "Kiss me, my brother: I am your true born sister." Monday at vespertide: "Are you then my brother-in-law, Willame? If I had known that at l'Archamp, much use as I was to you, I would have helped you all the more!"

Notes

1 The MS gives lines 1 and 1a continuously. By comparison with other epics we would expect the first line to be completed either by an invocation of divine blessing (e.g. 'que Deus vus salt, seignur') or a statement of the worth of the song (e.g. 'chançun de grant valur'), or of its power to uplift the audience (e.g. 'chançun de grant baldur').

14 Much ink has been spilled over the site of Deramed's invasion, since it is related to the identification of the battle site of l'Archamp. The MS reads 'amund girunde' at l.14 and 'a munt girunde' at l.40. Wathelet-Willem (1975, pp.731, 735) transcribes as I do, suggesting an identification with Gerona, although she translates using the name of the French river Gironde. She explains (p.610) that the preserved reference, which she takes to be to the river, disguises an original reference to Gerona. In this judgement she concurs with Frappier (1955, pp.168–71). Although 'Munt Girunde' is otherwise unknown as a toponym in the *chansons de geste*, 'Gironde' meaning Gerona is common, and I incline to that identification here for two reasons: firstly, as Wathelet-Willem points out, 'amunt' is predominantly an adverb in the twelfth century, not a preposition, favouring an analysis of the verb phrase in l. 14 as 'en venir a' which implies arrival at a location (Godefroy, 1937–38, VIII, 172c — examples from *Roland*; X, 840b — example from Le Ménestrel de Reims) and unlikely to refer to passage up a waterway; secondly, when Girard relays his message to Willame (*laisse* 77) the reference to 'Girunde' is missing from what is otherwise a textual reprise of the message taken to Tedbald in Bourges. Significantly the poet has just told us of Willame's return from a battle 'a Burdele sur Girunde' (l. 935) and it is not improbable that a copyist or revisor, failing to realise that the two Girundes were different places, excised the reference to the location of Vivien's battle because of the improbability it appeared to introduce of sending Willame back whence he had just come. Although the geography of the poem, which places Bourges, Orange and Barcelona within easy reach of each other, has more poetic than logical appeal, it is appropriate to interpret our MS reading as referring to a battle site in Catalonia, since, as Frappier points out 'Cette tradition est bien la plus

ancienne; si elle est effacée dans le poème d'*Aliscans*, ses traces subsistent encore dans la *Chevalerie Vivien*, dans les *Enfances Vivien* et dans *Foucon de Candie*' (1955, p.171).

60a   This line appears as a continuation of l. 60 in the MS with a point separating the two 'halves' of the line, indicating that the scribe realised that he had copied the second line in the wrong place. The formula 'al regne' ending the scribe's l. 60 seems to require a genetive or adjective to complete it. Like Wathelet-Willem I have chosen to add the name of the emperor.

85   For the only time in the poem Willame is referred to by the epithet 'al curt niés' ('with the short nose'), although at l. 55 the form 'cur niés' could hide a lost 't' from 'curt' as well as a lost 'b' from 'curb'. The use of the adjective 'curt', probably used inadvertantly by the thirteenth-century scribe, refers to the tradition established from *Le Couronnement de Louis* onwards, in which the hero's nose was truncated by a sword blow from the giant Saracen Corsolt (Lepage, 1978, *Rédaction AB*, l. 1041). That this tradition was also known to the poet of *G2* is clear from ll. 2310–12 where Guiburc asks Willame to show her the *bump* on the nose acquired in battle against Tedbald l'Escler. This allusion seems to derive from *Le Charroi de Nîmes* (McMillan, 1978, ll. 142–47) which unifies the 'Hooknose' and 'Shortnose' traditions by explaining that the *bump* (forming the hook) was the result of the incompetence of the surgeon who sewed back the *sliced off end* of the nose after the battle with Corsolt. Since the reading 'al curt niés' is isolated in the *Willame* I have translated it 'Hooknose' in keeping with the otherwise unanimous usage of the poem, in both *G1* and *G2*.

103   The reference to the presence of Saracens makes no sense in the context of this *laisse*. It appears to be an inadvertent intrusion produced by a scribe aware of developments in *laisse* 14, where Tedbalt spies the Saracen fleet. Suchier (1911) inserted a line of his own invention before this one ('De la poür quidat que ço fust presse' [104a]) to justify the line in the manuscript. McMillan (1949–50) printed the line without comment. Wathelet-Willem (1975) and Suard (1991) both reject the line while maintaining the line-numbering established by McMillan. I have followed this practice, since so much published research refers to lines of the text by these numbers, while being convinced that there is no text to fill the gap between lines 102 and 104 of the poem.

154 Most editors correct the MS's *navries* to *naviries*; however it seems that the scribe has produced his form by conflating the Continental form with the Anglo-Norman *navie*. Since this form produces acceptable sense and metre I have preserved it in this edition.

164 Wathelet-Willem prints 'En cuntreval' and McMillan 'Encuntre val' at this point. Word division in the MS is not clear, but the regularity of spacing suggests one word as I have printed. Whatever the word division it seems plain that Willame's advice to Vivien has been of a military and tactical nature: to keep himself and his troops hidden from the enemy until the moment of the charge, and not to expose his position by riding on to high ground unnecessarily (cf. Tedbald's order to Vivien, ll. 196–99). This is also Wathelet-Willem's interpretation. The implications of humility to be drawn from riding with head bowed, found in Suard's and Fassò's translations, seem totally out of place in this context.

280 Although it is possible to interpret the line as 'our standards have fallen', it seems preferable to maintain strict parallelism with l. 278 and interpret *gunfanun* as *standard-bearers* (a double metonymy, since the banners stand for those who carry them, who in turn stand for the commanders of the army).

297 The nickname 'Cornebut' which I have translated as 'Hornchest' (suggesting that he wore body armour of horn?) is attached to a character found only in this poem and named only here and at l. 1437 in a parallel passage. It is likely that it was included by the person to whom we owe the Gui episode to tie his revision in with earlier material.

404 Wathelet-Willem (1975, p.771) and Fassò (1995, p.121) both arbitrarily change the construction of this line in their translations, firstly by replacing the definite article with the indefinite, then by changing the infinitive construction to provide a verb in the pluperfect subjunctive. I prefer to follow Suard's interpretation (1991, p.29), which respects the reading of the MS. The line could have two meanings, which have possibly become conflated: the poor man (the shepherd) could not afford to lose his sheep, or as an aphorism, the poor man (who lost the material possession of the sheep) would not have had to lose what Tedbald lost — his reputation.

521a Although a lacuna of only one line is signalled here, at least two lines must be missing: the first completes the construction 'Qui dunc veist...' probably with an expression of the type 'dunc peust de vasselage penser';

the second, less easily guessable, probably referred to binding other serious wounds, in the head or bowels.

548   The exclamation 'ei, ore' has a distinctly colloquial tinge. I have chosen to render it by the second part of the Duke of Wellington's famous (but probably apocryphal) command at Waterloo: 'Up, Guards, and at 'em!'

674   'Deus aïe!' was in fact the Norman warcry: *et* is probably an error for *ço est*, read as one syllable.

677   Wathelet-Willem and Suard correct arbitrarily to 'alues'/'alués'; Fassò translates 'saluz' to imply that Vivien is calling on his uncle to save or rescue him, which greatly diminishes the hero. I take the word 'saluz' to mean 'the place where we find salvation', since death in battle against the Infidel was equated with martyrdom in the ideology of the crusade.

717   (also 721, 724, 728) The MS presents third-person verbs in ll. 717 and 721 and a first person in ll. 724 and 728. Wathelet-Willem corrects the first two to agree with the last two and reads the emphatic negative 'nen' as 'n'en' (including the third-person agent pronoun). Suard and Fassò both print the original verb forms, but translate them all as first persons. They also use the second person ('avec toi' — Suard, 'Con te' — Fassò) to render 'en' and 'nen' respectively. It seems to me that the poem offers a consistent set of apostrophes to the various arms, and that all these verbs are really second persons, and that in the apostrophe 'nen' really is an emphatic negative.

890   All recent editors, including McMillan, read *plein e* (dividing the last letter of what is clearly one word in the manuscript from the rest of the word). This maintains the 'correct' gender for *escalberc*, although there are many other examples of shifts of gender in this Anglo-Norman text, but it also introduces a unique example of the co-ordinating conjunction written out in full in the body of a line, rather than being represented by the conventional sign of a 'barred seven'. I have therefore decided to adhere strictly to the manuscript reading, including the word division.

939   In a medieval castle the *soler* was an upper chamber with large windows and possibly a balcony open to the sun, similar in purpose to the Renaissance Italian *loggia*, which is used to render the term here. The *estre* of a building is usually an outer area (from Latin *extera*), but the word is also used of an upper appartment, so that the whole line may be pleonastic.

1021 This line does not appear to make sense as it stands. Wathelet-Willem corrects 'fort' to 'fors' understood as a synonym of 'loinz', a solution adopted by Fassò. Suard understands 'fort' as 'rebelle' ('unwilling to serve'). The two lines 1020-21 seem to be a parenthesis between the two parts of Willame's admission of his recent failure and consequent depression ('I have lost my war band and cannot face another battle') in which he momentarily reasserts his own status as commander of broad territories and powerful warriors.

1074 This statement seems odd since Girard has already appeared in the poem equipped as a knight. However, Vivien remarked on this 'self-knighting' (l. 459) and symbolically all the signs of that first elevation have been abandoned during his walk to Barcelona. Now he is formally equipped and made a knight for the first time by his overlord and/or head of clan, Willame. There was no knighting ceremony in the twelfth century as it came to be understood later, but it was already accepted that to be a knight one had to receive at least one's sword from an overlord.

1182 The construction *le aie de prodom* is difficult, both because it uses a wrong case at the rhyme (subject for oblique) and because it suggests that the call for help comes from a man of valour. This could only be understood ironically in Guischard's case (and may indeed be an ironical allusion to the Normans' warcry used by the French elsewhere in this poem). It is probably better to interpret the line, as do both Suard (1991) and Fassò (1995), as a call for help addressed to a brave warrior.

1188 The correction of 'entreis' to 'entereies' also adopted by Suard (1991, pp.80 and 237) appears to restore a correct conditional form, although it replaces a hypometric line by a hypermetric one (eleven syllables instead of nine). The line could be construed as an Anglo-Norman alexandrine with a lyric caesura dividing 5+7 (Bennett, 1987). A further complication is the possibility voiced by Jacques Roubaud during discussion at the Saintsbury Colloquium 'Poetry, Culture and Translation' (Edinburgh, 1995) that unstressed 'e' has been highly unstable in the realisation of French poetry from very early times, so that the form 'entreis' may represent a phonetic realisation of the conditional.

1206ff. For the rare use of *lasseté* to mean 'cowardice' see Godefroy, 1937-38, IV, 734b. Previous translators choose to ignore the negative 'ja...ne' in l. 1207, and make Willame say that Guischard is too weak to prevent the hero from carrying him home as promised to Guiburc. The following lines make clear, however, that Willame's first intention is to force Guischard to ride home in a position of disgrace (on the crupper of the horse), wounded as he is. This ploy is frustrated by the Barbarin who kills Guischard, thus obliging Willame to carry the corpse before him and so keep his word to his wife.

1387 Suard and Fassò accept the apparently personal reference of the MS and translate by expressions equivalent to 'capture those men'. However, since in the rest of the poem killing rather than capturing pagans is the goal of the French, I prefer to follow Wathelet-Willem and interpret *icés* as 'those things' (i.e. the gold and silver currently in the hands of the pagans).

1387a There is a lacuna of indeterminate length here completing the conditional probably by indicating the wealth accruing to those going, and stressing Willame's gratitude.

1406 This line has caused translators many problems. The pronoun in the first hemistich should be *le* referring to the verb 'mangat'; the final word may be 'a[a]te ('rapid', 'lively') or 'ate' ('suitable'). Wathelet-Willem, Fassò and Suard all seem to take the meaning from the last form ('tendre', 'ben cotta', 'à point') even though Wathelet-Willem corrects to *aate*. They are also unanimous in taking 'tant cum' to mean 'as if' instead of 'while'. I take 'ate' to be the Anglo-Norman form of *aate* in a metaphoric sense of 'hot'. In an age where eating with the fingers normally meant that food was allowed to cool, the double indication that Willame ate hot food straight from the spit is a sign of his voraciously impatient appetite.

1421 Although it is not absolutely clear, it is probable that the possessive *sun* refers to the subject rather than to the object of the clause; *romanz* refers as usual to a vernacular language. Lynette Muir's translation (Price, 1975, p.159) 'the French language' is unwarranted. It is more likely that the poet intended to imply that he was transcribing in French a conversation held in Occitan, if, indeed, we are not faced with a conversation held in Guibourc's native 'sarazineis'. Compare l. 1331 where, conversely, Willame is described as addressing Guibourc 'en sun romanz'.

1438 The MS has 'aemeris' all in small letters, and most editors choose to print 'Aemeris' with one capital and one small letter. However, since the digraph 'ae' is clearly meant to represent [ɛ] as normal in Anglo-Norman orthography under the influence of Latin usage (Pope, 1934, § 1219), I have printed the name with a capitalised diphthong.

1502   This line provides one of the many instances in the text of the total confusion between the spear or lance (*espié*, masc.) and the sword (*espee*, fem.) respectively in Continental Old French. The translation here as elswhere follows the logic of the narrative in deciding which is meant.

1502a   A lacuna of at least one line describing Willame's mounting his horse with Guiburc holding his stirrup is probable.

1705ff.   (*laisse* 115)   This *laisse*, which brings the pagan commander Deramé 'onstage' for the first time in the song, is probably an interpolation by the redactor to whom we owe the addition of *G2* to the poem. One of its purposes seems to be to insert the scene in which a number of French heroes are captured by the Saracens. This scene belongs to *Aliscans* (Régnier, 1990, ll. 318–22). Although the list of those captured differs slightly in the two poems (Bertram, Guielin, Guischard, Galter, Reiner in *G1*; Bertran, Guichart, Girart, Guielin, Huon, Gaudin, Gautier in *Aliscans*), the two lists have enough in common for us to be sure of the borrowing. Later references to these prisoners in the *Willame* reveal just how much difficulty redactors had with the borrowed episode, especially since some characters also had their stories, and personalities, revised during the evolution of *G1*. While in *Aliscans* (Régnier, 1990, ll. 5582–85) the list of those released is identical with that of the captured (except that 'Huon' has by metathesis become 'Hunaut'), we have two versions of the names of those released in *G2*: Bertram, Walter, Reiner, Guielin, Guischard (ll. 3034; 3055–56); Bertram, Walter, Guielin, Guischard, Girard (ll. 3153–55). It is notable that 'Reiner' never appears in the poem again, and seems to have been substituted for 'Girard' in the earlier lists by someone aware that Girard was supposed to be dead. A similar embarrassment is shown by another copyist-redactor, however, who changes the descriptor 'quis cadele' ('who leads them' — i.e. 'the captain') given to Girard by Alderufe in his list of Narbonnais heroes (l. 2100) to 'fiz cadele' ('son of the captain'): the substitution of an identically named son for a supposedly dead father, when that father died as a young, unmarried knight first seen in the poem as a squire, reveals that we are in fact dealing with one character, that scribe-redactors were also aware of that fact and that they tried to reduce to logical order a story becoming increasingly incoherent as a result of successive revisions. Similar lessons can be drawn from the fates of Guischard and Gui. Guischard is referred to as a member of the 'fere geste' (ll. 2100–01) and constantly named as a pair with Girard, as if his natural companion. He is called 'l'enfant' in *Aliscans* (l. 320), which fits with the reference to his recent knighting in *Willame* (l. 1035). The *G2* redactor seems not to care about this character's temporary shift from Willame's to Guiburc's family and ignores his unwilling death as a double apostate, parodying the deaths of both Vivien and Girard, but also acting as a foil to the noble Saracen converts (Guiburc and Reneward). Gui (captured as 'Guielin' at l. 1722) is captured a second time as 'Guiot' in a scene virtually identical to *laisse* 115 in which fifteen new pagan kings attack Willame immediately after he has administered the last rites to Vivien (ll. 2056-90). It is likely that these lines (which, of course, have no equivalent in *Aliscans*) were also added by the revisor linking *G2* to *G1*. That he had to do his work twice shows both his care to tie up as many loose ends as he could, and that he could not ignore the role given to Gui in the revised ending of *G1*. The fact that, unlike 'Guielin', 'Guiot' is never released nor heard of again in the poem indicates that the *G2* redactor did not regard these 'two' characters as really distinct, and was satisfied by having a 'Gui' restored to his rightful place at his uncle's side at the end of the poem.

1762-63 (*Laisse* 117a) I have habitually maintained the *laisse*-divisions indicated in the manuscript by capital letters. However, since lines 1763-79 follow immediately a refrain plus its associated line assonating in *è....e* (which is also the standard assonance of *laisses* beginning with the refrain), but assonate in *-ir*, it seems most probable that the scribe has on this occasion failed to observe a new *laisse* in his model.

1782ff   The repetition of 'terre' in ll. 1782, 1783, 1784 suggests a corruption in the MS. Suard corrects to 'tertre' ('hill') in his revised 1781 and 1784 (where Wathelet-Willem — followed by Fassò — keeps 'terre') but translates Suchier's hypothetical correction 'presse' ('battle[field]'). Wathelet-Willem and Suard correct to 'Chastele' ('Castile') in 1783. I have followed the MS literally, as any correction is subjective.

1879   This line is a model of the confusion referred to in the note to l. 1502. Although the manuscript naturally has no accent on the last syllable of *mustre* it is impossible given the assonance of the *laisse* not to read the word as a past participle, requiring the addition to the line of the auxiliary. All editors agree on this, although not on where to insert the missing verb. In order to restore the proper ten syllables of a continental text to the line Wathelet-Willem (1975, p.917) prints 'Sa bone espée ad a cel colp mustré'. This procedure is unnecessary, as the Anglo-Norman writer undoubtedly expected *espee* to be read in two syllables, with the final *-ee* representing (as normal for him) a stressed [e].

1884 *entre le punz et le brant* is a very odd circumlocution for 'hilt', and as such may be intended to be comic. However, it may be meant to indicate that Willame is holding his sword point-forward (like a lance), bracing it by gripping the hand-guard.

1919a This line is written as a continuation of the previous one in the manuscript. However the scribe has inserted a point after *mecresdi* (l. 1919) indicating a missed line break. Suard (1991) prints the line as in the manuscript, while indicating that Suchier (1911) and Wathelet-Willem (1975) both complete the line with different readings. Fassò (1995), printing McMillan's text, replaces the full stop in the middle of the line by a comma. Suard follows Wathelet-Willem in starting a new *laisse* immediately after this line, in keeping with the habits of the Vivien-poet who allows only one feminine line after the refrain line when the refrain comes at the end of a laisse, and ignoring the fact that the Gui-revisor like the Reneward-continuator accepts multi-line extensions to the refrain.

2115 Literally: 'not worth a medlar'. The expression is one of an open series of picturesque expressions of depreciation in Old French.

2171 The manuscript reading *aleis* offers no obvious meaning, although it is kept by all editors. I have followed Suard (1991) in assuming the loss of an initial *g* from *galeis* ('Welsh'). The presence of this language in Willame's repertoire suggests that the poet was aware of the *matière de Bretagne*. Unlike prevous editors, however, I have kept the poet's distinction between *tieis* (approximately corresponding to High German) and *alemandeis* (a variety of German spoken in the areas of Alsace and Franche-Comté in modern France, and in Switzerland).

2286a There must be a lacuna of two lines here (or more probably of one here and of one more after l. 2287). The first missing line recounts the death of Willame's first victim, and the second refers to the second (or rather third) enemy he killed. Suard translates *altre* as 'troisième', which is not convincing (one expects a sequence 'premer...altre...terz'), although more acceptable than Fassò who follows Wathelet-Willem in interpreting *altre* as 'the next two'.

2318 The 'adverser' causing Willame trouble is both the Devil and the enemy (Alderufe) who forced Willame to fight him, and is now taking a sort of posthumous revenge for having his armour stolen to be used as a disguise enabling Willame to escape from l'Archamp.

2438   Wathelet-Willem's correction of *lui* to *Loun* is misconceived, especially from her own standpoint, as it introduces an Anglo-Norman rhyme not in the manuscript into a poem she saw as Continental. One must, however, suspect a corruption at this point as not only is the syntax incoherent but the next line (2439) also contains a false assonance in [ei].

2469a There appears to be a lacuna of some lines here, introducing the 'bachelers' (young knights) to whom Willame habitually distributed his Spanish gold.

2651   Although 'tinel' is generally taken in the broad sense of 'club', it is important to understand that it is, as Wathelet-Willem (1967) points out, a domestic implement designed for carrying buckets. The fact that, except in one short scene where he is 'reduced' to using a sword, Reneward only ever fights either with the sign of his servitude or with the roof-tree of a peasant's hut establishes the carnavalesque atmosphere of this part of the *Willame*.

2691   Reneward is here identifying the head cook with the 'hob-goblin', a malicious sprite haunting the fireplace and held responsible for inexplicable losses in the household.

2718   Here and at the start of *laisses* 161, 162, 167 and 168 the name of the hero is spelt with a capital 'U'. This feature occurs only when the name is the initial word of the *laisse* and may indicate the intervention of a different rubricator, possibly making good blanks left by the main rubricator. Although in general 'u' before another vowel is transcribed 'v', I have kept the 'U' in these cases to reflect the probable pronunciation [w] in the scribe/rubricator's Anglo-Norman dialect.

2803   The blatant discrepancy between this line and the scene we have just witnessed (which took place in Laon) may constitute part of Willame's 'lie', or may simply be introduced at the dictates of assonance. It is unlikely that the two references belong to different strata of the epic tradition, since both fall clearly within the *G2* (or 'Reneward') section. In *Aliscans* the interview between Guillaume and Louis also takes place in Laon, but there is no equivalent of this exchange between the hero and Guibourc, which is replaced by a series of *laisses parallèles* in which Guillaume's clan lead in their respective contingents.

2911 In this line I take 'estage' to be 'estache'. Literally a 'stake', it seems to refer here to one of the shafts of which a composite pillar was constructed in Romanesque and Gothic architecture.

3058 This line appears to refer to a tradition of Bertram as master of a longship otherwise known only from *Aliscans* l. 152 and the 'Siège d'Orange' episode in MS *E* of Redaction *C(E)* of *La Prise d'Orange*, in which Guillaume's nephew is repeatedly called 'le timonier' ('the steersman') rather than 'le palasin' ('count palatine'), his usual epithet in the Guillaume Cycle.

3155 McMillan, Wathelet-Willem and Suard (silently) all correct the MS 'fiz cadele' to 'quis cadele', a reading borrowed from l. 2100, thereby identifying the Girard referred to by Alderufe with one of the prisoners. I have kept the MS version, translating it by the Anglo-French naming formula 'Fitz Captain' on the model of such twelfth-century names as Brian Fitz Count (son of Count Alain Fergant of Brittany and a supporter of Mathilda) and Henry Fitz Empress (Henry II, son of Mathilda).

3216 McMillan, followed by Suard, reads 'pereres' ('catapults'). The MS clearly reads 'peres' ('stones'), which might be a scribal error, or might be a metonymic usage. I have therefore not corrected the MS.

3344a There is a lacuna, probably of a single line here, which must have contained the idea that the Franks killed all the enemies they found.

3529 'Romant' has given editors and translators much trouble. Wathelet-Willem glosses it rather vaguely as 'nom d'un peuple chrétien', Suard as 'qui parle la langue romane' and Fassò as 'latino'. It appears to mean 'an occupant of the Roman Empire': its Latin equivalent is frequently used in the twelfth and thirteenth centuries to mean either an occupant of the western empire (and its heir the Holy Roman Empire) or of the eastern (Byzantine) empire. The form in *-an* (rather than *-ain*) is Anglo-Norman, and its appearance at the assonance suggests that the Anglo-Norman contribution to the production of the existing *Chançun de Willame* extended beyond mere copying into a manuscript.